# Lecture Notes in Computer Scien

T0238856

Commenced Publication in 1973
Founding and Former Series Editors:
Gerhard Goos, Juris Hartmanis, and Jan van Leeuwen

## Editorial Board

Massimo Villari   Wolf Zimmermann
Kung-Kiu Lau (Eds.)

# Service-Oriented and Cloud Computing

Third European Conference, ESOCC 2014
Manchester, UK, September 2-4, 2014
Proceedings

Springer

Volume Editors

Massimo Villari
Università di Messina
Dip. di Ingegneria Civile, Informatica, Edile, Ambientale
e Matematica Applicata (DICIEAMA)
C.Da Di Dio, No.1, 98166 Messina, Italy
E-mail: mvillari@unime.it

Wolf Zimmermann
Martin-Luther-Universität Halle-Wittenberg
Institut für Informatik
V.-Seckendorff-Platz, 06099 Halle (Saale), Germany
E-mail: zimmer@informatik.uni-halle.de

Kung-Kiu Lau
The University of Manchester
School of Computer Science
Oxford Road, Manchester M13 9PL, UK
E-mail: kung-kiu@cs.man.ac.uk

ISSN 0302-9743               e-ISSN 1611-3349
ISBN 978-3-662-44878-6       e-ISBN 978-3-662-44879-3
DOI 10.1007/978-3-662-44879-3
Springer Heidelberg New York Dordrecht London

Library of Congress Control Number: 2014948210

LNCS Sublibrary: SL 2 – Programming and Software Engineering

*Typesetting:* Camera-ready by author, data conversion by Scientific Publishing Services, Chennai, India

Printed on acid-free paper

Springer is part of Springer Science+Business Media (www.springer.com)

# Preface

Service-oriented computing – together with web services as its most important implementation platform – has become the most important paradigm for distributed software development and application for a number of years now. The former ECOWS (European Conference on Web Services) conference series addressed key issues of service-oriented computing, in particular web services, in nine successful conferences until 2011. In the meantime, as services are increasingly used remotely, i.e. in the "cloud", the focus of the conference series has shifted slightly. Accordingly, ECOWS was re-launched in 2012 as the "European Conference on Service-Oriented and Cloud Computing" (ESOCC) in Bertinoro, Italy, addressing the state of the art and practice of service-oriented computing and cloud computing. The second European Conference on Service-Oriented and Cloud Computing, ESOCC 2013, was held in Málaga, Spain, on 11–13 September 2013. This conference was the third conference of the series and was held in Manchester, UK on September 2–4 2014.

This volume contains the technical papers presented at the conference. The conference consisted of two tracks: Research Track and Industrial Track. There were a total of 38 submissions to the Research Track, from which 8 papers were selected (yielding an acceptance rate of 21%), together with 4 short papers, and one paper that has been shifted to the industrial track. The review and selection process was performed rigorously, with each paper being reviewed by at least three PC members (sometimes with the help of additional reviewers).

There were three excellent invited talks at the conference, given by Scharam Dustar (Vienna University of Technology, Austria), Simon Moser (IBM Germany), and Rob Cooper (BBC, U.K.).

Four workshops were co-located with the conference: The Cloud for IoT (CLIoT 2014), the 4th International Workshop on Adaptive Services for the Future Internet (WAS4FI 2014), The 2nd International Workshop on Cloud Service Brokerage (CSB 2014), and SeaClouds - Seamless adaptive multi-cloud management of service-based applications. A PhD Symposium was held on the first day of the main conference.

All in all, ESOCC 2014 was a successful conference, and we owe its success to many people: all the authors who submitted papers, and those who presented papers at the conference; all the PC members who took part in the review and selection process, as well as the additional reviewers they called on for help; all the invited speakers; the members of the Organizing Committee who chaired the industrial track, workshops and the PhD Symposium, as well as the people who

helped organize these events. Last, but not least, we are grateful to the local
Organizing Committee for their efficient organization and warm hospitality. To
all of you: we say a heart-felt 'Thank you'!

July 2014                                                                    Massimo Villari
                                                                         Wolf Zimmermann
                                                                           Kung-Kiu Lau

# Organization

ESOCC 2014 was organized by the the School of Computer Science of the University of Manchester, UK.

## Organizing Committee

### General Chair

Kung-Kiu Lau             University of Manchester, UK

### Program Chairs

Massimo Villari             University of Messina, Italy
Wolf Zimmermann         Martin-Luther-University, Halle-Wittenberg,
                                Germany

### Industrial Track Chair

Kenji Takeda             Microsoft Research, UK

### Workshop Chairs

Guadalupe Ortiz           University of Cadiz, Spain
Cuong Tran               University of Manchester, UK

### Ph.D. Symposium Chairs

Alexander Pokhar        University of Hamburg, Germany
Friederike Klan          Friedrich Schiller University, Germany

## Program Committee

Marco Aiello             University of Groningen, The Netherlands
Farhad Arbab            CWI and Leiden University, The Netherlands
Luciano Baresi           Politecnico di Milano, Italy
Judith Bishop            Microsoft Research, USA
Mario Bravetti           University of Bologna, Italy
Antonio Brogi            University of Pisa, Italy
Christoph Bussler        VoxeoLabs Inc., USA
Javier Cubo              University of Málaga, Spain
Flavio de Paoli           Università Milano Bicocca, Italy

# Additional Reviewers

Achilleas Achilleos        Pooyan Jamshidi        Jan Sürmeli
Raffael Dzikowski          Kai Jander              Pengwei Wang
Michela Fazzolari          Christos Mettouris
Kristof Hamann             Gabriel Orsini

# Table of Contents

# CloudDSF – The Cloud Decision Support Framework for Application Migration

Vasilios Andrikopoulos, Alexander Darsow,
Dimka Karastoyanova, and Frank Leymann

IAAS, University of Stuttgart,
Universitätsstr. 38, 70569 Stuttgart, Germany
{firstname.lastname}@iaas.uni-stuttgart.de

**Abstract.** Migrating existing applications to cloud solutions is a multi-dimensional problem that spans beyond technical issues and into the financial, security and organizational domains. The existing works in the field form a picture of a maturing but still incomplete research area, requiring the introduction of comprehensive solutions for the migration of enterprise systems and applications to cloud solutions. As part of this effort, in this work we focus on supporting decision makers in evaluating the need for migration, and guiding them along the decisions that need to be made before the actual migration process. For this purpose we build on existing work to provide an elaborated decision support framework that is available as a Web application. We discuss the evaluation of the framework by experts, identify its deficiencies and outline our future steps. {keywordsApplication migration, decision support, decision visualization.

## 1 Introduction

Cloud computing has become increasingly popular over the last few years both with the industry and the academia. The main driving factors for this popularity as discussed e.g. in [16], are the ease of infrastructure provisioning, the cost savings due to the transfer from capital to operational expenses, and the potential for elastic resource utilization to cope with fluctuating demand. In this context, it is a key requirement for enterprises to migrate partially or completely their existing systems and applications to a cloud solution [6]. However, the migration of existing software to the cloud poses a number of challenges both technical as well as financial, legal and organizational [1]. In recent years a number of experience reports have started appearing discussing the migration of existing systems to cloud solutions, e.g. [7,17,22], illustrating in all cases the multi-dimensionality of the problem. In a recent publication, Jamshidi et al. [16] provide a systematic review of the State of the Art on methodologies, techniques, tooling support and research directions. Their conclusion is that the field is still at a formative stage, and that cross-cutting concerns like security and effort estimation are not being addressed sufficiently.

M. Villari et al. (Eds.) : ESOCC 2014, LNCS 8745, pp. 1–16, 2014.

Along these lines, the work in [3] discusses the vision of a system that supports decision makers in deciding whether and how to migrate their applications to cloud solutions. Multiple decision points creating feedback loops with each other are identified and associated with tasks like cost analysis that not only depend on the decisions' outcome, but also affect these decisions in turn. However, the discussion in [3] stays on a high level and does not identify concrete decision outcomes that can be used in practice. This is a deficiency that we are addressing with this work.

More specifically, the contributions of this work can be summarized as follows:

- a publicly available Cloud Decision Support Framework (CloudDSF) which aims to assist decision makers during the migration of applications to the cloud, and
- an empirical evaluation of CloudDSF by a cohort of experts, together with a discussion on the steps required to realize a decision support system based on it.

The remaining of this paper is structured as follows: Section 2 summarizes the conceptual framework for cloud migration decision support discussed in [3]. Section 3 discusses the process of elaborating this framework into CloudDSF, the identified decisions and outcomes, and the visualization of CloudDSF as a Web application offering different interaction options to its users. Section 4 discusses the process of evaluating CloudDSF by means of a survey and summarizes the findings of the survey. Consequently, Section 5 provides a discussion on the aspects that need to be addressed in order to realize a decision support system based on CloudDSF. Finally Sections 6 and 7 close this paper with related work, and conclusions and future work, respectively.

## 2   Background

Figure 1 summarizes the vision for a Decision Support System for Cloud Migration as discussed in [3]. Two types of concepts are presented in the figure: *decision points* that identify high-level decisions that need to be made, and *tasks* that need to be performed in order to support these decisions. Four major decision points are identified:

1. *How to distribute the application* in logical and physical placement terms. This entails viewing the application as a set of components across different functional layers, and deciding which components are to be hosted in one or more cloud providers.
2. *Which is the elasticity strategy* that the application needs to implement in order to cope with current and future demand in the face of service level agreements (SLAs) and performance requirements of its users.
3. *What are the requirements of the application with respect to multi-tenancy,* i.e. to what extent the existing application is required to support resource sharing across different levels ranging from the bare metal to the application instance, to what degree it is designed for this purpose, and how it should be (re-)engineered to support multi-tenancy.

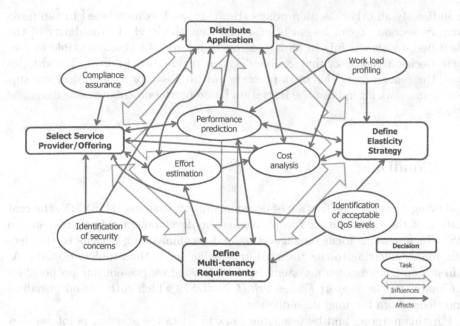

**Fig. 1.** The Decision Support Framework for Cloud Migration [3]

4. *How to select an appropriate (cloud) service provider and offering* that fits
   the application needs in terms of cost, expected performance, compliance
   and security requirements etc.

Relations between these decision points are illustrated with transparent block
arrows in Fig. 1. In addition, the set of tasks that were identified in [3] to be
related to these decisions points are:

a) *workload profiling* of the application,
b) *performance prediction* based on the workload profile of the application,
c) *effort estimation* for any necessary adaptations to the application during the
   migration process,
d) *cost analysis* that builds on the pay-per-use model of the cloud services,
   including the cost for the estimated adaptation effort,
e) *identification of acceptable QoS levels* in order to cope with existing or future
   SLAs,
f) *compliance assurance* with respect to organizational regulation, and national
   and international law, and
g) *identification of security concerns* with emphasis on critical data communication and storage.

Tasks and decision points therefore form a network of relationships with decisions made on one point, e.g. which elasticity strategy to use, affecting directly

or indirectly all other decision points. However, and as mentioned in the introductory section, it can be easily observed that the level of granularity of the identified decision points in [3] is too coarse in order to be connectible to concrete decision outcomes that enable decision making in the field. Toward this goal, the remaining of this work presents our proposal for a cloud decision support framework for application migration based on elaborating the one discussed above.

# 3   CloudDSF

Following Power's classification of decision support systems (DSS) [23], the realization of the vision outlined in [3] means the development a *knowledge-driven DSS*. Such systems focus on suggesting and recommending actions to the decision maker referring to the gathered knowledge about the problem domain. As a first step towards such a system, in the following we present our proposal for a *Cloud Decision Support Framework (CloudDSF)* which gathers and visualizes knowledge from the migration domain.

For this purpose, and by using the work in [3] as the starting point, we conducted a thorough literature review focusing on the areas of decision support for application migration to the cloud e.g. [5,8,14,18,21], and application migration and cloud computing [4] in general, with the explicit goal of verifying and elaborating the already identified decision points. The gathered knowledge was initially captured in a spreadsheet which recorded potential (concrete) *decisions* affiliated with each *decision point*, their possible *outcomes*, as well as the relevant literature sources[1]. The result of this process serves as the *Knowledge Base* of CloudDSF, based on which a *Visualization* component was developed to enable interaction with users. Both of these components are presented in the following.

## 3.1   Knowledge Base

The Knowledge Base of CloudDSF capturing the results of the elaboration process is summarized in Table 1. A total of 17 decisions are identified for the existing 4 decision points (application distribution, elasticity strategy, multi-tenancy requirements and provider selection). For each decision, a set of outcomes is provided for a total of more than 50 outcomes, ranging from very specific, e.g. which pricing model is offered by the service provider (*Select Pricing Model*), to more coarse, e.g. whether a single or multiple components are to be hosted in the cloud (*Select Application Components*). More specifically, the identified decisions are:

---

[1] The same process also resulted in the refinement of tasks, as well as the identification of additional tasks to be considered. However, for reasons of space we omit the discussion on task elaboration and postpone it for future work.

**Table 1.** The CloudDSF Knowledge Base

| Decision Point | Decision | Outcomes |
|---|---|---|
| Application Distribution | Select Application Layer | – Presentation/Business/Data Layer<br>– Multiple Layers |
| | Select Application Tier | – Client/Application/Data Tier<br>– Multiple Tiers |
| | Select Application Components | – Single Component<br>– Multiple Components |
| | Select Migration Type | – Type I, II, III or IV |
| Elasticity Strategy | Define Scalability Level | – Instance/Container/VM/Virtual Resource/<br>Hardware Level<br>– Multiple Levels |
| | Select Scaling Type | – Vertical/Horizontal Scaling<br>– Hybrid Scaling |
| | Select Elasticity Automation Degree | – Manual Scaling<br>– Semi-automatic Scaling<br>– Automatic Scaling |
| | Select Scaling Trigger | – Event-driven<br>– Proactive |
| Multi-Tenancy Requirements | Select Kind of Multi-Tenancy | – Multiple Instances Multi-Tenancy<br>– Native Multi-Tenancy |
| | Select Multi-Tenancy Architecture | – Any of the Possible Combinations |
| Provider/ Offering Selection | Select Cloud Deployment Model | –Private/Community/Public/Hybrid Cloud |
| | Select Cloud Service Model | – S/P/IaaS |
| | Define Cloud Hosting | – On Premise/Off Premise<br>– Hybrid Hosting |
| | Define Roles of Responsibility | – Ownership/Operation/Management Role<br>– Any Combination of Roles |
| | Select Pricing Model | – Free/ Pay-per-Use/-Unit/Subscription<br>– Combined Model |
| | Select Cloud Vendor | – Evaluated Vendor |
| | Define Resource Location | – Evaluated Physical Resource Location |

**Application Distribution** Four decisions are associated with application distribution. The first two follow Fowler et al.'s distinction between physical tiers and functional layers in the application architecture [9]. They are concerned with which application layer(s) and which application tier(s) are to be moved to the cloud (*Select Application Layer* and *Select Application Tier*, respectively). More than one layers or tiers at a time are of course also possible. The next decision (*Select Application Components*) becomes essential if finer granularity than a layer or tier is required and refers to deciding which specific application component(s) are to be migrated. Finally, the last decision (*Select Migration Type*) refers to the type of migration to be used for the migration using the classification of Andrikopoulos et al. [1]: Type I — component(s) replacement, Type II — partial migration of functionality, Type III — full application stack migration (virtual machine-based), or Type IV — cloudification of the application. As such, the outcome of this decision may have an effect on the possible outcomes of all other decisions concerning the distribution of the application.

**Elasticity Strategy** The first decision concerning elasticity strategy refers to the scalability level required for the application (*Define Scalability Level*). For this purpose we discern between three different system levels: the physical *hardware* one, the *virtualization* level built on top of it, and the *application* level on top of that. The virtualization level itself can be distinguished into *virtual resources*, e.g. the hypervisor used, and *virtual machines* allocated to these virtual resources. Similarly, the application level discerns between the application *instances* and the middleware *container* hosting these instances (e.g. application servers or database management systems). The scalability options for each level increase as we traverse the levels: while on the physical level there are only few choices (i.e. bringing in another server or updating the existing one with more powerful hardware), on application level potentially unlimited application instances can be added to cope with additional demand. The remaining decisions refer to the type of scaling that can be used i.e. vertical (adding/removing computational resources), horizontal (adding/removing instances or replicas) or hybrid combinations [28] (*Select Scaling Type*), how much automation is achievable by existing solutions [25] (*Select Elasticity Automation Degree*), and which type of trigger is used (*Select Scaling Trigger*): the more common event-driven type based on monitoring rules, or a proactive one which combines log files with real-time data to dynamically predict scaling actions [27].

**Multi-tenancy Requirements** Following Guo et al.'s [13] classification of multi-tenancy, there are two kinds of multi-tenancy in cloud applications (*Select Kind of Multi-tenancy*): *multiple instances*, where each application tenant (application user) is working on a dedicated application instance, or *native* multi-tenancy where tenants share a single application instance and its underlying resources. Furthermore, and looking at the different system levels previously discussed (hardware, virtualization, application), different possibilities appear on which resources are to be shared between tenants. An application for example may rely on a single hardware and virtualization level for all tenants, but provide multiple instances for each tenant on the level of application or database management server (middleware). One database schema with separate tenant data spaces could be used, or different tenants may even share the same tables in the database. As a result, multiple combinations are available as outcomes of this decision (*Select Multi-Tenancy Architecture*).

**Provider/Offering Selection** Deciding on which cloud provider and which particular offering to be used depends fundamentally on the type of cloud solution that is appropriate for the enterprise. Towards identifying this solution we consider a series of decisions based on the definition of the different cloud solution types as provided by NIST (as updated and extended in [4]). In particular, it needs to be decided which of the private, public, community or hybrid deployment models is more suitable (*Select Cloud Deployment Model*), which of the *\*aaS*, that is Software, Platform or Infrastructure as a Service delivery models fits the application migration (*Select Cloud Service Model*), as well as where the application is to be hosted: on premise (in-house on e.g. a private cloud solution) or off premise (*Define Cloud Hosting*).

Depending on the deployment, delivery and hosting decisions, different responsibility roles are available to be distributed between application stakeholders and cloud providers (*Define Roles of Responsibility*). In principle there are three fundamental roles to be performed [4]: resource owner (i.e. to whom the infrastructure belongs to), resource operator (i.e. who hosts and makes sure that the application is running) and resource manager (i.e. who is responsible for managing the resources, rolls out updates etc.) Any combination of these roles is possible; for example in an off premise private cloud scenario, the enterprise may be the resource owner but not the resource operator or manager (roles to be performed by the cloud provider).

While cloud computing is usually associated with the "pay as you go" pricing model of utility-style charging for resource consumption [4], in practice many cloud offerings use alternative pricing models [27]. For this purpose we adapt the pricing model classification discussed by Suleiman et al. [27] to distinguish between free, pay-per-use, pay-per-unit (of time), or subscription-based charging, e.g. for reserved instances offered by the Amazon EC2 service[2] (*Select Pricing Model*). Finally, the remaining two decisions (*Select Cloud Vendor* and *Define Resource Location*) are concerned with the evaluation of the reputation of the cloud provider in the manner discussed e.g. in [12], and of the physical location of the migrated data for regulatory compliance purposes [10] (*Select Cloud Vendor* and *Define Resource Location*, respectively).

## 3.2   Visualization

Aiming for a modern, user friendly, cross-platform visualization of CloudDSF we opted for a Web-based solution which we made publicly available at http://www.clouddsf.com. The resulting Web application uses basic Web technologies like HTML, CSS and SVG in order to provide an interface to the users through their browsers. The decision points, decisions and possible outcomes, together with the identified tasks and their relations, as discussed in the previous section are stored in a JSON[3] file, which is used as input for the visualization logic. The latter is written in Javascript, based on the D3[4] and jQuery[5] libraries that offer out of the box a number of features like network graph visualization and dynamic graph manipulation. The Bootstrap framework[6] was used for layout rendering purposes.

---

[2] Amazon Elastic Cloud Computing (EC2): http://aws.amazon.com/ec2/
[3] JavaScript Object Notation (JSON): http://www.json.org/
[4] D3.js — Data Driven Documents: http://d3js.org/
[5] The jQuery library: http://jquery.com/
[6] Bootstrap: http://getbootstrap.com/

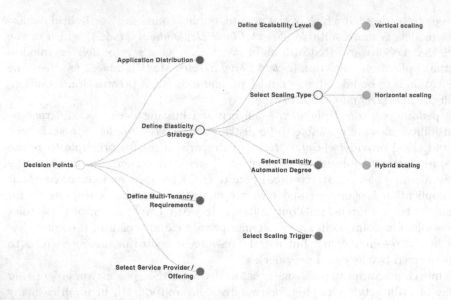

**Fig. 2.** CloudDSF Visualization Options: Tree View

As a result, a series of hierarchical and network-based visualization options are available at http://www.clouddsf.com. Figures 2 and 3 show an example for each one of these options: a (hierarchical) tree view of the possible outcomes of the "Select Scaling Type" decision (Fig. 2), and a (network) partition view of all the decisions (Fig. 3) which reconfigures the ring to zoom to a decision point or to a decision and its outcomes when selected. Cluster, treemap and partition layouts are also offered to the user, allowing for different types of interaction with the application.

## 4   Evaluation

Given the fact that CloudDSF is meant to be part of a knowledge-driven DSS, evaluating the framework focuses on the *understandability*, *suitability* and *completeness* of the decision points, decisions and outcomes in its knowledge base. In the following we present the evaluation procedure towards these objectives and report on our findings.

### 4.1   Procedure

The instrument of a Web-based survey by means of questionnaire was used for the evaluation of CloudDSF. More specifically, a questionnaire of 86 questions was designed following the guidelines discussed in [19], combining open (free text responses) and closed (choice from an ascending rating scale) questions towards the identified evaluation objectives (understandability, suitability and

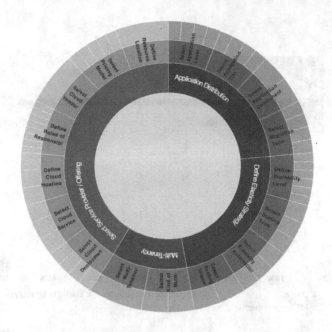

**Fig. 3.** CloudDSF Visualization Options: Partition View

completeness). The questionnaire was then realized using the open source survey application LimeSurvey[7] and made available online for a period of two weeks in February 2014. A group of academic researchers, system developers, operations managers and IT consultants with expertise in cloud computing were invited by email to participate and provided with the credentials to access the survey. A completion rate of 42,9% was achieved among the participants of the survey for a total of 6 completed surveys (consisting of 4 academic and 2 industrial participants). The results of the survey including the posed questions — after discarding incomplete (unfinalized) questionnaires and anonymizing the participants — are also available online[8]. Only completed questionnaires are considered in the following discussions on the findings of the survey.

## 4.2   Findings

Figures 4, 5 and 6 summarize the results of the conducted survey with respect to the objectives of understandability and relevance (suitability)[9]. With respect to the former, it can be seen from Fig. 4 that the understandability of the decision points ('Overall' in Fig. 4) is perceived as good from the survey participants, while the (average) understandability of individual decisions per decision point is actually ranked higher. This is expected since the finer granularity of the

---

[7] LimeSurvey: http://www.limesurvey.org

[8] http://www.clouddsf.com/survey/questionnaire_results.zip

[9] *Note:* In all figures the scale is from worse (0) to best (4).

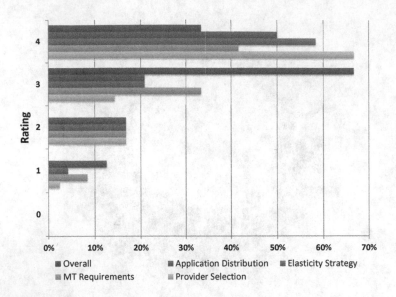

**Fig. 4.** Understandability of Decisions per Decision Point (Average)

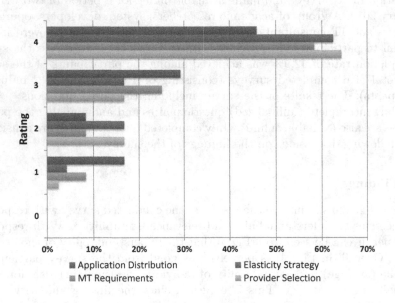

**Fig. 5.** Relevance of Decisions per Decision Point (Average)

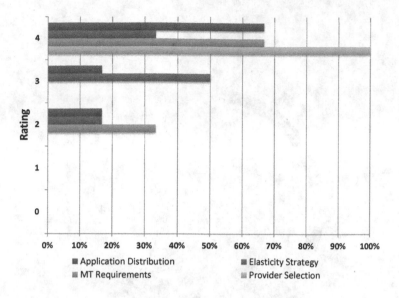

**Fig. 6.** Relevance of Decision Points

decisions in the CloudDSF allows for better understanding of the decisions involved. In terms of suitability, Fig. 5 shows that the vast majority of decisions are deemed as relevant to the decision point that they are associated with, with only the application distribution decisions rated lower than the rest. Furthermore, in Fig. 6 all decision points with the exception of elasticity strategy are viewed as highly relevant for migration to the cloud, with elasticity strategy perceived as simply relevant. In terms of completeness, an average of around two additional decisions was pointed out by the survey participants as relevant for each decision point. The provided suggestions will be used in the future for further improving and elaborating CloudDSF.

## 5  Discussion

The evaluation of CloudDSF as discussed in the previous section showed that the framework contains a suitable and representative amount of knowledge for guiding decision makers during the migration of applications to the cloud. One aspect of the accumulated knowledge that was not discussed sufficiently however in the previous section is that of the relationships between decisions, and between decisions and tasks. A number of relationships are already identified in Fig. 1 distinguished between two types: what is the *influence* of a decision type to another, and how a task *affects* the decisions at a decision point (and vice versa). The elaboration of the decision points of [3] into concrete decisions in CloudDSF results naturally into a significant increase in the number of these relationships, as shown by the cluster diagram of Fig. 7 (using one of the available visualization options in CloudDSF).

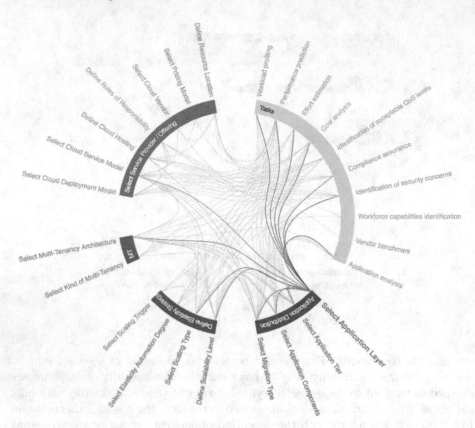

**Fig. 7.** Cluster View of the Decisions and Tasks in CloudDSF

As shown in Fig. 7, there is a strong interplay between decisions (and decisions and tasks) forming a dense network of relationships with each other. In turn, this means that selecting any of the available outcomes for each decision has a direct or indirect impact to the possible outcomes in other decisions. Furthermore, the result of any of the identified tasks may end up constraining significantly the available outcomes across many of the related decisions, as well as potentially contradicting already taken decisions. A formal representation of these relationships that allows this type of reasoning on them is therefore required for the realization of the knowledge-driven decision support system discussed in [3]. The other major task is the linking between the decisions to be taken and the representation of the enterprise applications to be migrated to the cloud in order to translate decision outcomes into concrete actions. This linking is anyway required for most of the tasks (e.g. cost calculation) associated with the decisions. These two tasks are part of our future steps.

# 6   Related Works

A series of works on decision support for the migration of applications to the cloud have appeared in the literature. The Cloudward framework [14], for example, was developed in collaboration between academic and industrial partners with the goal of migrating applications to hybrid cloud solutions. The framework takes into account cost savings, communication costs, transaction delays and constraints like security. CloudGenius [21] provides an automated decision making process towards identifying the optimal selection of a combination of IaaS offerings and VM image types for single-tier web application migration. The focus of the system is however on technical requirements and does not address organizational or other enterprise concerns. The Cloud Adoption Toolkit [18] provides a framework specifically aimed at enterprise stakeholders. For this purpose it provides the means for tasks like technology suitability analysis based on the profile of the enterprise, cost modeling and energy consumption analysis for the "to be" model of the migrated systems, as well as responsibility modeling distinguishing between operation, maintenance and management roles for migrated and non-migrated system components. These tasks are meant to be performed in a sequential manner, forming a decision making process.

In a similar fashion, the Cloudstep [5] approach provides a decision process consisting of nine activities including enterprise, legacy application and cloud provider profiling, constraint identification analysis and alternative migration scenarios evaluation and ranking. Constraints that are taken into consideration are categorized in seven areas: financial, organizational, security, communication, performance, availability and suitability. Finally, Chauhan and Babar present in [8] a high level seven step process built on best practices and lessons learned from the migration of legacy application to service-oriented architectures. As discussed in Section 3, the process of elaborating the decision points identified in [3] was based on these works.

A related research field to decision support for application migration is cloud service selection based on multi-criteria decision making (MCDM) techniques. Approaches like [15,24,26] and [11] provide the means to users to provide a set of requirements against which existing cloud service offerings are evaluated and ranked. Similarly, in [20], a resolution engine is presented that matches user-provided criteria with available offerings from a cloud service marketplace in order to identify suitable business-level offerings. In [12], the authors discuss a feature-based model for the description of service offerings that can be used for decision making towards offering selection. These works can be used as the basis for the implementation of a decision support system around CloudDSF.

# 7   Conclusion

While cloud computing has been increasingly successful with adoption by the industry, the migration of existing systems to cloud solutions has proven to be a more complicated problem than cloud vendors and proponents would admit. A big part of the problem is the multi-dimensionality required to deal with a series of technical, financial, legal and organizational issues. Towards supporting enterprise stakeholders in deciding whether and how to migrate their applications, in previous work we outlined the vision for a decision support system that incorporates different aspects of migration. The current work expanded on this vision to propose CloudDSF, a framework in which knowledge about the problem domain (i.e. migration to the cloud) was gathered, organized, visualized and offered as a publicly available Web application. The empirical evaluation conducted in collaboration with experts on cloud computing, while limited in scope, showed that the resulting framework is sound and suitable for migration-oriented decision making. However, in order to translate it into a full blown decision support system there are still important issues to be addressed.

In terms of future work the focus is on the tasks already identified in the previous sections, i.e. the incorporation of the evaluation results, the formalization of the relationships between decisions, and decisions and tasks, as well as the linking from the application model to the decisions that need to be taken. Part of our plans is also a larger scale evaluation of CloudDSF with a wider profile of participants, as well as additional evaluation by means of case studies in industrial migration projects. To this purpose, we need also to work on the elaboration of the relationships between tasks and decisions, and the connection between decisions outcomes and inputs and outputs of tasks. Cost calculation facilities provided e.g. by the Nefolog system [2] will be used as the pilot for this effort.

**Acknowledgment.** This work is partially funded by the FP7 EU-FET project 600792 ALLOW Ensembles.

# References

1. Andrikopoulos, V., Binz, T., Leymann, F., Strauch, S.: How to Adapt Applications for the Cloud Environment. Computing 95(6), 493–535 (2013)
2. Andrikopoulos, V., Reuter, A., Mingzhu, X., Leymann, F.: Design Support for Cost-efficient Application Distribution in the Cloud. In: Proceedings of the 7th IEEE International Conference on Cloud Computing (CLOUD 2014). IEEE Computer Society (to appear, 2014)
3. Andrikopoulos, V., Strauch, S., Leymann, F.: Decision support for application migration to the cloud: Challenges and vision. In: 3rd International Conference on Cloud Computing and Service Science (CLOSER 2013), pp. 149–155. SciTePress (2013)
4. Badger, L., Grance, T., Patt-Corner, R., Voas, J.: Cloud computing synopsis and recommendations - recommendations of the national institute of standards and technology. NIST Special Publication 800-146 (2012)
5. Beserra, P.V., Camara, A., Ximenes, R., Albuquerque, A.B., Mendonca, N.C.: Cloudstep: A step-by-step decision process to support legacy application migration to the cloud. In: Maintenance and Evolution of Service-Oriented and Cloud-Based Systems (MESOCA 2012) Workshop, pp. 7–16. IEEE (2012)

6. Buyya, R., Broberg, J., Gosćinśki, A.: Cloud computing: principles and paradigms. Wiley (2011)
7. Chauhan, M.A., Babar, M.A.: Migrating service-oriented system to cloud computing: An experience report. In: International Conference on Cloud Computing (CLOUD 2011), pp. 404–411. IEEE (2011)
8. Chauhan, M.A., Babar, M.A.: Towards process support for migrating applications to cloud computing. In: 2012 International Conference on Cloud and Service Computing, pp. 80–87. IEEE Computer Society (2012)
9. Fowler, M., et al.: Patterns of Enterprise Application Architecture. Addison-Wesley Professional (November 2002)
10. Gagliardi, F., Muscella, S.: Cloud Computing–Data Confidentiality and Interoperability Challenges, pp. 257–270. Springer (2010)
11. Garg, S., Versteeg, S., Buyya, R.: Smicloud: A framework for comparing and ranking cloud services. In: 2011 Fourth IEEE International Conference on Utility and Cloud Computing (UCC), pp. 210–218. IEEE (2011)
12. Gudenkauf, S., Josefiok, M., Goring, A., Norkus, O.: A reference architecture for cloud service offers. In: 2013 17th IEEE International Enterprise Distributed Object Computing Conference (EDOC), pp. 227–236. IEEE (2013)
13. Guo, C., Sun, W., Huang, Y., Wang, Z., Gao, B.: A Framework for Native Multi-Tenancy Application Development and Management. In: Proceedings of CEC/EEE 2007, pp. 551–558. IEEE (2007)
14. Hajjat, M., Sun, X., Sung, Y., Maltz, D., Rao, S., Sripanidkulchai, K., Tawarmalani, M.: Cloudward bound: planning for beneficial migration of enterprise applications to the cloud. In: ACM SIGCOMM Computer Communication Review, vol. 40, pp. 243–254. ACM (2010)
15. Hussain, O.K., Hussain, F.K., et al.: IaaS cloud selection using MCDM methods. In: 2012 IEEE Ninth International Conference on e-Business Engineering (ICEBE), pp. 246–251. IEEE (2012)
16. Jamshidi, P., Ahmad, A., Pahl, C.: Cloud Migration Research: A Systematic Review. IEEE Transactions on Cloud Computing 1(2) (2013)
17. Khajeh-Hosseini, A., Greenwood, D., Sommerville, I.: Cloud migration: A case study of migrating an enterprise it system to iaas. In: International Conference on Cloud Computing (CLOUD 2010), pp. 450–457. IEEE (2010)
18. Khajeh-Hosseini, A., Greenwood, D., Smith, J.W., Sommerville, I.: The cloud adoption toolkit: supporting cloud adoption decisions in the enterprise. Software: Practice and Experience 42(4), 447–465 (2012)
19. Krosnick, J.A., Presser, S.: Question and Questionnaire Design, pp. 263–314. Emerald (2010)
20. Menychtas, A., Gatzioura, A., Varvarigou, T.: A business resolution engine for cloud marketplaces. In: 2011 IEEE Third International Conference on Cloud Computing Technology and Science (CloudCom), pp. 462–469. IEEE (2011)
21. Menzel, M., Ranjan, R.: Cloudgenius: decision support for web server cloud migration. In: Proceedings of WWW 2012, pp. 979–988. ACM (2012)
22. Pahl, C., Xiong, H., Walshe, R.: A comparison of on-premise to cloud migration approaches. In: Lau, K.-K., Lamersdorf, W., Pimentel, E. (eds.) ESOCC 2013. LNCS, vol. 8135, pp. 212–226. Springer, Heidelberg (2013)
23. Power, D.J.: Decision Support Systems: A Historical Overview, pp. 121–140. Springer, Heidelberg (2008)
24. ur Rehman, Z., Hussain, F.K., Hussain, O.K., et al.: Towards multi-criteria cloud service selection. In: 2011 Fifth International Conference on Innovative Mobile and Internet Services in Ubiquitous Computing (IMIS), pp. 44–48. IEEE (2011)

25. Sallam, A., Li, K.: Virtual machine proactive scaling in cloud systems. In: 2012 IEEE International Conference on Cluster Computing Workshops (CLUSTER WORKSHOPS), pp. 97–105. IEEE (2012)
26. Saripalli, P., Pingali, G.: Madmac: Multiple attribute decision methodology for adoption of clouds. In: 2011 IEEE International Conference on Cloud Computing (CLOUD), pp. 316–323. IEEE (2011)
27. Suleiman, B., Sakr, S., Jeffery, R., Liu, A.: On understanding the economics and elasticity challenges of deploying business applications on public cloud infrastructure. Journal of Internet Services and Applications 3(2), 173–193 (2012)
28. Vaquero, L., Rodero-Merino, L., Buyya, R.: Dynamically scaling applications in the cloud. ACM SIGCOMM Computer Communication Review 41(1), 45–52 (2011)

# Windows Azure: Resource Organization Performance Analysis

Marjan Gusev[1], Sasko Ristov[1], Bojana Koteska[1], and Goran Velkoski[2]

[1] Ss. Cyril and Methodius, Faculty of Computer Science and Engineering,
Rugjer Boskovikj 16, 1000 Skopje, Macedonia
{marjan.gushev,sashko.ristov,bojana.koteska}@finki.ukim.mk
[2] Innovation LTD,
Vostanichka 118, 1000 Skopje, Macedonia
goran.velkoski@innovation.com.mk

**Abstract.** Cloud customers can scale the resources according to their needs in order to avoid application bottleneck. The scaling can be done in two ways, either by increasing the existing virtual machine instance with additional resources, or by adding an additional virtual machine instance with the same resources. Although it is expected that the costs rise proportionally to scaling, we are interested in finding out which organization offers scaling with better performance. The goal of this paper is to determine the resource organization that produces better performance for the same cost, and help the customers decide if it is better to host a web application on a more "small" instances or less "large" instances. The first hypothesis states that better performance is obtained by using more and smaller instances. The second hypothesis is that the obtained speedup while scaling the resources is smaller than the scaling factor. The results from the provided experiments have not proven any of the hypotheses, meaning that using less, but larger instances results with better performance and that the user gets more performances than expected by scaling the resources.

**Keywords:** Cloud Computing, Microsoft Azure, Performance, SaaS.

## 1 Introduction

One of the customers' motivations to migrate their applications onto a cloud is the cost. Currently cloud service providers (CSPs) use a linear "pay-by-the-drink" cost model, where the costs are proportional to the rented resources.

Although the cloud offers a possibility to reduce the costs, we are eager to find a platform that will offer the best performance for the same price. The customers can choose among various possibilities, such as using large or small instances. When the web services are hosted on the cloud, the performance is usually discrepant due to several reasons, such as the additional virtualization layer, cloud multi-tenant and shared resources environment. The overall web service performance depends on the quantity and capacity of rented hardware

M. Villari et al. (Eds.) : ESOCC 2014, LNCS 8745, pp. 17–31, 2014.
© IFIP International Federation for Information Processing 2014

resources, platform environment, the number of active virtual machines (VMs) on a physical server, the total number of active VMs in the cloud, and so on.

One of the advantages of the cloud compared to the traditional IT hosting platforms is that cloud is scalable and elastic. In this paper we analyze the performance trade-off to make conclusions about which resource organization of the cloud offers the maximum performance for a given cost.

A typical scenario that initiates a huge dilemma for the customer happens with scaling. Imagine that the customer has migrated the web service onto a cloud and measures the response time of the applications. Increased popularity of the web service might initiate a need for more transactions, and soon the rented resources will not be sufficient to keep the response times low enough to ensure a good quality of service. A typical CSP answer is that the customer should rent more resources, usually expressed with more CPU cores. For example, let the initial configuration be a small single tenant VM with one CPU core and the customer would like to rent 2 CPU cores instead of one. The dilemma is due to the fact that the customer faces several options, such as a medium VM with 2 CPU cores, or two small VMs with 1 CPU core each. The dilemma increases if the customer decides to use 4 CPU cores, or higher number of cores. In this case, the possibilities are even higher, for example, for 4 CPU cores, the options are 1x4, 2x2, and 4x1, corresponding to one large VM, or 2 medium VMs, or 4 small VMs. CSP is using a linear cost model, so all the configurations using a total of 4 CPU cores will approximately cost the same. In this paper we conduct experiments on Azure, as one of the most commonly used commercial clouds.

The research problem is to find out the Azure resource organization that performs the best and scores the highest performance trade-off. In addition, we set a hypothesis that renting more "smaller" VMs for the same cost is better than renting less "greater" instances, hoping that the tasks will be completed faster if we distribute them to more smaller instances. The second hypothesis is that the performance is smaller than the scaling factor. For example, it means that by renting double size resources, we will not obtain double performance. This is set due to virtualization and Gustafson's bounded linear speedup [10].

The paper is organized as follows. Related work in the area of cloud performance is given in Section 2. Section 3 presents the testing methodology, plan and infrastructure. The results from the experiments are described in Section 4. Section 5 is dedicated to a discussion of the outcome and performance trade-off, comparison of the results and analysis which environment provides the best performance. The conclusion and future work are specified in Section 6.

## 2   Related Work

The performance of various cloud applications and services is analyzed by many authors. For example, Brebner and Liu conducted empirical evaluations of different cloud infrastructures using a suite of cloud testing applications [2]. They also use those experimental evaluations to predict the resource requirements in terms of application performance, cost and limitations of a realistic application for different deployment scenarios. Gao et al. proposed formal graphic models and metrics in order to preform SaaS evaluation and analyze system scalability in clouds [3]. Their case study is Amazon's EC2 cloud technology.

Several papers analyze the performances on Azure. Hill et al. [11] present the results of the performance experiments conducted on Azure. They present a detailed performance evaluation and give some recommendations for Azure users. Scaling as performance measure was analyzed by Mao et al. [14]. They present a cloud auto-scaling mechanism which scale computing instances automatically based on workload information and performance desire. They have also implemented their mechanism in Azure platform and made evaluations of simulations and real scientific cloud application.

The performance trade-off was also analyzed in the literature. A comparison between the performance and monetary cost-benefits of clouds for desktop grid application was reported by Kondo et al. [12]. They conducted performance measurements and monetary expenses of real desktop grids and the Amazon elastic compute cloud. Ostermann et al. evaluated the usefulness of the cloud computing services for scientific computing [16]. They found that current cloud services need performance improvement in order to be used in scientific community.

Other performance aspects were also analyzed, such as storage services, data transfer etc. For example, Agarwal and Prasad describe a benchmark suite for the storage services of Azure platform called AzureBench [1]. Tudorian et al. concluded that Azure can support the efficient TCP data transfers and it can decrease the costs and time for deployment [17]. Several pitfalls in the Azure cloud are examined during several days of performing the experiments: Instance physical failure, Storage exception, System update [13]. The authors also discovered several pitfalls resulting in waste of active VM idling.

Recently, Gusev and Ristov [8] have reported that it is better to use many smaller VM instances for a web service hosted in the cloud. They achieved similar result for parallel implementation of cache intensive matrix multiplication algorithm [7], i.e., maximum speedup is obtained if matrices are scattered and multiplied on 8 concurrent (XS) VMs using a single thread in a VM, rather than using OpenMP with 8 threads in a single XL VM. This was the initial motivation to define the hypothesis in this paper and to check if this holds for a real web service that includes transactions in a 3-tier architecture, using a database server, a web server and an application server.

In this paper, we measure the performance of the 3-tier cloud SaaS application hosted on Azure. It acts as a transaction based application, where a database transaction is started and then the results are transferred back to the customer. The application is loaded with different number of requests, while it is being hosted in different number of instances with different resources.

## 3    Testing Methodology

This section describes the testing environments of Azure cloud, test cases and design implementation.

## 3.1  Test Goal

We are trying to determine which organization of the resources in the Azure cloud will provide the best performance for the most common 3-tier application using Web, Application and Database Servers.

The idea is to conduct three experiments. The first is about analyzing large ($L$) and small ($S$) configurations for the same amount of resources. By large configuration, we define a configuration that uses a small number of large VMs with greater number of CPUs. Correspondingly, a small configuration will be the one that uses more small VMs, where each VM consist of 1 or 2 CPUs. The results would give answer to the first hypothesis.

The next two experiments should provide an answer for the second hypothesis, whether the scaling of CPUs or the number of VMs will benefit with proportional performance. These experiments will also confirm which is better, to increase the number of CPUs or number of VMs when scaling is desired.

Let the number of VMs be $v$ and the number of CPU cores $c$. Then the total number of CPU cores $n$ used in a given configuration will be $n = v \cdot c$.

To answer the research questions and confirm validity of both hypotheses we conduct three experiments. Experiment 1 provides the tests with different configurations by keeping the same total number of CPU cores ($n$), as defined by (1); Experiment 2 provides the tests with different configurations by keeping the same number of VMs and scaling the number of CPU cores in each VM, as defined by (2); and Experiment 3 provides the tests with different configurations by keeping the same number of CPUs in each VM and scaling the number of VMs, as defined by (3).

$$\text{change } v, c \qquad n = const \tag{1}$$

$$\text{scale } c \text{ (and thus } n), \qquad v = const \tag{2}$$

$$\text{scale } v \text{ (and thus } n), \qquad c = const \tag{3}$$

## 3.2  Cloud Testing Environment

The testing environment is a client-server environment hosted on Windows Azure. The server side consists of the SaaS application "PhluffyFotos" [15], as a sample cloud application developed for public use under the Microsoft Public License (Ms-PL). The application uses the following technologies: ASP.NET MVC 4, Azure SQL Databases and Azure Storage, including Tables, Blobs, and Queues. This application is used because it frequently interacts with cloud storage services [18].

The PhluffyFotos is a Picture Gallery Service which can be accessed by web or mobile device. Users can create new albums, upload photos and share their photo albums. They must register and login in order to perform these actions. Unregistered and unlogged users can see all albums and search photos by tag, but they neither can create their own albums nor upload photos. There are database records for 100 albums, each containing one picture.

This web system is programmed specially for the Azure platform, which means that it is designed to be scaled by using different number of VMs and CPUs offered by the cloud service. The images and their meta-data are sent over to Windows Azure for processing. The information stored in Azure Storage Queues is picked up and processed by the the Cloud Service. After that, it is stored in Azure Table Storage. The content of the image is stored in binary blobs using Azure Blob Storage. Multiple user profiles can be stored in a Azure SQL Database and accessed by using the Universal Profile Providers. Everything image-centric is stored in Azure Storage, once it has been processed via the Cloud Service [4].

We created a storage, web site, cloud service and 1 GB SQL database. Another storage was created when the project was published. Also, the worker role was added in the cloud service. Each storage contains three services: Blobs, Queues and Tables.

The client uses Apache JMeter to test the performance by varying the load (the number of requests) and using different number of instances with various number of resources. To minimize the network latency, both the client and the cloud are placed in the same data center (the West Europe's center).

In order to perform the load testing we add a Thread Group element to configure the number of clients that will send HTTP requests. Each user sends one HTTP request. HTTP requests of all clients are processed in parallel. The Rump-up period value is set to 0 seconds in order to immediately start all clients' requests.

The experiments consist of accessing a web page which displays the albums created by other users. The web page retrieval includes reading information from the SQL database that is common for all application instances, and can be assumed as an IO intensive operation, like most of 3-tier web applications.

## 3.3 Test Cases

Each test case is denoted with $v$ x $c$, expressing the corresponding number of VMs and CPU cores per VM in each configuration.

We tested all possible configurations, where the total number of VMs is less or equal to 10, and the number of CPUs per VM is at most 4, explicitly expressed with $1 \leq v \leq 10$ and $1 \leq c \leq 4$.

In addition we have also tested several configurations that are beyond this threshold, required to realize necessary comparisons for the scaling experiments. The list of all test cases covers at least the following configurations: 1x1, 1x2, 1x4, 2x1, 2x2, 2x4, 3x1, 3x2, 3x4, 4x1, 4x2, 4x4, 5x1, 5x2, 5x4, 6x1, 6x2, 6x4, 8x1, 8x2, 8x4, 10x1, 10x2, 10x4.

Each test case is executed at least 5 times with different number of HTTP requests $N = 1$, 50, 100, 150, 200, 250, 300, 350, 400, 450, 500, 550, 600, 650, 700, 750, 800, 850, 900, 950 and 1000. JMeter deals with the server load until 1000 requests are complete, since it reports an error message for increased load.

For each test case, we measure the average response time when all requests will be completed.

Our goal is to obtain reliable tests in each cloud environment by changing the number of application instances and CPU cores. The Azure load balancer decides how to serve the concurrent HTTP requests.

Each experiment realizes two different cloud configurations denoted as $L$ and $S$ testing various total numbers of CPU cores. For example, a part of the first experiment assumes that the application will serve the HTTP requests with such a capacity that will require a configuration with a total of 16 CPU cores. Fig. 1 (left) depicts the test case defined as large configuration, denoted by $L$, where 4 instances of the SaaS application are hosted on 4 VMs, each allocated with 4 CPU cores. Fig. 1 (right) presents the test case defined as small configuration, which is denoted by $S$. It is a cloud environment where 8 instances of the SaaS application are hosted on 8 VMs, each allocated with 2 CPU cores.

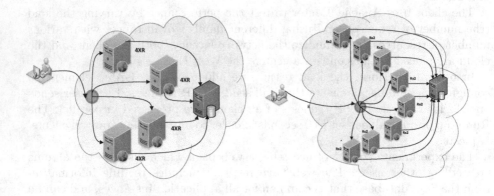

**Fig. 1.** 4x4 (left) and 8x2 (right) environments

Now, the dilemma a customer might have, is to decide what is better, a configuration in Fig. 1 (left) or in Fig. 1 (right). Our hypothesis assumes that the configuration with a bigger number of small VMs (Fig. 1 right) performs better for the same price.

## 3.4   Test Data

The performance of the SaaS application is calculated by measuring the average response time $T$ for experiments. Denote by $T_{vc}$ the measured average response time in each test case using $v$ instances of the SaaS application hosted on $v$ VMs, each with $c$ CPU cores.

In the evaluation of results we usually compare two configurations denoted by indexes $L$ and $S$. We calculate the *Relative Speedup* as ratio of average times measured for $S$ configuration over $L$ by relation $R = R(v_S, c_S, v_L, c_L) = T_{v_S c_S}/T_{v_L c_L}$.

Value $R > 1$ will mean that response times of the $L$ configuration are smaller than those of the $S$ configuration, and we can conclude that the $L$ configuration is $R$ times better than $S$.

In Experiment 1 we realize test cases where (1) is satisfied, keeping the total number of CPUs $n$ in analyzed pair of configurations the same. Our first hypothesis in this case assumes that we will obtain $R < 1$.

Let us compare two experiments and find the scaling factor. Denote the number of required CPUs in the configuration by $n_L$ and $n_S$ corresponding to the configurations $L$ and $S$. In order to analyze the scaling relation between these two experiments there should be a positive integer number $m$, such that $n_L = m \cdot n_S$ is valid. In this case, $m$ is the scaling factor.

Scaling speedup $S$ is the ratio of obtained relative speedup $R$ and scaling factor $m$ when two configurations $L$ and $S$ are compared, that is, $S = R/m$. It means that the scaling speedup $S$ will give information how much the $L$ configuration performs better than $S$ with factor compared to the scaling factor.

Suppose that the $L$ configuration uses $m$ times more resources than the $S$ configuration. One will expect that the performance will also scale with at most the same factor. A value of scaling speedup $S > 1$ will mean that the performance is at least $m$ times better, meaning that it is worth enough to scale. Hypothesis 2 assumes that $S < 1$.

## 4    Analysis of Experimental Results

In this section, we present and analyze the experimental results of the three conducted SaaS performance experiments. We have measured response times for each configuration and in the next sections we will elaborate the relative speedup and scaling speedup, along with explanation of obtained results.

### 4.1    Experiment 1: Same Total Number of CPUs $n$

For this experiment we define $L$ configuration to be the large configuration which uses less number of large VMs, each with large number of CPUs. The $S$ configuration will be the small configuration using more small VMs, each with small number of CPUs. We assume that (1) is valid, keeping the same total number of CPUs. The formal definition of criterion for this experiment is given in (4).

$$n = v_L \cdot c_L = v_S \cdot c_S, \quad v_L < v_S, \quad \text{and} \quad c_L > c_S \tag{4}$$

Table 1 presents the test cases and their identification as large and small configurations. For example, the first comparison assumes using a total of 4 CPUs, and the $L$ configuration is a single VM environment with 1 application instance hosted on a VM with 4 CPU cores, while the $S$ configuration is a multi VM environment with 4 application instances hosted on 4 small VMs, each with 1 CPU.

We have provided analysis on the following relative speedups $R_4 = R(4,1,1,4)$; $R_6 = R(6,1,3,2)$; $R_8 = R(8,1,2,4)$; $R_{10} = R(10,1,5,2)$; $R_{12} = R(6,2,3,4)$;

**Table 1.** $L$ and $S$ configurations for Experiment 1

| CPUs $n$ | 4 | 6 | 8 | 10 | 12 | 16 | 20 |
|---|---|---|---|---|---|---|---|
| $L$ configuration $v_L$ x $c_L$ | 1x4 | 3x2 | 2x4 | 5x2 | 3x4 | 4x4 | 5x4 |
| $S$ configuration $v_S$ x $c_S$ | 4x1 | 6x1 | 8x1 | 10x1 | 6x2 | 8x2 | 10x2 |

$R_{16} = R(8, 2, 4, 4)$; and $R_{20} = R(10, 2, 5, 4)$, which correspond to pairs of $L$ and $S$ configurations in Table 1. The index denotes the total number of used CPU cores for the analyzed configurations.

The performance of the SaaS, measured for a total of 4 CPU cores is presented in Fig. 2 (left). The response time is presented on the Y axis, measured in seconds. The input parameter, which is the number of requests sent to the server is presented on the X axis. Blue bars present the results for large configurations, and red for small configurations. For example, in $L$ configuration, the time to complete 1000 requests is 8.916 seconds, while in the $S$ configuration is 10.401 seconds. We conclude that for all tests, $L$ configuration performs better. The differences rise when the number of concurrent HTTP requests rises.

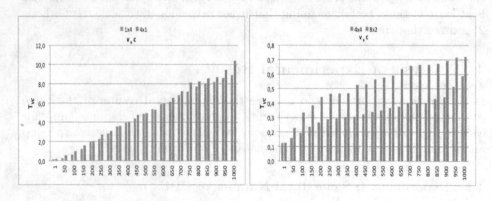

**Fig. 2.** Response time for test cases with a total of 4 (left) and 16 CPU cores (right)

The behavior of the response time is similar for all the cases. For example, the results for test cases, which use a total of 16 CPU cores, are presented in Fig. 2 (right). In all tests the $L$ configurations perform better, and in this case the differences are bigger than in previous example.

Fig. 3 depicts the relative speedup for all experiments. We can clearly observe that the relative speedup is always greater then 1, for all experiments, meaning that the large $L$ configurations perform better than the small $S$ configurations. Therefore, our first hypothesis, does not hold, and renting less more powerful VMs is better than renting more smaller VMs in Azure.

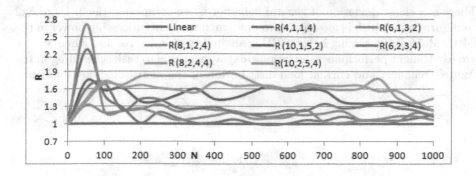

**Fig. 3.** Relative Speedup between large and small configurations for all experiments

## 4.2 Experiment 2: Scaling the Number of CPU Cores $c$

In the previous section we concluded that $L$ configurations perform better than their corresponding $S$ configurations, expressing the cases with same number of CPU cores, as defined by (1). In this section we will analyze what happens when the number of CPUs is increased by a scaling factor $m > 1$ keeping the number of VMs the same, as expressed in (2).

**Scaling $c$ from 1 to 2.** The first part of the experiment consist of analysis of the case when the number of VMs $v$ is constant and the number of CPU cores $c$ is doubled from 1 CPU core to 2 CPU cores, or choosing the scaling factor to be $m = 2$. We assume that each application instance runs on a separate VM and the customer decided to use more powerful VMs upgrading the number of CPUs in each VM.

Table 2 presents the $L$ and $S$ configurations. For example, the first test case assumes using $S$ configuration with a total of 3 CPU cores, and the $L$ configuration with 6 CPU cores. Both configurations are multi VM environment with 3 application instances hosted on 3 VMs, where the $S$ configuration specifies a VM with 1 CPU and the $L$ configuration a VM with 2 CPUs.

**Table 2.** $L$ and $S$ configurations for Experiment 2a: CPU cores doubled from 1 to 2

| CPU increase $n_S \to n_L$ | $3 \to 6$ | $4 \to 8$ | $5 \to 10$ | $6 \to 12$ | $8 \to 16$ | $10 \to 20$ |
|---|---|---|---|---|---|---|
| $S$ configuration $v_S$ x $c_S$ | 3x1 | 4x1 | 5x1 | 6x1 | 8x1 | 10x1 |
| $L$ configuration $v_L$ x $c_L$ | 3x2 | 4x2 | 5x2 | 6x2 | 8x2 | 10x2 |

Fig. 4 (left) presents the scaling speedup for all test cases defined in Table 2 comparing configurations when the number of CPU cores is doubled from 1 to 2 CPU cores per each VM. The results show that it is worthwhile to upgrade from 1 to 2 CPUs and the performances will mostly scale more than the scaling factor.

There is a slight deviation of general behavior when comparing the 3x1 and 3x2 configurations, which is mostly due to unaligned usage of processing power in the CPU. Most of the scaling in the CPU is aligned to 2 or 4 cores and when 3 cores are used, slight performance deviations may appear due to task scheduling in the Azure's balancer and current load distribution of the distributed environment.

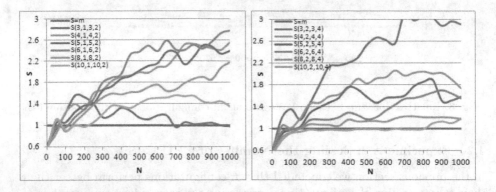

**Fig. 4.** Scaling speedup when $c$ is doubled from 1 to 2 (left) and 2 to 4 (right)

The average behavior shows that an upgrade of a VM from 1 to 2 CPUs makes an impact of approximately 94,5% more than the scaling factor (in this case the scaling factor is 2, the average speedup 3.89 and the average scaling speedup 1.945). We can notice that higher speedup is reached by increasing the workload, and the obtained impact stabilizes for $N > 200$.

**Scaling $c$ from 2 to 4.** The second part of this experiment analyzes the case when the number of CPU cores is doubled from 2 to 4 per VM. Test cases for $L$ and $S$ configurations are presented in Table 3. For example, the first test case defines the $S$ configuration 3x2 with a total of 6 CPU cores, and the $L$ configuration 3x4 with 12 CPU cores, doubling $c$ from 2 to 4.

**Table 3.** $L$ and $S$ configurations for Experiment 2b: CPU cores doubled from 2 to 4

| CPU increase $n_S \rightarrow n_L$ | $6 \rightarrow 12$ | $8 \rightarrow 16$ | $10 \rightarrow 20$ | $12 \rightarrow 24$ | $16 \rightarrow 32$ | $20 \rightarrow 40$ |
|---|---|---|---|---|---|---|
| $S$ configuration $v_S$ x $c_S$ | 3x2 | 4x3 | 5x2 | 6x2 | 8x2 | 10x2 |
| $L$ configuration $v_L$ x $c_L$ | 3x4 | 4x4 | 5x4 | 6x4 | 8x4 | 10x4 |

The results are presented in Fig. 4 (right). Once again we observe it is worth to upgrade the VMs from 2 to 4 CPUs. The impact is similar to the previous case with upgrade from 1 to 2 CPUs. An average of 69,2% better performance than the scaling factor is obtained.

The results show that the same trend is also observed for these cases. The workload has impact on the overall performance. Note that the impact factor is smaller for configuration using greater number of CPUs, and it can also be observed for increased workload. This happens due to the processing power of measured configurations. For example, the 10x2 configuration is quite powerful in handling the workload, and the 10x4 configuration achieves a scaling speedup equal to the scaling factor 2 for almost complete domain of testing when $N \leq 800$. The analyzed trend starts to rise for heavier workload when $N > 800$. In all other cases the achieved speedup is much higher than the scaling factor of 2.

We have not analyzed the cases when the number of CPU cores is upgraded from 1 to 4, since the value can be easily calculated as a multiple of the two previous values. The average impact in this case is even higher than 2.5 times more than the scaling factor (in this case 4).

The conclusion from the experiments 2a and 2b is that the scaling with upgrade of the CPU cores in a VM will impact more than the scaling factor, contrary to our hypothesis 2. Next we analyze the scaling speedup by scaling $v$.

### 4.3   Experiment 3: Scaling the Number of VMs $v$

The case when (2) is satisfied for scaling with upgrade of the number of CPUs per VM was discussed in the previous section. Here we analyze the scaling when the number of CPUs per VM $c$ is fixed and scaling is obtained by increasing the number of VMs, as specified in (3). We conduct three parts of the experiments, each part defined with different number of CPUs.

**Scaling $v$ with 1 CPU per VM.** The first part of the experiment consists of analysis of the case when doubling $v$, with 1 CPU per VM. We assume that each application instance runs on a separate VM and the customer decided to use more VMs instead of upgrading the number of CPUs in each VM.

Table 4 presents the $L$ and $S$ configurations for the experiment. For example, the first test case assumes using $S$ configuration with a total of 3 CPU cores, and the $L$ configuration with 6 CPU cores. Both configurations are multi VM environment where a VM is defined with 1 CPU, and the $S$ configuration with 3 application instances hosted on 3 VMs, and the $L$ configuration with 6 VMs.

**Table 4.** $L$ and $S$ configurations for Experiment 3a: $v$ is doubled, $c = 1$

| CPU increase ($n_S \rightarrow n_L$) | $S$ configuration ($v_S$ x $c_S$) | $L$ configuration ($v_L$ x $c_L$) |
|---|---|---|
| $3 \rightarrow 6$ | 3x1 | 6x1 |
| $4 \rightarrow 8$ | 4x1 | 8x1 |
| $5 \rightarrow 10$ | 5x1 | 10x1 |

Fig. 5 (left) presents the scaling factors comparing the configuration when the number of VMs is doubled and each VM has 1 CPU core. A deviation from the trend exposed in all analyzed cases is observed for the configuration 3x1. We have previously discussed that this deviation happens due to alignment of processing power in real CPUs, since most of the configurations demand 2 or 4

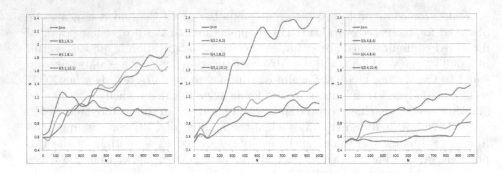

**Fig. 5.** Scaling speedup with doubled number of VMs $v$, each with 1 (left), 2 (middle), and 4 CPU cores (right)

CPUs and it depends on current cloud workload. In all other cases the upgrade by doubling the number of VMs makes an impact with average value of 32,2% more than the scaling factor, so it is worth to upgrade. Even in the case where a deviation is observed we measure the achieved speedup to be equal to the scaling factor as average behavior.

**Scaling $v$ with 2 CPUs per VM.** The second part of the experiment analyses the case with $c = 2$ CPUs per VM and the upgrade is done by doubling the number of VMs $v$. The test cases are presented in Table 5.

**Table 5.** $L$ and $S$ configurations for Experiment 3b: $v$ is doubled, $c = 2$

| CPU increase ($n_S \rightarrow n_L$) | $S$ configuration ($v_S$ x $c_S$) | $L$ configuration ($v_L$ x $c_L$) |
|---|---|---|
| $6 \rightarrow 12$ | 3x2 | 6x2 |
| $8 \rightarrow 16$ | 4x2 | 8x2 |
| $10 \rightarrow 20$ | 5x2 | 10x2 |

The results of the second part of Experiment 3 are shown in Fig. 5 (middle). Also in this case the upgrade makes a good impact better than the scaling factor, which is slightly better than in the previous case with the configuration using VMs with 1 CPU. The rising trend depends on the workload. Higher number of concurrent messages will show better performance of $L$ configurations, rather than the $S$ configurations. We can also observe that, for example, the configuration 5x2 can handle a sufficient number of concurrent messages, and the 10x2 configuration can achieve speedup more than the scaling factor only for heavier workload, such as for $N > 700$.

**Scaling $v$ with 4 CPUs per VM.** The last part of Experiment 3 analyses powerful VMs with $c = 4$ CPUs each and the scaling is done by doubling the number of VMs $v$. Table 6 presents the $L$ and $S$ configurations.

**Table 6.** $L$ and $S$ configurations for Experiment 3c: $v$ is doubled, $c = 4$

| CPU increase $(n_S \rightarrow n_L)$ | $S$ configuration $(v_S \times c_S)$ | $L$ configuration $(v_L \times c_L)$ |
|---|---|---|
| $12 \rightarrow 16$ | 3x4 | 6x4 |
| $16 \rightarrow 32$ | 4x4 | 8x4 |
| $20 \rightarrow 40$ | 5x4 | 10x4 |

Fig. 5 (right) presents the scaling speedup comparing the configurations of Table 6. In this case the impact is lower than in the previous cases, which is due to the reasons explained previously that the configurations are capable to handle large number of concurrent messages. The speedup is obvious (more than 0.5 means it is positive but still under the value of scaling factor 2). Desired speedup greater than the scaling factor happens for heavier workload, when, for example, the configuration 10x4 can have greater impact over 5x4.

As a conclusion of analysis in Experiment 3, we realize that the second hypothesis is also disproved as in Experiment 2. We obtain better performance when scaling the number of VMs keeping fixed number of CPU cores.

## 5  Discussion

Experiment 1 showed that the first hypothesis is not valid and Azure performs better with large sized VMs with 4 CPUs. Both experiments 2 and 3 covered all cases to show that the second hypothesis is also disproved, meaning that by scaling the resources, a customer gets more performance than the scaling factor.

We can also conclude from experiments 2 and 3 that it is better to scale in such a way to use more powerful VMs instead of using more VMs, a fact that also is shown by the Experiment 1 for comparing different configurations with same number of CPUs. So we have concluded that the linear cost model is not unfair to the customer, once the customer needs more power, the solution by renting more resources achieves performance higher than the scaling factor.

The results of Experiment 1 oppose the findings [8] where the test cases are performed for compute intensive and memory demanding web services instead of a transactional web service. Gusev et al. [9] also achieved opposite results for transactional web services without using worker role on Azure. The authors believe that a great role in this behavior is mostly due to the Azure's balancer and organization of the system using a predefined database. The results show that the balancer for transactional web services using databases should be improved because internal VM web server's task scheduler handles the load much better.

We have observed two side effects. The first one addresses the alignment to the number of CPU cores. This is highly dependent on the CSP availability and the current cloud workload. The alignment of needs is mostly to the 2 or 4 CPU cores per active CPU, meaning that the requests for 3 CPU cores are rare. In this case depending on the availability, the CSP may schedule 3 CPU cores in one CPU or several CPUs, which can change the obtained performance. We have provided a lot of experiments and the average performance (with very small discrepancy among each repeated test case) is presented in this paper. We have concluded that with this configuration there is a deviation in trend behavior which was observed for other test cases.

The second side effect was the capability to handle the number of requests. More powerful configurations (with higher number of CPUs) were capable to provide a good throughput and processing speed. Scaling the resources for these cases will produce speedup equal to the scaling factor. A speedup bigger than the scaling factor (superlinear) is observed for heavier demands and number of requests. A superlinear speedup is a well known phenomenon achieved in distributed environment for cache intensive algorithms [6], where more CPU cache memory is used in parallel implementations with low inter-CPU communication, despite the Azure's virtualization layer [5]. Obviously, the superlinearity in this distributed environment is totally different. We believe that increasing the incoming requests over-utilizes smaller VMs faster than a greater VM.

## 6   Conclusion and Future Work

In this paper we have conducted three experiments to conclude about the performance trade-off for transactional web services on Azure cloud.

We concluded that when a customer wants to scale the existing configuration it is better to choose a configuration which is using less number of larger instances, i.e. to choose VMs with 4 CPUs if possible. Also we have concluded that by scaling the resources, a customer usually gets more performance than the expected scaling factor, i.e. if there is an upgrade which doubles the number of CPU cores in the configuration, then the achieved performance is more than double. In this case, a customer should choose configurations that use powerful instances with 4 CPU cores.

These results will solve the customer's dilemma to choose the most optimal configuration that performs the best. For example, if the customer is using a 4x4 configuration with total of 16 CPUs and would like to upgrade to total of 20 CPU core, should chose 5x4 having advantage over the 10x2 or 20x1 configurations.

Although most offers follow the linear pricing model we have observed that the number of CPU cores is not the only parameter that a customer should analyze. A customer can choose among great variety of available RAM and storage, or throughput etc. Although there are a lot of available online calculators for this purpose, we plan to make deeper analysis of impact of these factors on the overall performance.

We will continue to realize the same and similar experiments on different environments and clouds.

## References

1. Agarwal, D., Prasad, S.K.: AzureBench: Benchmarking the storage services of the Azure cloud platform. In: Proc. of the IEEE 26th Int. Parallel and Distributed Processing Symp. Workshops & PhD Forum, IPDPSW 2012, pp. 1048–1057 (2012)

2. Brebner, P., Liu, A.: Performance and cost assessment of cloud services. In: Maximilien, E.M., Rossi, G., Yuan, S.-T., Ludwig, H., Fantinato, M. (eds.) ICSOC 2010. LNCS, vol. 6568, pp. 39–50. Springer, Heidelberg (2011)
3. Gao, J., Pattabhiraman, P., Bai, X., Tsai, W.: SaaS performance and scalability evaluation in clouds. In: 2011 IEEE 6th International Symposium on Service Oriented System Engineering (SOSE), pp. 61–71 (2011)
4. Gaster, B.: PhluffyFotos on Windows Azure (October 2012), http://www.bradygaster.com/post/phluffyfotos-on-windows-azure
5. Gusev, M., Ristov, S.: Superlinear speedup in Windows Azure cloud. In: 2012 IEEE 1st International Conference on Cloud Networking (CLOUDNET), Paris, France, pp. 173–175 (2012)
6. Gusev, M., Ristov, S.: A superlinear speedup region for matrix multiplication. Concurrency and Computation: Practice and Experience 26(11), 1847–1868 (2013), http://dx.doi.org/10.1002/cpe.3102
7. Gusev, M., Ristov, S.: Resource scaling performance for cache intensive algorithms in Windows Azure. In: Zavoral, F., Jung, J.J., Badica, C. (eds.) IDC 2013. SCI, vol. 511, pp. 77–86. Springer, Heidelberg (2013)
8. Gusev, M., Ristov, S., Velkoski, G., Simjanoska, M.: Optimal resource allocation to host web services in cloud. In: Proceedings of the 2013 IEEE 6th International Conference on Cloud Computing, CLOUD 2013, CA, USA, pp. 948–949 (June 2013)
9. Gusev, P., Ristov, S., Gusev, M.: Performance analysis of SaaS ticket management systems. In: 2014 Federated Conference on Computer Science and Information Systems (FedCSIS) (SCoDiS-LaSCoG'14 Workshop) (in press, September 2014)
10. Gustafson, J.L.: Reevaluating Amdahl's law. Communication of ACM 31(5), 532–533 (1988)
11. Hill, Z., Li, J., Mao, M., Ruiz-Alvarez, A., Humphrey, M.: Early observations on the performance of Windows Azure. In: Proc. of the 19th ACM International Symposium on High Performance Distributed Computing, HPDC 2010, pp. 367–376 (2010)
12. Kondo, D., Javadi, B., Malecot, P., Cappello, F., Anderson, D.: Cost-benefit analysis of cloud computing versus desktop grids. In: IEEE International Symposium on Parallel Distributed Processing, IPDPS 2009, pp. 1–12 (2009)
13. Lu, W., Jackson, J., Ekanayake, J., Barga, R.S., Araujo, N.: Performing large science experiments on Azure: Pitfalls and solutions. In: CloudCom 2010, pp. 209–217 (2010)
14. Mao, M., Li, J., Humphrey, M.: Cloud auto-scaling with deadline and budget constraints. In: 2010 11th IEEE/ACM International Conference on Grid Computing (GRID), pp. 41–48 (2010)
15. Microsoft: Picture gallery service (April 2008), http://phluffyfotos.codeplex.com/
16. Ostermann, S., Iosup, A., Yigitbasi, N., Prodan, R., Fahringer, T., Epema, D.: A performance analysis of EC2 cloud computing services for scientific computing. In: Avresky, D.R., Diaz, M., Bode, A., Ciciani, B., Dekel, E. (eds.) Cloud Computing. LNICST, vol. 34, pp. 115–131. Springer, Heidelberg (2010)
17. Tudoran, R., Costan, A., Antoniu, G., Bougé, L.: A performance evaluation of Azure and Nimbus clouds for scientific applications. In: Proc. of the 2nd Int. Workshop on Cloud Computing Platforms, CloudCP 2012, pp. 4:1–4:6. ACM (2012)
18. Zhang, L., Ma, X., Lu, J., Xie, T., Tillmann, N., de Halleux, P.: Environmental modeling for automated cloud application testing. IEEE Software 29(2), 30–35 (2012)

# Cloud Standby: Disaster Recovery of Distributed Systems in the Cloud

Alexander Lenk[1] and Stefan Tai[2]

[1] FZI Forschungszentrum Informatik, Berlin, Germany
lenk@fzi.de
[2] Technische Universität Berlin, Berlin, Germany
tai@tu-berlin.de

**Abstract.** Disaster recovery planning and securing business processes against outtakes have been essential parts of running a company for decades. As IT systems became more important, and especially since more and more revenue is generated over the Internet, securing the IT systems that support the business processes against outages is essential. Using fully operational standby sites with periodically updated standby systems is a well-known approach to prepare against disasters. Setting up and maintaining a second datacenter is, however, expensive. In this work, we present Cloud Standby, a warm standby approach for setting up and updating a standby system in the Cloud. We describe the architecture of Cloud Standby and its methods for deploying and updating the standby system. We show that by using Cloud Standby the recovery time and long-term costs of disaster recovery can significantly be reduced.

**Keywords:** Cloud Standby, IaaS, Warm Standby, Disaster Recovery, Distributed Systems.

## 1    Introduction

Since the industrial revolution, protecting critical business processes against potential risks like earthquakes, fire, power outages, theft, illness, floods, and similar events has been a major concern of companies. Therefore, disaster recovery planning and preparing contingency plans for disaster preparedness have always been an integral part of running a company. To be prepared for these worst-case scenarios, disaster recovery plans are made in order to resume operations as soon as possible. These measures to keep up critical business processes in case of an emergency are often referred to as Business Continuity Management (BCM) [5] or, in the context of IT, as IT Service Continuity Management (ITSCM) [13]. The effectiveness of BCM can be controlled via the key figures Recovery Time Objective (RTO) and Recovery Point Objective (RPO) [5]. RPO refers to the maximum acceptable time between two backups whereas RTO defines the maximum reasonable time a business process may be interrupted (see also Fig. 1).

M. Villari et al. (Eds.): ESOCC 2014, LNCS 8745, pp. 32–46, 2014.
© IFIP International Federation for Information Processing 2014

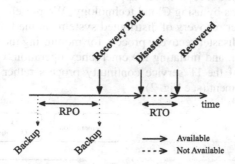

**Fig. 1.** Recovery Point Objective and Recovery Time Objective in the context of IT

To reduce the downtime of a system after an outage, it is common to replicate the whole system to another standby site [18] or even better, to another provider [14]. This is an established but very expensive approach that comes in different types: *hot standby* is a failover mechanism where all relevant data is consistently and continuously mirrored to a second data center with equivalent infrastructure almost in real-time. The main disadvantage of this procedure is the high costs. In addition to the operating costs of both systems, there are also the costs for mirroring. In contrast, there is *Cold standby*. Cold standby sites are updated only at times of low load such as nights or weekends and no standby systems are prepared. Therefore, in a case of a disaster, the standby system has to be ordered, deployed and equipped with the last backup. Therefore an RPO of days or weeks and an RTO of days or months are common. The third replication mechanism, warm standby, is positioned between cold and hot standby. A warm standby system has, similar to a hot standby system, an identical copy of the primary systems infrastructure but does not mirror data immediately. Instead, warm standby systems replicate the data periodically in short timeframes. Thus the primary and the secondary systems can have small amounts of different data that needs to be recreated in case of an outage. In general, warm standby systems have an RTO and RPO between minutes and hours.

To reduce operating costs of infrequently used IT components like warm standby systems, it is possible to use Cloud Computing [4, 16]. Cloud Computing provides the user with scalable, configurable IT resources over the internet with a pay-per-use pricing model [8, 12]. This means that the user only pays for resources he actually needs and unused resources can be used by other users. In the case of warm standby systems this pricing model makes Cloud Computing an ideal platform for hosting replication sites at reasonable prices with high availability [20]. Using a Cloud Computing datacenter as a standby site is especially interesting for small and medium companies that have all their servers in a single datacenter and do not have the possibility to run their own colocation center. Many of these small and medium-sized companies, however, should prepare for disaster with a standby system at another location or provider: according to recent studies [17], downtime costs in small and medium companies sum up to $12,500-23,000 per day and even data centers that are considered as highly available have reported downtimes [11].

In this work we introduce a novel approach for securing a distributed system against provider outages by using Cloud technology. We present Cloud Standby as a new method for disaster recovery of distributed systems in the Cloud. This method is composed based on a disaster recovery process for monitoring the standby site, updating the standby system, and initiating the emergency operation. Our focus thereby is on technical aspects of the IT service continuity process rather than on regulatory aspects or risk management (see Fig. 2).

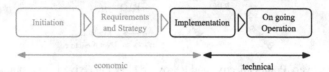

**Fig. 2.** IT service continuity process (cf. [13]) – the focus of this paper lies on the parts marked in black

The subsequent chapters of this paper are structured as followed: In Chapter 2, we refer to existing works. Chapter 3 introduces the novel Cloud Standby approach. We present the results of an evaluation with the company "barcoo" in Chapter 4. The final Chapter 5 concludes the findings and provides an outlook for our future work.

## 2      Related Work

In the following we describe state of the art warm and hot standby approaches that are using Cloud Computing as standby sites. We exclude cold standby in this discussion, because in cold standby no standby system is prepared.

### 2.1      Warm Standby in the Cloud

Wood et al. [20] analyze the cost reduction by having a Cloud provider as standby site. In contrast to our work, this paper focuses on the economic part and does not present a concrete warm standby system. The authors, however, identify that the pay-as-you-go Cloud computing billing is especially effective in the warm standby. Pokharel et al. [14] reach the same conclusion. They also recommend that the primary system and replication system should be deployed geographically apart. This ensures that if a whole datacenter goes down, one of the systems will still be available and the business can continue with only a short interruption. In their approach they describe an algorithm that allows identifying outages and initiating the emergency operation.

Klems et al. [6] present a concrete warm standby approach that is using Cloud technology to run the replication system. Also, Klems at al. point out that using Cloud Computing in the context of warm standby systems can lead to a reduction of costs and deployment time. In their work they focus on single servers rather than on distributed systems and present a mechanism for backing up the primary virtual machine. Thus, for every primary virtual machine they provision two virtual machines in the Cloud, leading to an unnecessary overhead if there are already data backup mechanisms in place.

## 2.2    Hot Standby in the Cloud

The hot standby approach PipeCloud [21] replicates virtual machines to the cloud by copying all writing operations to the virtual hard disk. To get access to these writing operations, this approach needs access to the hypervisor. All the writing operations are asynchronously sent to the cloud and stored in a queue where they are applied to the virtual images stored there. This allows this approach to be used if the RPO is very small; however, it also introduces the problem that the primary system cannot run on a public cloud since there is no access to the hypervisor and the disk-writing operations themselves in the public cloud. It also introduces a huge traffic overhead as every single writing operation has to be packaged and sent to the Cloud over the Internet. Similar approaches are called Remus[3]  and SecondSite [15]. Both of them rely on access to the hypervisor for copying the writing operations and sending them over the network. Remus, though, is not focusing on the Cloud but rather on replicating the virtual machine to another hypervisor within the same datacenter, and with the additional SecondSite it is possible to copy one or more virtual machines to the hypervisor of another datacenter. None of the presented approaches, however, are applicable in the public Cloud due to their requirement to have low level access to the hypervisor.

In conclusion it can be noted that in the related work there are approaches for warm and hot standby but none of them can be used to easily setup and update a standby system of a distributed system in the public Cloud.

## 3    Cloud Standby

In this section we describe Cloud Standby, a novel approach for replicating a distributed system in the Cloud to another Cloud. In the following subsections we describe the components and possible states of the Cloud Standby system, and the process for replicating the primary system to the Cloud.

### 3.1    Components and Methods

The Cloud Standby method consists of several different components and methods. An overview of the Cloud Standby method can be found in Fig. 3.

- **Primary System (PS)** – The primary system is the distributed system that needs to be secured by the warm standby approach. This system, with its given architecture and features like failure tolerance is secured as a whole, so that the same architecture and features are still present after the disaster. The primary system is backed up repeatedly using a state of the art data backup method as to meet a desired RPO.
- **Standby System (RS)** – The standby system is a copy of the primary system, which takes over the operation in the case of an emergency. The Cloud Standby approach aims to deploy this system and keep it up to date. In order to enable the standby system to take over the operation, the requests of the users of the distributed system must also reach the emergency system. There are various methods for

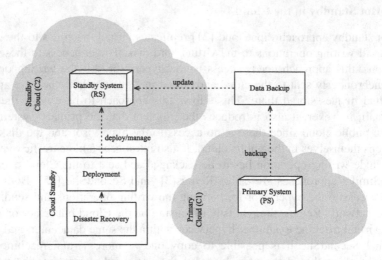

**Fig. 3.** Overview of the combination of methods

handing over external requests to the standby system, for example the use of virtual IP addresses or dynamic DNS entries. These methods are not part of this work, but established methods of the state of the art like the work of Ayari et al. [2] can be used in this case.

- **Cloud (C1 and C2)** – The exact location of resources like virtual machines or storages are often veiled in Cloud Computing. In this paper, "Cloud" describes the location of a Cloud data center and refers to a logical unit where computing power and memory is supplied. Within this Cloud, transaction costs like traffic are not charged. The Cloud is a runtime environment for virtual machines and provides storage. These Cloud resources can be maintained with the Cloud Management Interface. Typical management tasks are creating, reading, updating and deleting resources.

In the following we describe the methods that are applied to the components. The tools and implementations supporting these methods can be located anywhere. We, however, recommend having them hosted in the Standby Cloud for availability and cost reasons: If the primary cloud becomes unavailable the Standby System can still be started with the last version of the backup. Also many Cloud providers do not charge data transfer within a single datacenter, so the data transfer during the update cycle of the standby system is free of charge.

- **Data Backup** – The data backup method includes a central database that contains all backups for the distributed system and is filled by backup software of the respective virtual machines of the primary system. The backup interval has to match the RPO. The RPO applies to the superordinate business process, hence to every system and virtual machine involved in the process. We assume that the current backup status is adequate for the RPO. Therefore, the backup ensures that the replicated data is consistent. Only after every virtual server has saved its data, is the backup completed and unlocked for restoration. The backup serves as a consistent central data source that can be accessed from the primary as well as from the standby system. By using the backup as a common component, existing solutions are integrated and it is ensured that the standby system can be updated to a condition that matches the RPO.

- **Deployment** – Besides the Disaster Recovery Method, the Deployment Method is a key part of Cloud Standby. It coordinates and maintains the infrastructure like virtual servers and network configurations that are involved in the distributed system[1]. The Deployment Method has all information about the distributed system like IP addresses or access data and serves as the information source for other components. As a deployment method, a state of the art Cloud provider-independent deployment method like TOSCA [23] can be used. We, however, recommend to use our tailored Cloud Standby deployment model [7, 9] that has native support of Cloud federation and data backup and is thereby ready for the usage with the disaster recovery method presented in this paper. Our deployment method is available online[2].

- **Disaster Recovery** – Tasks of the Disaster Recovery Method are updating the standby system, and initiating and terminating the emergency mode. Therefore, it uses the deployment method for every task that effects the administration of single entities. The disaster recovery method consists of the emergency backup process and the update protocol.

In the following, we further describe the disaster recovery method by detailing valid state transitions and the disaster recovery process. We design our system as a warm standby approach. That is, the standby systems gets updated periodically with the data backup available within the data backup store as part of the data backup method. So, setting up the data backup correctly is a preliminary requirement for our method. Fig. 4 gives an overview of the backup and update process and illustrates the independence of the two. While the backup process depends on the RPO, the update of the standby system happens afterwards and is defined as $t_{updateInt}$.

In order to do the periodic updates necessary in a warm standby approach we start the system with the deployment method, restore the last backup, and save the updated images. Therefore, in the next run, only the changed data has to be updated on the image which reduces the time until the instance is fully available. In the following section we describe the states of a Cloud Standby system during the disaster recovery process.

---

[1]  Cloud infrastructure specific features like availability zones, firewall configurations, or external storage are specified with the deployment method and are not in the focus of this paper.

[2]  https://github.com/alexlenk/CloudStandby/
tree/master/org/cloudstandby/model

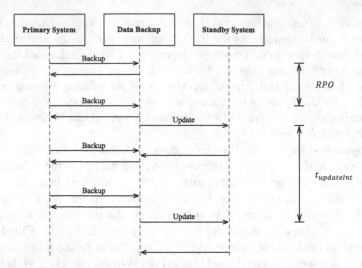

**Fig. 4.** Exemplary representation to show the independence of the update and backup interval as a UML sequence diagram

## 3.2    Disaster Recovery States

Cloud Standby is based on a warm standby approach where a Primary System (PS) running in the Primary Cloud (C1) is periodically synchronized as a Standby or Replica System (RS) to Standby Cloud (C2). The states and state transitions of our Cloud Standby approach are depicted in Fig. 5.

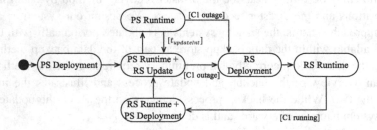

**Fig. 5.** UML state chart of a Cloud Standby system (c.f. [9, 10])

- **PS Deployment** – The PS is deployed on C1 at first. The deployment time depends highly on the structure of the deployment. For each use case, the deployment time can be determined by experimentation. It depends, however, on the amount of data that has to be copied to the virtual machine. If the deployment contains a stateful server, causing a lot of data changes over time, the deployment time can rise quickly (see section 4.2). After the initial deployment a RS update is performed to ensure the RS can take over immediately in the case of a disaster.

- **PS Runtime + RS Update** – Periodically (after $t_{updateInt}$) the RS is updated. This ensures that the deployment time of the RS is reduced when an actual disaster occurs.
- **PS Runtime** – During PS runtime, the RS is turned off and generates no costs. The PS data are, however, backed up using standard backup methods. This ensures the RPO can be met in case of a disaster (see Fig. 4).
- **RS Deployment** – When C1 fails the RS is started and takes over the service. The time for the deployment is $t_{replDepl}$. The deployment time varies with the amount of data that needs to be installed or stored during the deployment process. This means that $t_{replDepl}$ decreases with a decreasing $t_{updateInt}$. The correlation between $t_{replDepl}$ and $t_{updateInt}$ can be determined through experiments or monitoring over time.
- **RS Runtime** – In the case of an outage on C1, the RS takes over and only if during this time an outage also takes place on C2 is whole system unavailable.
- **RS Runtime + PS Deployment** – As soon as C1 is up again, the PS can be redeployed and then takes over the service.

In the following section we describe a high level process that implements the states described in this section.

## 3.3  Disaster Recovery Process

The main purpose of the process described in this section is to provide all the functionality and parallel tasks that are necessary for the Cloud Standby approach. The process ensures that the primary Cloud is monitored, the emergency mode is activated and deactivated, and that the update of the standby system is triggered. The disaster recovery process is depicted in Fig. 6 as an UML activity diagram.

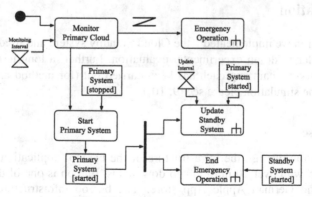

**Fig. 6.** Disaster recovery process

There are two parallel activities that are executed while the primary system is running: monitoring of the primary Cloud, and the update of the standby system. Both of these activities run continuously and are periodically restarted. Each of them has its own timer and can be externally controlled, but both depend on the state of the standby system - for example, updating the standby system is only possible if the primary system is in the state 'started'. Once the primary system is stopped, this activity can't be executed, but the failure of the monitoring activity also automatically triggers the emergency operation. Once the primary Cloud is available again, but the primary system is still stopped, the primary system is started and the operation is switched back to normal mode so that the update can be executed.

The updating process is depicted in Fig. 7. After the standby system is started, the update of the system is initiated by restoring the last backup with the standard backup method. Once the restoring process has finished, the current state is saved and the deployment is stopped again. When using our model-based deployment method [7] the update of the standby system can be modelled within the deployment. Therefore, it can be ensured that the update cycle is always executed and no data is lost. Even if all presented processes and methods are applied correctly, it is however crucial to test the disaster recovery process from time to time. We therefor recommend including live testing during ongoing operation as part of the ITSCM (see section 1).

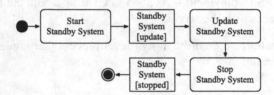

**Fig. 7.** Update Standby System Process

So far, we described the Cloud Standby approach comprising a set of methods and the disaster recovery process. In the following section, we evaluate this new method with a real world use case.

# 4     Evaluation

For the evaluation we implemented[3] the Cloud Standby system and used a real world use case in order to do an experimental evaluation. Further, a long term simulation based on a Markov chain approach has been carried out (for method and further information on the simulation please see [9, 10]).

## 4.1     Use Case

For our evaluation, we use the infrastructure of the barcoo[4] application. Barcoo is a German startup with over 10 million app downloads. Barcoo is one of the most famous apps in the German Apple App store. The barcoo infrastructure consists of four components: a load balancer, a set of application servers, a MySQL database, and a NoSQL database (for caching). The components and their dependencies are shown in Fig. 8.

---

[3]   Implementation available at: https://github.com/alexlenk/CloudStandby
[4]   http://www.barcoo.com

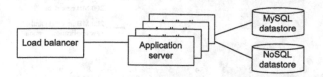

**Fig. 8.** Barcoo application components (c.f. [19])

The load balancer is used as an access point for all clients (browser, smartphone app, etc.). Here, the requests are forwarded to each application server. Each application server uses data from the MySQL database or NoSQL-cache in order to make the appropriate information available to the user. Data in the NoSQL store comes mainly from external providers (price service provider, warnings about food scandals, etc.) and are cached only for performance and bandwidth reasons.

Besides non-critical cache data, the production system of barcoo also includes mission-critical and privacy-related data. For the unlimited use of this data, special precautions and consents to third parties are required, which cannot be obtained in the evaluation. For this reason, not all data of barcoo is available for evaluation and will be replaced by non-critical data for the evaluation of this paper. Thus, it is also possible to reproduce the findings of this work without access to the internal data of barcoo.

**Data and Application Changing Rate.** The business data of barcoo is subject to permanent changes: new products are constantly added to the database, prices are updated, new users are included, and so on. The requests that are addressed to the database are a mixture of insert, update, and delete operations. The examination of the data in the MySQL database for several years revealed a trend towards a continuous increase of the amount of data. Therefore, only insert operations are considered in this evaluation. Due to the historical data available it is assumed that the database is growing by 400 MB within one week.

The barcoo application is subject to a continuous development. As part of the agile Scrum development process, there are a number of minor and major releases of new versions. In the context of this evaluation, it is assumed that, as usual for Scrum, a new and bigger version is published every two weeks, which makes it also necessary to update the underlying software packages of the operating system. Fig. 9 once more illustrates the relationship between the change of the MySQL data and the application server updates.

**Simulation of Critical Business Data.** In the context of this evaluation, sensitive business and customer data are replaced with publicly available data sets and applications. However, to receive realistic results, the amount and the structure of the data were adjusted in close relation to the real data. More precisely, the MySQL database is filled with data of the Ensembl gene database [22]. These data include both large quantities of numbers that are comparable to the prices stored in the barcoo database as well as longer texts that correspond to other data stored.

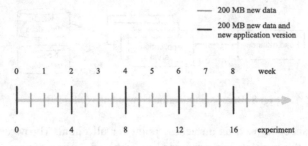

**Fig. 9.** Sequence of the experiments

The Ensembl database contains the data in the form of databases, where each database comprises the genetic code of a form of life. Initial analyses of the data showed that parts of the data can be faster imported than others. This can be due to the fact that some tables only consist of numbers whereas others consist of larger amounts of text. In order to prevent that these different import times distort the measurements, all data of an Ensembl database were converted into MySQL import commands and written into a large MySQL file. Each line corresponded to an import command in the data file. Subsequently, the lines of the large, multi-gigabyte file were randomly mixed. The result was divided into small files, which can be individually imported into an existing schema and enlarge the final database to 100 MB. For reasons of better transportation, these 100 MB parts were packed with GZip[5].

The data of the NoSQL database are kept in the main memory and are not of crucial importance for the operation, it just reduces the number of requests to external providers over the time. In an emergency, the NoSQL database is deployed empty and gradually fills itself.

As the barcoo application is the company's main core business, its publication would definitely harm the business. Thus, for this evaluation, every installation step for setting up a Ruby-on-Rails server that is capable of running the barcoo-application has been available but the application itself has not. To simulate the application, the github project "diaspora" was used. We chose diaspora because it is an open-source Ruby-on-Rails application and there are several versions available, so the development of several versions over a certain time can be simulated.

## 4.2   Results

With the given use case we set up the Cloud Standby system and by applying the changed data according to the description in the use case, we simulated a 24 week runtime of the system by repeating it 48 times within a short period of time. To evaluate the deployment times, we measured the time when the first startup call was sent to the cloud provider until the last installation package of the last server was installed. The results are shown in the following sections.

We first compared the startup time of the distributed system with increasing business data and new application versions over time with and without Cloud Standby replica-

---

[5]  https://www.gnu.org/software/gzip/

tion. By measuring the starting time without replication we created a reference on how the startup time develops with increasing data. We used a curve estimation regression on the measured data point to fit a function that we can use in our simulation later. Since the Cloud Standby replication comes with a price that has to be paid to the Cloud provider when updating the standby system, we used the data we gained from the experiments to calculate the overhead in costs for a given RTO. With this information we then simulated the long term costs of the Cloud Standby system using a Markov chain based approach that also takes the outages costs into account and can thereby estimate in which cases our Cloud Standby approach is useful and in which it is not.

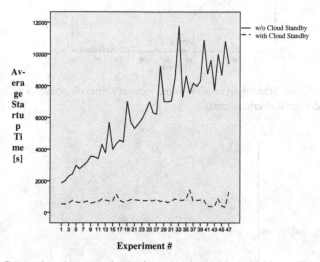

**Fig. 10.** Comparison between the deployment time with and without Cloud Standby

**Reduction of the RTO.** Considering the deployment time of a system with and without Cloud Standby Fig. 10 shows that the difference between the deployment time of the respective system rises with the size of the backup.

By doing a fit on the measured data points we determined the following function:

$$f(x) = 1234.742x^{0.519} \tag{1}$$

**Additional Costs.** The costs for this approach arise from the starting of the standby system consisting of 7 virtual machines[6] for update reasons. Thereby the standby costs are linked to the configured update interval (see section 3.3). The update interval also defines what RTO can be achieved. So, we used interpolation on the startup times in Fig. 10 and with the resulting function and a cost function for periodic Cloud updates (see [9, 10]) we calculated the costs of running a standby system. Apart from breakdown costs, these costs are solely overhead. In our case, the overhead for RTO is between 2-5 % of the primary system hosting costs (see Fig. 11).

---

[6] Usage cost for the used virtual machines types on Amazon EC2: 0.68€/h [1]

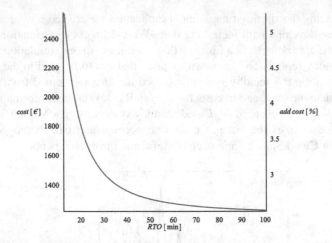

**Fig. 11.** Costs for Cloud Standby in relation to the recovery time objective as an absolute value and percentage additional overhead costs

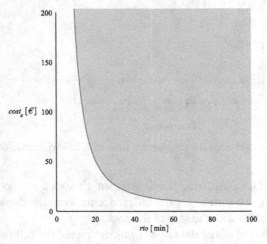

**Fig. 12.** Area (grey) in which Cloud Standby is cheaper than risking an outage (c.f. [9, 10])

**Long-term Savings.** Taking the outage probability of the primary provider, the outage costs ($cost_e$) of the business processes, and the startup time (see formula 1) into account, we can calculate for the given use case when Cloud Standby should be used and when not[7]. As shown in Fig. 12, Cloud Standby is not useful in the case of very high or very low outage costs. When these costs are very high a hot standby approach should be considered and when they are very low it might be better to not use any standby approach at all. However, as shown in Fig. 12, in many cases our approach is beneficial (grey area). In our use case this approach should be used when the outage costs are between 4.88€ and 2989.97€ per hour.

---

7   For calculating the long term savings we used the calculation method presented in [9, 10]

# 5     Conclusion

In this paper we presented a novel approach for warm standby in the cloud. We introduced Cloud Standby and its methods and processes for preparing, monitoring, and updating the standby system. We evaluated the system using a real-world use case where we deployed a multi-tier application several times with increasing data in the cloud. We showed that by using Cloud Standby, the startup time, and thereby the smallest possible RTO, can be significantly reduced. We also showed that in this use case, the cost overhead of the approach is between 2-5% and that when taking the outage costs of the business process into account, our approach should be used when these costs are between 4.88€ and 2989.97€ per hour.

In our future work we will lay additional focus on the deployment method and describe how a model-driven approach can be used to complement our disaster recovery method. We also plan to extent the implementation of our approach.

**Acknowledgements.** We would like to thank Tobias Bräuer, CTO of barcoo, for his help and the insights he gave us on the barcoo infrastructure.

# References

1. AWS Inc.: Amazon Web Services, Cloud Computing: Compute, Storage, Database, https://aws.amazon.com/
2. Ayari, N., et al.: Fault tolerance for highly available internet services: concepts, approaches, and issues. IEEE Commun. Surv. Tutor. 10(2), 34–46 (2008)
3. Cully, B., et al.: Remus: High Availability Via Asynchronous Virtual Machine Replication. In: Proceedings of the 5th USENIX Symposium on Networked Systems Design and Implementation, pp. 161–174 (2008)
4. Henderson, C.: Building scalable web sites. O'reilly (2008)
5. Hiles, A.: The definitive handbook of business continuity management. Wiley (2010)
6. Klems, M., et al.: Automating the delivery of IT Service Continuity Management through cloud service orchestration. In: 2010 IEEE Network Operations and Management Symposium (NOMS), pp. 65–72 (2010)
7. Lenk, A.: Cloud Standby Model Implementation, https://github.com/alexlenk/CloudStandby/tree/master/org/cloudstandby/model
8. Lenk, A., et al.: What's inside the Cloud? An architectural map of the Cloud landscape. In: ICSE Workshop on Software Engineering Challenges of Cloud Computing, CLOUD 2009, pp. 23–31 (2009)
9. Lenk, A., Pallas, F.: Cloud Standby System and Quality Model. Int. J. Cloud Comput. IJCC. 1(2), 48–59 (2013)
10. Lenk, A., Pallas, F.: Modeling Quality Attributes of Cloud-Standby-Systems. In: Lau, K.-K., Lamersdorf, W., Pimentel, E. (eds.) ESOCC 2013. LNCS, vol. 8135, pp. 49–63. Springer, Heidelberg (2013)

11. Li, Z., et al.: The Cloud's Cloudy Moment: A Systematic Survey of Public Cloud Service Outage. ArXiv Prepr. ArXiv13126485 (2013)
12. Mell, P., Grance, T.: The NIST definition of cloud computing. NIST Spec. Publ. 800, 145 (2011)
13. Menken, I., et al.: Itil V3 Malc-Managing Across the Lifecycle Full Certification Online Learning and Study Book Course: The Itil V3 Intermediate Malc Complete Certification Kit. Emereo Pty Limited (2009)
14. Pokharel, M., et al.: Disaster Recovery for System Architecture Using Cloud Computing. Presented at the July (2010)
15. Rajagopalan, S., et al.: SecondSite: disaster tolerance as a service. In: Proceedings of the 8th ACM SIGPLAN/SIGOPS Conference on Virtual Execution Environments, pp. 97–108 (2012)
16. Schmidt, K.: High availability and disaster recovery. Springer (2006)
17. Symantec: 2011 SMB Disaster Preparedness Survey - Global Results (2011)
18. Whitman, M., et al.: Principles of incident response and disaster recovery. Cengage Learning (2013)
19. Wittern, E., et al.: Feature-based Configuration of Vendor-independent Deployments on IaaS. In: 18th IEEE International Enterprise Distributed Object Computing Conference, EDOC (2014)
20. Wood, T., et al.: Disaster recovery as a cloud service: Economic benefits & deployment challenges. In: 2nd USENIX Workshop on Hot Topics in Cloud Computing (2010)
21. Wood, T., et al.: PipeCloud: using causality to overcome speed-of-light delays in cloud-based disaster recovery. In: Proceedings of the 2nd ACM Symposium on Cloud Computing, p. 17 (2011)
22. Ensembl Genome Browser, http://www.ensembl.org/index.html
23. Topology and Orchestration Specification for Cloud Applications Version 1.0, http://docs.oasis-open.org/tosca/TOSCA/v1.0/cs01/TOSCA-v1.0-cs01.pdf

# Weaving Aspects and Business Processes through Model Transformation

Heiko Witteborg[1], Anis Charfi[1], Daniel Colomer Collell[2], and Mira Mezini[2]

[1] SAP AG
Bleichstr. 8, Darmstadt, Germany
{firstname.lastname}@sap.com
[2] Software Technology Group
TU Darmstadt, Hochschulstr. 10, Darmstadt, Germany
lastname@informatik.tu-darmstadt.de

**Abstract.** Concerns such as logging, auditing and accounting need to be addressed already in the business process modeling phase and not only in the process implementation phase. Mostly, such concerns are modeled as part of the normal flow in business process models. However, the crosscutting nature of such concerns leads to complex, scattered, and tangled models that are hard to understand and to manage. The lack of appropriate means to modularize crosscutting concerns in business process modeling languages seriously affects understandability, maintainability and reusability. In a previous work we proposed AO4BPMN 1.0 as an aspect-oriented extension of BPMN that allows the modularization of crosscutting concerns. However, there were several open issues in that proposal. First, it lacks a concrete weaving mechanism for composing business processes and aspects. Second, it lacks a well-defined pointcut language to select join points. Third, it does not support BPMN 2.0, which was still under development at that time. In this paper we tackle these issues and present a weaver for AO4BPMN based on model transformation as well as an OCL-based pointcut language.

**Keywords:** aspects, business process, modeling, weaving, model transformation.

## 1 Introduction

With the rise of executable process languages such as the Web Services Business Process Execution Language (WS-BPEL) [11] and the Business Process Modeling Notation (BPMN) [13] the borders between process modeling and process implementation are blurring. A BPMN process model can be at the same time the process model and the process implementation as BPMN 2 is not only a modeling language but also an executable language. This requires such languages to allow expressing several concerns that are important for process implementation such as security, accounting, and auditing. However, these concerns have a crosscutting nature and using the current means of WS- BPEL and BPMN to specify them leads to complex process models with many activities that are not directly related to the core process logic. Without appropriate language constructs for supporting crosscutting concerns the process complexity increases

M. Villari et al. (Eds.) : ESOCC 2014, LNCS 8745, pp. 47–61, 2014.
© IFIP International Federation for Information Processing 2014

and the process models become hard to understand, to manage, and to maintain. For example, consider a business process for order fulfillment that involves the usage of external services with costs such as a delivery service. We need to extend the business process to collect accounting data whenever we use an external service with cost. To do this we need for each activity that calls an external service at least another activity for accounting. Obviously the process complexity will drastically increase and the activities belonging to one concern such as accounting will be mixed with activities addressing other concerns. In addition, the implementation of a given concern such as accounting will be scattered across several business process models.

In addition to the need for concepts to modularize crosscutting concerns in business processes, we motivated in [15] the need for concepts to modularize business process extensions as first-class entities. Consider for example an independent software vendor (ISV) who extends the standard business processes implemented by an ERP-System to adapt that software to the particular needs of a company or a domain. The process extension should be kept separate from the business process for several reasons. First, the extension is owned by the ISV whereas the core process is owned by the ERP provider. A separation of both entities avoids problems when the core process is updated by the ERP provider. Second, several extensions may be applied to the same business process and if they are not modelled as separate entities it would be very difficult to understand the new process that results after applying these extensions to the original core process.

In order to address the limitations of business process languages with respect to crosscutting concern modularity and process extension modularity, we introduced aspect-oriented workflow languages in [3] and as an instantiation thereof we proposed AO4BPEL [4], which is an aspect-oriented extension to WS-BPEL. A new implementation of that language based on Apache ODE was recently made available [9]. After AO4BPEL, we proposed AO4BPMN 1.0 [5] as an aspect-oriented extension to BPMN, which allows a better modularization of crosscutting concerns and process extensions. However, that work has three open issues. First, it lacks a concrete pointcut language. Second, no weaving mechanism was provided. Third, the language extension and the respective editor were based on BPMN 1.2 and not on BPMN 2.0, which was still in development at that time.

In this paper, we present the following contributions. First, we refine the language definition of AO4BPMN and make it compliant with BPMN 2.0 using a light-weight extension of BPMN 2.0. Second, we propose a concrete pointcut language based on OCL. Third, we present a weaving mechanism for composing aspects and processes, which is based on model-to-model transformation. Fourth, we present a new Eclipse based toolset for AO4BPMN 2.0 including a graphical editor, a weaving wizard, and a weaver. A variation of AO4BPMN was applied in an industrial context to modularize business process extensions as first class entities as presented in [15]. However in that work process extensions were extracted from modified business process models and modularized in aspects implicitly ·behind the scenes. In the current paper, we advocate a rather explicit approach for modeling aspects in business processes.

The remainder of this paper is organized as follows. Section 2 presents AO4BPMN 2.0 and illustrates its constructs by means of an example. Section 3 introduces the weaving mechanism and the underlying algorithms. Section 4 is dedicated to implementation and tooling. Section 5 discusses related work and Section 6 concludes the paper.

# 2   AO4BPMN 2.0

In this section, we first give a language overview focusing on the AO4BPMN concepts that were added or refined in version 2.0. Then, we shortly discuss the integration of these concepts into the metamodel of BPMN 2.0. After that, we present an example business process that we use throughout the paper for illustration.

## 2.1   Language Overview

*Base Process and Join Points:* In AO4BPMN, a *Base Process* is a business process model that ideally focusses on the core functional process logic, while the crosscutting concerns are captured separately in *Aspect* modules. The base process contains *Join Points*, which are distinct and uniquely identifiable points at which crosscutting concerns can be integrated. AO4BPMN per default defines base processes and joint points in an implicit and standard-conform way: any standard BPMN 2.0 process can serve as a base process. Any contained BPMN flow node, i.e., any BPMN element used to define events, activities and gateways, is available as an AO4BPMN join point. Hence, existing BPMN 2.0 processes are AO4BPMN-enabled by default. A base process modeler does not have to foresee or annotate possible AO4BPMN join points. However, while this gives the modeler flexibility and ensures the standard-conformity and reusability of the process models, there are use cases, in which certain process elements should be protected from being advised by aspects [15]. For example, this requirement arises when a core business process should not be adapted by a third-party to protect intellectual property or to ensure compliance with legal obligations. To cover these scenarios, AO4BPMN also supports the explicit exclusion of base process flow nodes from the join point set.

*Aspects:* Aspects are units for modularizing crosscutting concerns in business process models such as monitoring, accounting, or security. An aspect acts as a container for both the concern-specific business process logic, represented as *Advice*, and for the *Pointcuts*, which select the join points at which the advice will be integrated. An aspect can define multiple sets of pointcuts and advices. In addition, an aspect may define some state, i.e., data that can be accessed and modified by the advices contained in that aspect.

*Advice and Proceed Node:* An advice is a construct that holds a connected fragment of the process logic of a crosscutting concern. In case the concern is scattered over several join points in a business process (e.g., a timer that is started at the beginning of a process and is stopped at its end), the corresponding aspect will hold several advices. Apart from the concern's process fragments, an advice may also include the special flow node *Proceed*, which is a placeholder for the *Join Point* element that is selected by the pointcut. This node defines how the advice must be applied: everything implemented sequentially before the *Proceed* will be integrated before the selected join point; every-thing implemented sequentially after it will be integrated after the selected join point (cf. Section 3). If the *Proceed* flow node is not used the join point element is replaced by the advice content (or deleted without substitution, if the advice is empty). Com-pared to other AOP languages, where advice composition strategies are often limited to either before, after, or instead of the join points selected by the associated pointcut, AO4BPMN's *Proceed* concept allows more advanced advice composition strategies.

*Pointcut:* A pointcut allows selecting one or more related join points at which a certain advice will be integrated. Usually, a pointcut targets elements of a base process. Yet, as multiple aspects can be applied to the same base process, the pointcut belonging to a certain aspect may also target elements that were introduced by another aspect in a previous step, resulting in a dependency hierarchy of concerns. Pointcuts can be defined based on element characteristics both on the meta level (e.g., all activities that are typed as receive task) or on the model level (e.g., an activity with a certain id). The pointcut language should also be powerful enough to allow selecting elements based on different criteria such as their relationship to other model elements (e.g., the resource that will perform an activity), their containment information, or the existence of certain boundary events. To support weaving at execution time, the pointcuts may also include instance attributes, e.g., the state of an activity or the priority of a user task. Based on the alterna-tives sketched in [5], we opt for an OCL-based pointcut language for AO4BPMN 2.0 as OCL [12] provides the required expressiveness, flexibility and tool support. We lever-age OCL's usability and understandability by providing helper functions that facilitate the specification of query expressions, e.g., to enable the use of wild-cards.

## 2.2    Extending the BPMN 2.0 Metamodel with AO4BPMN Concepts

BPMN 2.0 introduces an extensibility mechanism that can be used to extend BPMN's metamodel in a standard-compliant manner [13]. The concepts *ExtensionDefinition* and *ExtensionAttributeDefinition* are at the core of this mechanism. We use these concepts to define AO4BPMN 2.0 as a light-weight extension of BPMN 2.0. Figure 1 shows using dashed arrows how the AO4BPMN metamodel elements extend to the BPMN meta-model elements. AO4BPMN *BaseProcesses* and *Aspects* are specialized *Processes*. An aspect contains possibly multiple *States* and *Advices*. An *Advice* is a specialized *SubPro-cess* that contains a *Pointcut* and optionally a *ProceedNode* in addition to the elements a standard *SubProcess* may contain. A *Pointcut* may reference multiple *JoinPoints*, which are specialized *FlowNodes* that are part of the *BaseProcess*.

## 2.3    Example Scenario: Agile Software Development

We consider the (simplified) scrum-like development process shown in Figure 2 that will be used as base process. This process covers the creation and presentation of a sprint backlog by the development manager, the execution of tasks during the sprint by the development team, and the review of the sprint results. While this development process looks plain and readable, it can easily become complex and tangled by adding

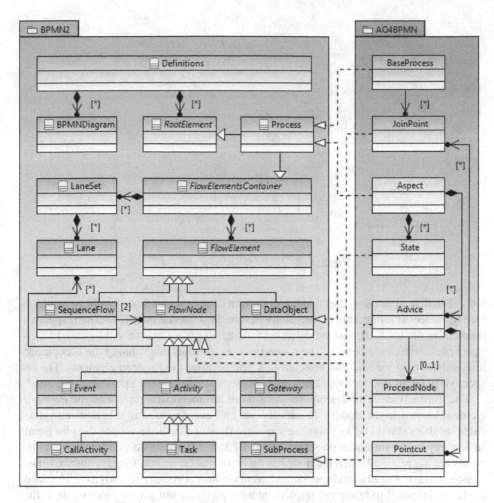

**Fig. 1.** Extending BPMN 2.0 with AO4BPMN concepts

activities to cover concerns such as quality assurance, test-driven development, monitoring or documentation. Other examples of crosscutting concers could involve activities related continuous integration or setup-specific activities e.g., regarding open-source development; activities related to other development approaches such as extreme programming practices; activities that might be of interest for other company-internal stakeholders like the HR, finance, or legal department. A business process model representing a realistic development setup would have to cover multiple concerns. Mixing the core process functionality and the other relevant crosscutting concerns leads to a complex process model that is difficult to understand and to maintain.

AO4BPMN helps addressing the issues discussed above. Figure 3 shows an AO4BPMN aspect that modularizes the process logic related to test-driven development (TDD) in the context of our example process. For demonstration purposes, two rather simple advices define the additional process fragments required for acceptance

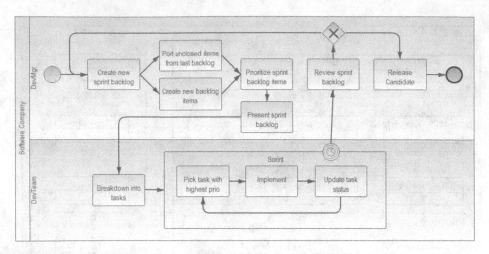

**Fig. 2.** Agile development base process

tests. The first advice specifies that the definition of acceptance tests should be done before the selected join points (sequentially before the *Proceed* element). The respective pointcut is the OCL expression `context Activity :: name = 'Prioritize sprint backlog items'`. The second advice specifies that running the acceptance tests should be done after the selected join points (after the *Proceed* element). The respective pointcut is `context BoundaryEvent :: name = 'SprintTimeOut'`.

The third advice, *Unit Testing*, shows a more advanced structure, with the *Proceed* element located in the middle. In addition, an end event is used in this advice to indicate that there should be an outgoing sequence flow to the successors of the join point. In analogy to the instantiation semantics of BPMN 2.0, these start and end event elements are not required when the node has no incoming (resp. outgoing) sequence flows. Hence, we do not need to add specialized events in the acceptance test advices. The third advice is intended to refine the implementation phase of our scrum process, thus, the corresponding pointcut is `context Activity :: name = 'Implement'`.

## 3   Composition of Processes and Aspects

As AO4BPMN aspects are separate modules a weaving mechanism is necessary to compose them with the BPMN base processes. In this section, we present a weaving mechanism that is based on model-to-model transformation together with the underlying algorithms and rules.

### 3.1   Weaving Mechanism

The weaving mechanism of AO4BPMN takes aspect models and business process models as inputs and produces BPMN 2.0 compliant business process models as output.

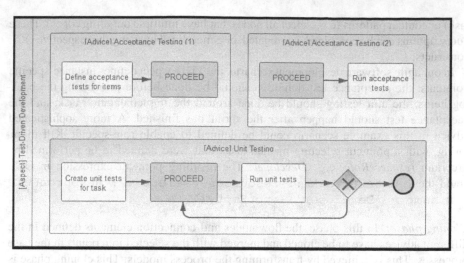

**Fig. 3.** Test-driven development aspect

Apart from evaluating the pointcut queries and identifying the matching join points, the weaving mechanism integrates the advice process fragments into the base processes via model-to-model transformation. Thereby, merging and branching restrictions need to obeyed and the newly inserted elements need to be re-linked with the base process flow. A simplified version of the weaving algorithm is shown in Listing 1. We elaborate on the core tasks of the weaving mechanism in the following.

```
public List<Process> weave(List<Process> baseProcesses, List<Aspect> aspects){
 List<Process> targetProcesses = new ArrayList<Process>();
 Process targetProcess;
 for (Aspect aspect : aspects) {
   for (Process baseProcess : baseProcesses) {
     targetProcess = cloneProcess(baseProcess);
     for (Advice advice : aspect.getAdvices()){
       List<JoinPoint> jps = identifyJoinPoints(baseProcess, advice.getPointcut());
       for (JoinPoint jp : jps){
         cloneAdvice(targetProcess, advice);
         relink(targetProcess, jp);
       }
     }
     targetProcesses.add(targetProcess);
   }
 }
 return targetProcesses;
}
```

**Listing 1.** Weaving algorithm

*Join point identification phase:* The first phase in the weaving process is the evaluation of the pointcuts contained in the aspect. This phase identifies the join points at which the advices have to be integrated in the subsequent phases. Depending on the OCL expressions used in the pointcuts the join point selection can be based on different characteristics of the flow nodes, such as instance-specific properties (e.g., select a node based on its id or name), properties on the meta-level (e.g., select all nodes of type user task) or context patterns (e.g., select all nodes that have multiple outgoing edges). These query options can be combined, aggregated, or generalized by using the respective OCL constructs.

In our agile software development scenario, the TDD aspect defines instance-specific pointcuts: the acceptance test definition should be done before prioritizing the backlog items; the unit testing should be done around the implementation task; and the acceptance test should happen after the sprint has finished. A more sophisticated advice in this example scenario could be defined to enable role-specific KPI monitoring, with a pointcut selecting manual tasks that were defined to be performed by a certain *resourceRole*, e.g., *Developer*. The resulting pointcut expression in OCL could be: `context Task :: resources->select(r : ResourceRole | r.name = 'Developer')->notEmpty()`.

*Cloning phase:* In this phase, the flow nodes and connection elements defined in the different advices have to be cloned and merged with the selected join points in the base processes. This is achieved by transforming the process models. This cloning phase is responsible for copying the needed information and process elements from the aspect model to the process model. Given a join point and a *Proceed* element as input, the weaver knowledge is limited to whatever is directly attached to these elements. For this reason, the weaver clones level by level. In this context, a level is defined as the set of all the elements that are at the same distance from the *Proceed* element. The distance between two elements is defined as the number of associations in the shortest path that links these two elements.

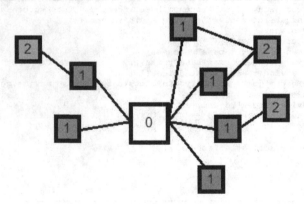

**Fig. 4.** Abstract structure with the elements and their distance to the central element

For illustration Figure 4 shows an abstract structure with elements and their distance to the central element (element with distance 0). The weaving algorithm clones first all the elements at distance 1, then all elements at distance 2, and so on until the last level is reached. In the unit testing advice of our example, apart from the *Proceed* element itself, all elements have distance 1 except the end event, which has distance 2.

Besides flow nodes, other BPMN 2.0 elements can occur in the advice definition and need to be handled appropriately in the cloning step. Connections are elements of particular interest for the cloning phase. In fact, in a BPMN process diagram the different flow objects and other elements such as data objects are related by means of connecting elements such as sequence flow and association. Moreover, boundary events can be used to interruptively branch the process flow. Regarding the process transformation, these connecting elements are taken into account by the weaver as explained in the following.

– Everything that is linked by means of a sequence flow connection belongs semantically to the process itself as part of its sequence of steps. The weaving algorithm supports this flow level as it is the level that contains the semantic part of the process.
– Everything related by means of an association connection is used to express relevant information that is found along the steps of the process; but it does not belong to the normal flow. Both data associations targeting flow nodes and sequence flows, as well as the data objects themselves are considered by the weaving algorithm, as they contain relevant information that contribute to the semantics of the process.
– Boundary events indicate that the activity to which they are attached should be interrupted when the event is triggered. The weaving algorithm reflects this by copying the aspect boundary events into the composed process.

*Re-linking phase:* After cloning the content of the advice (i.e., the flow nodes and connecting elements) in the context of the selected join point, the original connections of the join point potentially need to be re-routed to or from the newly cloned elements.

As a first step after the cloning is performed, the weaver needs to identify the elements that are candidates to be targets or sources of the so called re-linking phase. In analogy to the instantiation semantics of BPMN 2.0 we identify nodes with either only incoming or only outgoing edges as candidates. Yet, there may be the need for an explicit candidate specification, as shown in the unit testing advice of our example. Here, the contained gateway cannot be automatically detected as a final flow node of the advice process but this can be indicated using an end event. Note that these start and end events have to be removed at the end of the weaving process.

The re-linking strategy has to cover various composition setups, e.g., the combination of an advice with multiple tasks without successor and a selected join point with multiple outgoing sequence flows. An example of such a join point could be the *Create new Sprint backlog* task, as depicted in Figure 5. As an example aspect targeting this join point we consider a monitoring aspect that starts two timers after the backlog is initialized as shown in Figure 6.

In this situation (multiple outgoing edges and multiple end candidates), the re-linking strategy needs to merge the cloning structure with the original process and needs to keep the semantics, without overloading the composed model with edges. A full clone of the succeeding process fragment for each re-linking candidate of the advice would not be a practically scalable solution. To tackle this problem we leverage two BPMN 2.0 equivalences. In fact, the BPMN 2.0 specification defines an equivalence relationship between multiple outgoing sequence flows and a split using a parallel gateway as well as an equivalence relationship between multiple incoming sequence flows and a merge

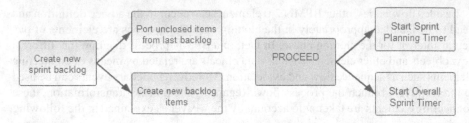

**Fig. 5.** Join point with multiple outgoing connections

**Fig. 6.** Aspect with multiple end candidates

using an exclusive gateway. Taking this into account, the weaver applies the following generic re-linking strategy: All cloned elements that are candidates for re-linking will be connected to the originally steaming out elements through the use of an exclusive gateway connected to a parallel gateway. Figure 7 depicts the result of applying this strategy to the monitoring aspect shown in Figure 6.

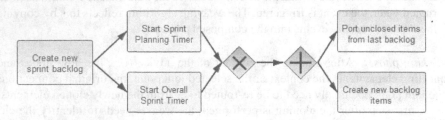

**Fig. 7.** Composed process in a scenario with multiple branches

The same strategy can be applied to multiple incoming join point edges and multiple re-linking start candidates. In the case of single edges and candidates we can avoid the creation of the intermediate gateways and simplify the re-linking using a direct connection via a sequence flow link.

### 3.2   Example Scenario Revisited

Figure 8 shows the result of weaving the TDD aspect shown in Figure 3 and the agile software development process depicted in Figure 2.

The integration of the first acceptance testing advice, the creation task, demonstrates the re-linking of multiple incoming sequence flows. As we do not have multiple start candidates in the advice there is no need to insert an additional merging gateway explicitly. The second acceptance testing advice with the *Run acceptance tests* task shows that not only activities but also other flow nodes can be valid join points. In this case the join point is a boundary timer event. The composition with a more complex process fragment is illustrated through the integration of the unit testing advice. Here, during the re-linking phase, the end event was replaced by the outgoing edges of the selected join point (i.e., the task *Implement*).

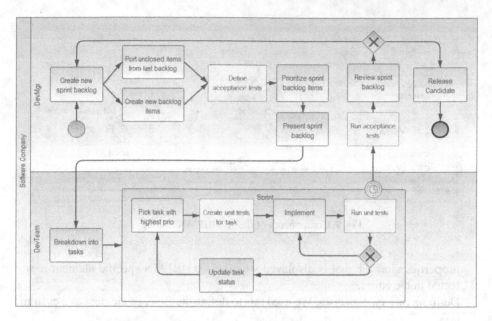

**Fig. 8.** Test-driven development process

## 4   Implementation and Tooling

Figure 9 gives a high level overview of the AO4BPMN toolset components. In the middle of this figure we see a *Repository*, which allows persisting and accessing aspect and process models. The *Navigator* can be used to browse processes and aspects; both types of models can be edited using a completely re-implemented new editor that extends the *BPMN2 Editor*. In addition, a *Weaving Wizard* is provided to support the selection of the base processes and aspects that should be composed by the weaver.

### 4.1   Editor

The editor shown in Figure 3 allows defining aspect models that are separated from the business process models, giving support to the AO4BPMN language. This editor is based on the tool BPMN2 modeler[1], which is an open source component of the Eclipse subproject Model Development Tools (MDT). The BPMN2 subproject aims at providing a metamodel implementation of the BPMN 2.0 specification and a corresponding modeler component. We extended and adapted the BPMN2 modeler to support AO4BPMN constructs making use of the powerful extension point provided by that tool. This extension point offers amongst others the following extension possibilities:

- Extending the property tabs of any modeling element defined in the BPMN2 metamodel (the actual eclipse implementation). We used this to add an AO4BPMN

---

[1] http://eclipse.org/bpmn2-modeler/

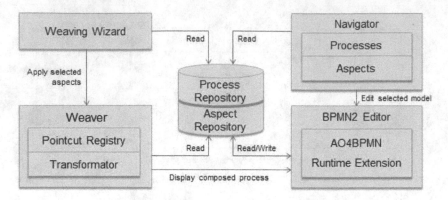

**Fig. 9.** Components of the AO4BPMN tooling

properties view tab that is displayed when an AO4BPMN-specific element is selected in the editor.
- Defining own custom tasks. We used this to define the *Proceed* element as a custom
  task.
- Defining own model extensions. That is, to extend the metamodel with new specialized BPMN elements. We used this extension point parameter to e.g., add the
  *Pointcut* attribute to the properties view of an *Advice*.
- Providing own feature containers for available modeling elements to override part
  of the default behavior. This offers a means to adapt the rendering and containment
  restrictions of e.g., *Advices*.
- Defining own style sheets. We used this to define styles for the adapted tool, e.g.,
  the background color of the *Proceed* element.

The editor allows defining aspects, OCL-based pointcuts, and advice including also
the proceed activity. A pointcut can be specified using the AO4BPMN property tab of
an advice. Moreover, it is possible to extend the tool to add support for other pointcut languages. A mechanism to switch between multiple pointcut languages is already
implemented.

## 4.2 Weaver and Weaving Wizard

As part of the toolset a weaver that implements the algorithms presented in Section 3 is
integrated with the editor described above. Hence, the weaving process can be started
directly from the editor. Furthermore, a weaving wizard is provided to support the selection of the processes and aspects that should be composed by the weaver. As shown in
Figure 10, the weaving wizard allows selecting on the left side the diagrams containing
the aspects to be woven and on the right side the diagrams containing the base processes.
If the aspects are in the same diagram as the base processes the checkbox with the label
*Use the same Diagrams* should be ticked. Once the button labeled *OK* is clicked the
wizard calls the weaver.

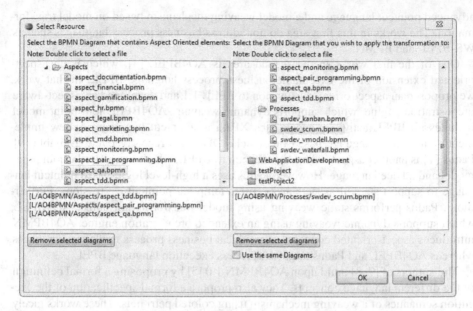

**Fig. 10.** Weaving wizard (Selection of base processes and aspects)

For implementing the weaver we used operational QVT[2], which is part of the OMG standard QVT. The reason for choosing QVTo and no other parts of the QVT language family is the operational nature of QVTo, which helped us in implementing the clone and merge algorithm in a rather straight-forward manner.

## 5  Related Work

We discuss in this section related work from two areas. The first area addresses the general topic of aspect-oriented modeling mainly in the context of object-oriented design. The second area addresses specifically the topic of aspect-oriented business process management.

An extensive survey on aspect-oriented modeling approaches is presented in [2], which is a deliverable of the AOSD-Europe network of excellence. That survey covers both works that extend UML diagrams with aspect-oriented constructs and works that are based on domain-specific languages. Another more recent survey is presented in [14] and it focuses specifically on approaches that are based on UML. As examples of works in that context we mention [16] and [6]. In [16], the authors present an aspect-oriented extension to UML state machines. In [6] an aspect-oriented extension to UML activity diagrams is proposed. Another similar work in this area is [10], which proposes a UML 2 profile for aspect-oriented modeling and uses UML 2 actions to define advice behavior in a platform independent manner. In addition that work defines an

---

[2] http://projects.eclipse.org/projects/modeling.mmt.qvt-oml

advanced pointcut language and a model weaving mechanism based on model transformation. The works in this first area do not address business process languages such as WS-BPEL and BPMN.

One of the first works in the second area is AO4BPEL [4], which is an aspect-oriented extension of the executable business process language BPEL. In that work, we proposed an aspect-oriented extension to BPEL 1.1 and developed an aspect-aware orchestration engine, which supports dynamic weaving. AO4BPEL join point model includes all BPEL activities and it uses XPath as pointcut language. A new implementation of that language based on Apache ODE was recently made available [9]. Padus [1] is another aspect-oriented extension to BPEL, which has a similar join point model and advice language. However, Padus uses a high-level logic-based pointcut language to support stateful aspects and express temporal pointcut expressions. Furthermore, Padus performs static weaving using model transformation unlike AO4BPEL, which supports dynamic weaving using an extended orchestration engine. AO4BPMN introduces aspect-oriented concepts to graphical business process modeling languages whereas AO4BPEL and Padus target the process execution language BPEL.

The authors of [7, 8] build upon AO4BPMN 1.0 [5] by proposing a formal definition of the different language concepts. They also propose a formal specification of the execution semantics of a weaving mechanism using colored petri nets. These works nicely complement AO4BPMN by providing a formal foundation. Furthermore, the authors of [8] also validate the usefulness of AO4BPMN in practice by presenting a banking case study. Another validation of AO4BPMN in the context of business software can be found in [15], where we use aspects behind the scenes to modularize and manage business process extensions as first-class entities in an industrial context. In that work, aspects are used as means to support extensibility and encapsulate business process extensions which are developed by software companies (e.g., as add-ons) that extend standard business applications. Unlike in that work, in the current paper we advocate an explicit approach to aspect-oriented business process modeling.

## 6   Conclusion

To improve the modularization of crosscutting concerns and process extensions in business process models, we proposed in a previous work an aspect-oriented extension to BPMN called AO4BPMN. However, that extension had some open issues especially with respect to the lack of a concrete pointcut language and the lack of a weaving mechanism. Furthermore, it was based on an older version of BPMN as BPMN 2.0 was still under development at that time. In the current paper, we addressed these issues and presented a concrete OCL-based pointcut language for AO4BPMN as well as a powerful weaver based on model-to-model transformation. We also refined the language definition to make it compatible with BPMN 2.0. In addition, we presented a new Eclipse based tooling for AO4BPMN including a graphical editor and a weaver. An application of an AO4BPMN variant for modularizing process extensions was presented in [15]. Another application in the context of a banking case study was presented in [8]. Our future work will focus on mapping AO4BPMN aspects to AO4BPEL as an alternative to weaving by model transformation and also on facilitating the definition of pointcuts to users that are not familiar with OCL for instance by providing a form-based query builder.

**Acknowledgments.** The work presented in this paper was performed in the context of the Software-Cluster project SINNODIUMIt was partially funded by the German Federal Ministry of Education and Research under grant no. 01IC12S01. The authors assume responsibility for the content.

# References

[1] Braem, M., Gheysels, D.: History-Based Aspect Weaving for WS-BPEL Using Padus. In: Proc. of the 5th European Conference on Web Services (ECOWS), pp. 159–167 (November 2007)

[2] Brichau, J., et al.: Report describing survey of aspect languages and models, AOSD-Europe Deliverable D12

[3] Charfi, A.: Aspect-Oriented Workflow Management. VDM Verlag Dr. Müller (2008)

[4] Charfi, A., Mezini, M.: AO4BPEL: An aspect-oriented extension to BPEL. World Wide Web Journal: Special Issue: Recent Advances in Web Services 10(3) (March 2007)

[5] Charfi, A., Müller, H., Mezini, M.: Aspect-oriented business process modeling with AO4BPMN. In: Kühne, T., Selic, B., Gervais, M.-P., Terrier, F. (eds.) ECMFA 2010. LNCS, vol. 6138, pp. 48–61. Springer, Heidelberg (2010)

[6] Cui, Z., Wang, L., Li, X., Xu, D.: Modeling and Integrating Aspects with UML Activity Diagrams. In: Proc. of the ACM Symposium on Applied Computing, SAC 2009, pp. 430–437. ACM, New York (2009)

[7] Jalali, A., Wohed, P., Ouyang, C.: Aspect oriented business process modelling with precedence. In: Mendling, J., Weidlich, M. (eds.) BPMN 2012. LNBIP, vol. 125, pp. 23–37. Springer, Heidelberg (2012)

[8] Jalali, A., Wohed, P., Ouyang, C., Johannesson, P.: Dynamic weaving in aspect oriented business process management. In: Meersman, R., Panetto, H., Dillon, T., Eder, J., Bellahsene, Z., Ritter, N., De Leenheer, P., Dou, D. (eds.) ODBASE 2013. LNCS, vol. 8185, pp. 2–20. Springer, Heidelberg (2013)

[9] Look, A.: Ao4bpel 2 server (2011), https://github.com/alook/ao4bpel2

[10] Mosconi, M., Charfi, A., Svacina, J., Wloka, J.: Applying and Evaluating AOM for Platform Independent Behavioral UML Models. In: Proc. of the 12th International Workshop on Aspect-Oriented Modeling, AOM 2008, pp. 19–24. ACM, New York (2008)

[11] OASIS: Web Services Business Process Execution Language Version 2.0., http://docs.oasis-open.org/wsbpel/2.0/wsbpel-v2.0.html

[12] OMG: Object constraint language (ocl) version 2.3 (2012), http://www.omg.org/spec/OCL/2.3.1/

[13] Object Management Group (OMG): Business Process Model and Notation (BPMN) Version 2.0., http://www.omg.org/spec/BPMN/2.0/

[14] Wimmer, M., Schauerhuber, A., Kappel, G., Retschitzegger, W., Schwinger, W., Kappsammer, E.: A Survey on UML-based Aspect-oriented Design Modeling. ACM Comput. Surv. 43(4), 28:1–28:33 (2011), http://doi.acm.org/10.1145/1978802.1978807

[15] Witteborg, H., Charfi, A., Aly, M., Holmes, T.: Business Process Extensions as First-Class Entities — A Model-Driven and Aspect-Oriented Approach. In: Liu, C., Ludwig, H., Toumani, F., Yu, Q. (eds.) ICSOC 2012. LNCS, vol. 7636, pp. 763–770. Springer, Heidelberg (2012)

[16] Zhang, G., Hölzl, M., Knapp, A.: Enhancing UML State Machines with Aspects. In: Engels, G., Opdyke, B., Schmidt, D.C., Weil, F. (eds.) MODELS 2007. LNCS, vol. 4735, pp. 529–543. Springer, Heidelberg (2007)

# Domain Objects for Dynamic
# and Incremental Service Composition

Antonio Bucchiarone, Martina De Sanctis, and Marco Pistore

Fondazione Bruno Kessler, Via Sommarive, 18, Trento, Italy
{bucchiarone,msanctis,pistore}@fbk.eu

**Abstract.** A key feature of service-based applications (SBAs) is the capacity to dynamically define the composition of services independently available, which is required to achieve user goals. For this reason, to effectively deal with the obstacles due to continuous context changes, an incremental refinement of provided services is needed. We propose a new model that allows service functionalities to be defined partially, through the use of abstract activities. The refinement of these activities is postponed and performed incrementally at runtime, using the actual context as a guide. Our approach lets a service provider avoid the hard-coding of all service functionalities and their possible compositions at design time, delaying their refinement until the execution phase. Consequently the whole SBA's design becomes modular and flexible to better meet the typical dynamism of SBA. We illustrate the approach through an example scenario from the urban mobility domain.

## 1 Introduction

The high dynamism of the environments in which *service-based applications* must operate, together with their context continuously changing, make the deployment and maintenance of complex distributed applications a hard task to accomplish in a really efficient way. Services may enter or leave the system at any time. Moreover, the situation in which they are executed may be different each time or it may change during their execution. Besides the end-users may change their preferences and emergent requirements can arise. In many situation it often occurs that the only way the application can manage such changes is at run-time, since current situations, available services and users needs are not known priori. *Incremental and dynamic service composition*, hence, becomes the key point to address the problem of continuously changing environment.

The existing approaches of service composition [19], have some crucial limitations. Most of them are based on the assumption that during the composition requirements specification, the application designer knows the services to be composed. Consequently, it often occurs that composition requirements include specific implementation details of the services with which they are supposed to be used. Thus, requirements are strongly linked to particular service implementations and they cannot further be used with similar but different services. However, in dynamic systems, both the composition requirements and the available services change frequently. For these reasons, a static specification of composition requirements upon services is not adequate. In this setting, it is necessary to be able to produce service compositions consistent with the surrounding context and

M. Villari et al. (Eds.) : ESOCC 2014, LNCS 8745, pp. 62–80, 2014.

to quickly manage emerging user requirements during the services execution [20]. To fulfill this purpose, a service model reflecting the contextual environment of services has to be provided. Moreover, the model has to be flexible enough to cope with the typical dynamism of service-based applications. This objective can be reached by avoiding the need of hard-coding every features of the context and/or services at design time [3], but rather leaving the application to dynamically discover the context around and, thus, to incrementally make service compositions.

In this paper we propose an approach, the unified service description "domain objects", that allows a partial definition of such services in order to enable their incremental composition when the context is discovered or when context changes are detected. In addition, the idea is to allow autonomous, heterogeneous and distributed services to be presented in a standard, open and uniform way. The incremental composition task is made by defining *abstract activities*, which are activities that have not a concrete implementation but they are defined in terms of a *goal* to be reached, in the context space. They represent the *opening points* in the application design in which the incremental refinement process can take place during the run-time phase. As concern the management of the dynamism of SBAs, the domain object model allows the designer to model a hierarchically structured conceptual network of services, which are modeled in a modular way that guarantees an efficient management of the continuous entrance and exit of services in the system, avoiding the need of re-designing of the application. The modularity feature is also given by the concept of *fragment* that is used to represent the protocols which have to be performed to execute the services, in a customizable and portable way. Fragments play a key role also in the process of the incremental composition of services because they are used to replace the abstract activities, by making them able to reach their goal using the service available in the context.

The paper is organized as follows: we start with a motivating scenario to understand the requirements that a service-based application must satisfy, in Section 2. Section 3 describes the general approach, firstly, in Section 3.1, by defining how the services are modeled using our approach; then, in Section 3.2, by explaining how to design a service-based application using the domain objects model; and, finally, by clarifying how the bottom-up approach for the incremental and dynamic refinement process is realized, in Section 3.3. Section 4 is devoted to the definition of the formal framework, followed by the implementation discussion of a prototype in Section 5. Related work are discussed in Section 6. Finally, our conclusions and directions for future work are presented in Section 7.

## 2 Motivating Scenario

In last years, the concept of smart-cities is increasingly catching on. In this context, in which each city is assumed as a system of systems, we focus on the *urban mobility domain*. The urban mobility system is a network of multi-modal transport systems (e.g., buses, trains), services (e.g., car sharing, bike sharing, car-pooling) and smart technologies (e.g., sensors for parking availability, smart traffic lights) strongly interconnected to better manage mobility by offering smart services. Today, also modern transportation services are increasingly prevalent, such as the *Flexi-bus* service that combines the features of the taxi and the regular bus service. A Flexi-bus system defines a network of pickup points and provides passengers with a way to get around between any of these points, on demand. In other words, a passenger can request a transit between any two points at a given time. The basic idea of the service is to organize bus routes in such a way that all requests are served with minimal number of buses/routes. A urban mobility application is made of autonomous and heterogeneous services, which are offered by different service providers, that can be composed in order to achieve specific user needs. The providers are *autonomous* from each other in the system, as they can take decisions in an independent and distributed manner. Each service may enter or leave the system at any time, as well as it may change its offered functionalities or it may offer new ones, making the system open and dynamic. The dynamism is also given by the system's context, whose change can affect the operation of the system (e.g., traffic jams, bus delays, on-line payment services unavailable, strikes). During the system execution, all these aspects may generate new properties when combined together, maybe bringing to different mobility solutions because of the enabling or disabling of services. However these informations are only known at runtime, therefore it is no possible to predict every potential solution that can be offered, in terms of services composition, because of the incomplete knowledge at design-time. A urban mobility application is essentially made of *entities*, which provide services, and *relations* between them. The model of the scenario is based on the idea of an extended service model, properly hosted by SCA [18]. SCA comes with built-in extensibility capabilities. The SCA assembly model is defined such that extensions can be added for new interface types or for new implementation types, or new binding types. However, the definition of extensions is left to the implementor. This is witnessed by different SCA implementations (e.g., Apache Tuscany [13]), but many of these specialties are not available at programming level. The *entities* can be organized in two main categories: (i) the **service consumers**, which comprises the *end users* that daily make use of mobility services, *private or public companies* that might want to create value-added services (VASs) by exploiting the urban mobility environment's services; (ii) the **value-added service (VAS) providers** that, by exploiting and composing more basic services or VASs available in the environment, create new VASs to be forwarded in the system. A VAS provider can play both roles of consumer, if it does not forward the new created service in the system, and provider, if it does, as we will see later. As regard *services*, we already said that we can have basic services available in the domain (e.g., smart traffic lights, flexi-bus service, train service, on-line payment service, parking service) or VASs (e.g., *route planner* able to provide a list of flexi-buses optimized routes, calculated by exploiting some basic services in the environment, such as those giving information on the current situation of traffic, pollution and weather together with the current number of requests coming from users). The different entities must be able to *collaborate* in the creation of services optimizing the resources or the quality of the system (e.g., reduction in traffic and emissions of $CO_2$). Moreover, there are the mobility solutions eventually provided to the requesting entities, possibly coming from the composition of different services. These must be customized on the needs expressed by requesters (e.g., user preferences and profile must be taken into account when choosing the services to compose). The need for customization also implies the need of *adaptive* services, capable of adapting their behavior dynamically. All the entities must interact together, each with different roles and purposes. As we said before, being the context continuously changing, these interactions must be *dynamic* and *context-aware* with respect to the surrounding environment (e.g., the application must be able to detect new available services or the unavailability of existing ones). In conclusion, a urban mobility application must meet specific requirements, as revealed by the scenario, such as: (i) *dynamism* to manage continuous changes; (ii) *openness* to address the problem of the services that can enter or leave the system at any time; (iii) *autonomy of the entities* to reflect the independence of the providers and their services; (iv) *context-awareness* to consider the availability/unavailability of services during the composition phases and the users profiles and preferences; (v) *adaptivity of services* to reflect the dynamic behavior of involved services; (vi) *collectivity* to allow entities to collaborate for realizing optimized services; (vii) *customization* to offer services which are not general and statically defined but services customized for each user on the basis of their specific needs. Those requirements are fundamental to really fulfill the main features of a modern and dynamic urban mobility application.

## 3   General Approach

In this Section, we discuss an approach at a conceptual level, by introducing all the main concepts through the exploration of the scenario depicted in Figure 2. In Section 3.1, we explain how the entities in the environment are modeled; in Section 3.2 , we explain how to design a service based application using *domain objects*, while, in Section 3.3 we define how the services are incrementally refined and composed during the execution phase.

### 3.1   Entity Representation

Firstly,the approach is designed around the concept of *domain object* (DO). The DOs are used to model the entities, both humans and systems (e.g., users, service providers), with their features and their behavior, in a *standard*, *open*, and *uniform* way. To describe the model of a DO, we refer to the *FlexiBus Manager (FBM)* DO, in Figure 1, which comes from to the *Urban Mobility Application (UMA)* scenario depicted in Figure 2 and whose design is illustrated in the next Section. A DO is represented as a model made of two layers, namely the *core layer* and the *fragments layer* (see Figure 1). Briefly, the business of the FBM mainly consists in the management of the flexi-bus service, the definition of optimal routes for flexi-buses and the management of requests for on line ticket payments. The core layer defines the *structure*, the *interface* and the internal *behavior* of a DO. The structure represents the state of the DO and it is made of:

– a set of *variables*, which represents its features. For example the state of the FBM is made of the optimized *routes* dynamically defined, the information about the *flexibuses* in action in the city, the *TicketStatus* related to the payment of the ticket by a user for the booked Flexi-bus, etc..
– a set of *relations* to model domain objects' direct connections. For example, the FBM holds relations with the instances representing the real flexi-buses running around the city, as shown by the *fbInstances* relation.

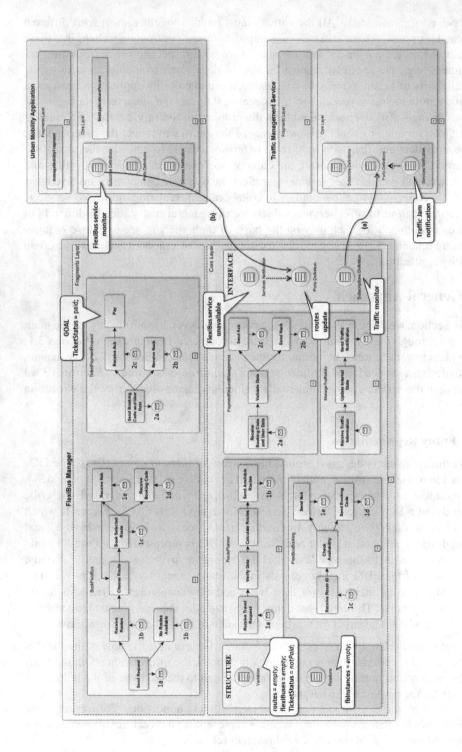

**Fig. 1.** FlexiBus Manager Domain Object

The interface, as depicted in the right side of the core layer, consists in:

- a set of *subscriptions definition* that associates reaction functions to some events coming from other DOs. As an example, the *Traffic monitor* subscription in the FBM triggers the execution of the *ManageTrafficInfo* process by reacting to a *Traffic Jam Notification* forwarded by the Traffic Management Service (TMS). This subscription is shown by the arrow labeled with (a).
- a set of *ports* that define *custom events* that a domain object may generate. They carry information and represent changes in the domain object's structure. As an example, the FBM publishes on the *routes update* port to notify that new routes are available. It is then possible that other DOs subscribe to this port to be triggered in case of the availability of new routes. This subscription is represented by the arrow labeled with (b), which shows that the UMA has made a subscription to the *routes update* port of the FBM.
- a set of *service notifications* that are used to propagate events and/or updates from a service, without an explicit request. This is realized by publishing the events on specific ports, as shown by the dashed arrows in the Figure. Examples of service notification are the *FlexiBus service unavailable* notification forwarded by the FBM and also the *Traffic Jam Notification* of the TMS.

The behavior of a DO represents all the processes that it implements to execute its services. A process is represented as a sequence of activities, also complex with loop and/or conditional steps. The FBM, for example, has three main processes such as *RoutePlanner*, *PaymentRequestManagement* and *FlexiBusBooking*.

In the fragments layer, the set of services that the DO externally exposes are modeled. Each service is represented as a *fragment* [8] that represents the interface with an internal process in a DO. The FBM for example, provides two main fragments, namely the *BookFlexiBus* and the *TicketPaymentRequest*. As regards activities, they can be essentially of four types: *input*, *output*, *concrete* and *abstract*. While the first three are well known, the novelty is the use of the *abstract activities* to make fragments, and thus services, dynamic. An abstract activity is defined in terms of the *goal* it needs to achieve. The goal consists in a configuration of the state of the DO holding the abstract activity that has to be reached. For example, the *TicketPaymentRequest* fragment ends with the abstract activity *Pay*, which is drawn with a dashed border and which has the goal *"TicketStatus = paid"*. The TicketStatus is a variable in the state of the FBM and its initial value is *notPaid*. Each non abstract activity can be executed both autonomously by the fragment or by interacting with the processes in the core layer, through direct communication. For example, considering the *BookFlexiBus* fragment of the FBM, the activity called *Choose Route* performs its task with no interaction with the core layer. To the contrary, its output activity *Send Request* is aimed to trigger the internal process named *RoutePlanner*, by calling its input activity *Receive Travel Request*. In the Figure, this kind of connection between activities is identified by tagging them with the same label. Abstract activities, instead, stand for tasks whose implementation is not known a priori and must be produced at run-time through the composition of fragments (so-called activity refinement) [4]. The execution of these fragments leads the process to reach the goal defining the abstract activity. As regards interactions and cooperations between DOs, these can be realized in two ways:

1. since the interface of the core layer of a DO is public, a direct connection can be established by using the mechanism of subscriptions. Example of these connections are expressed by the arrow labeled with (a) and (b) in Figure 1. These connections are defined during the design phase of an application. They allow the engineer to construct a *hierarchically structured conceptual network* of domain objects, having possibly different levels of abstraction. In such a hierarchy, usually the DOs in a layer can *monitor* the DOs in the layers below. The connections highlighted in Figure 1 by the solid arrows define the hierarchy made of the Urban Mobility Application which monitors the FBM which monitors the TMS;

2. a second way consists in collaborations between DOs realized dynamically at runtime, through the exchange of fragments during the execution of abstract activities. In this case, the interacting DOs are not directly connected by explicit relations, but they interact during the runtime phase. For example, the *Pay* abstract activity of the *TicketPaymentRequest* fragment will be refined by using one ore more fragments of other DOs, as we will in Section 3.3.

### 3.2   Service Based Application Design

In this Section we present our approach to design a SBA through the definition of correlations and cooperations between a multitude of DO. Moreover we present how domain objects are able to refine incrementally their services, while executing them. The scenario depicted in Figure 2 drives us through the design of the application by showing how all the entities are modeled, how service providers are designed, how a domain objects hierarchy is build up using relations between DOs and, finally, how mobility solutions are provided to the end-users through the runtime selection and composition of different fragments coming from the involved domain objects. At the bottom of Figure 2, all the entities that may contribute to the overall application are shown. They frame the environment in which the application lives. It is composed by a multitude of entities, both humans and systems, which are autonomous and disconnected from each other. In the case of systems, the interaction exploits all the IT interfaces these systems expose on the web. These IT interfaces are however fragmented and heterogeneous, i.e., they consist of software designed independently from each other, and they are made available through a large variety of different technologies (web pages, web APIs, REST or SOAP services, feeds, open data, and so on). There is hence a need to encapsulate interactions with systems, so that they are presented in a standardized way. In our approach, this is achieved by a specific *wrapping* layer, which has the goal to cope with the encapsulation of fragmented and heterogeneous sources, aiming at presenting them as open, uniform and reliable *services*. In this scenario, there are people that make use of services by using applications on their mobile devices (e.g., journey planner app); many mobility service providers (e.g., flexi-bus, car pooling, parking service); municipalities that can offer smart services for citizens (e.g., the *city-card* that is a smart rechargeable card enabling discount and facilities to the owner); traffic and security management systems; pollution detection systems; weather forecast systems; systems for geo-location; banks

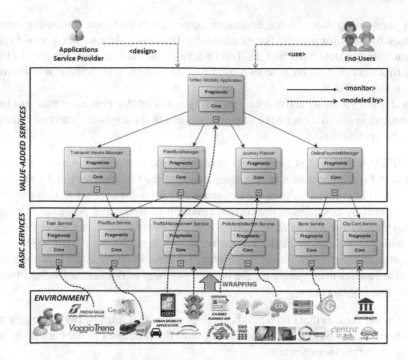

**Fig. 2.** Urban Mobility Application Scenario

and other public or private companies that can be involved in a urban scenario (e.g., banks offering on line payment facilities). For better comprehensibility, in our design, we show only the domain objects that are involved in the service composition.

**Basic Services.** The layer just above the environment shows the domain objects modeling the basic service providers. The flexi-bus service, just notify real-time information on the instances of flexi-buses all around (e.g., their position, their delay if any). While, the train service also offers a fragment, namely *trainBooking*, allowing the user to book a train and possibly to pay the ticket on line. The *Traffic Management Service* and the *Pollution Detection Service* domain objects essentially release information of real time traffic and pollution situations respectively. Finally, the *Bank Service* and the *City-card service* domain objects expose different fragments, all related to the management of the on line tickets payment and connected services. In detail, the bank service has one main fragment, namely the *onLinePayment*, while the city card service offers two fragments, the *payTransportMeansTicket* and the *RechargeCityCardOnLine*.

**Value Added Services.** Going up in the design of the scenario, there are the most interesting layers, in theDOs hierarchy containing the DOs modeling the *VAS providers*. These are the *Transport Means Manager*, the *Flexi-bus Manager*, the *Journey Planner* and the *Online payment Manager* in the middle layer, and the *Urban Mobility Application* in the top layer. These providers are characterized by the ability to offer value added services, in two possible ways:

1. by monitoring two or more basic service providers and then computing new services by exploiting them. For example the Transport Means Manager in Figure 2 monitors the DOs modeling the Train Service and the FlexiBus Service. In Figure 2, this kind of relation is shown by the solid arrows, which are marked with the <monitor >label.
2. by defining abstract activities in their fragments and/or processes that can be dynamically refined through the composition of others fragments currently available in the application.

The FBM introduced in Section 3.1 is an example of a VAS provider. Its business, depicted in Figure 1, consists in the management of the flexi-bus service by monitoring all the flexi-bus instances and in the definition of optimal routes for flexi-buses, which are calculated by considering the current situation of traffic and pollution. The routes are provided by the *RoutePlanner* process in the core layer. It is a clear example of VAS, which is realized by exploiting the services offered by the *FlexiBus Service*, the *Traffic Management Service* and the *Pollution Detection Service* in the layer below. The FBM also handles the requests for the on-line payment of the tickets for flexi-buses. It exposes two fragments:

1. the *bookFlexiBus* that corresponds to the protocol that must be performed by a user to book a flexi-bus. It works interacting with the processes in the core layer, as we said in the previous Section.
2. the *ticketPaymentRequest* that, by receiving the booking code of the chosen flexibus and the user data, triggers the internal process *PaymentRequestManagement* to verify if the user is allowed for the on line ticket payment. If so, the fragment execution can continue until the abstract activity *Pay*. The SBA will refine this abstract activity.

### 3.3 Incremental Service Composition

In this paper, starting from the domain object model proposed in [5], we extend it by introducing the concept of *fragment*, coming from [4], with its flexibility characteristic in modeling modular and dynamic services that can be easily composed. In particular, in this work we focus on the need for refining an abstract activity within a fragment/process instance. In our approach we model the incremental refinement process of an abstract activity by assuming that the adaptation engine [21] provides to the application the fragments composition on the basis of the goal of the abstract activity. In the majority of the approaches of service composition, *top-down* techniques are used. Essentially, a service composition is first defined and then deployed for being executed. This is not useful in a dynamic environment where services can enter or leave the system in any moment while end-users are constantly moving around, discovering new services and changing their needs. Our approach follows a *bottom-up* procedure. The fragments selected for the composition replace the abstract activities and are executed. To explain the approach, we present and example from our running scenario. Suppose that there are two end-users, namely Marco and Paolo, that use the urban mobility application. Its main fragment, namely the *manageMo-*

*bility* shown in Figure 3, consists in forwarding travel requests to its internal process that, after exploiting the monitored services, will send back the available applications in the environment that are able to manage multi-modal transport services.

The *journey planner* (JP) is a mobile application aimed at supporting sustainable urban mobility by offering multi-modal travel solutions. The JP allows users to send travel requests, by indicating different preferences (e.g., starting and destination's points, departure hour, preferred mode of transportation)

**Fig. 3.** manageMobility Fragment

and personal profile. After validating the request, the application is able to provide multi-modal transport solution(s) from which the user can possibly choose. Marco has both the city-card and the bank account while Paolo has not the city-card. In addition, Marco expresses the preference of moving by using a flexi-bus while Paolo prefers to go by train. We show how, following the bottom-up approach, two different final mobility solutions, customized for two different requests and user profiles, are incrementally defined. The urban mobility system receives the requests from Marco and Paolo. It replies by suggesting the usage of the JP application. The JP receives the two forwarded requests and it creates two customized transport solutions. As regards Marco, the incremental refinement process is shown in Figure 4. The process starts with the need of Marco of moving from a point A to a point B. This need corresponds to an abstract activity of the user DO. The *manage-Mobility* fragment of the UMA is executed. It provides the JP application, as response. Thus, in the second step, the *Plan* abstract activity of the *planJourney* fragment of the

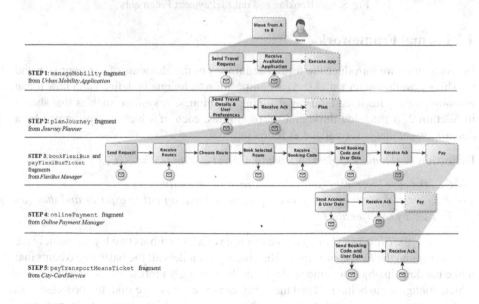

**Fig. 4.** Incremental Service Composition

JP has to be refined. Now, knowing that Marco prefers to go by flexi-bus, the selected fragments for the third step are the *bookFlexiBus* and the *TicketPaymentRequest* of the FBM, which are composed in sequence, giving the protocol to execute. But the *Pay* activity is abstract so, in the step number four, the fragment *onLinePayment* of the Online Payment Manager is provided to start the payment procedure. At this point is not yet known the real protocol to be performed for paying. In fact the fragment ends with an abstract activity also called *Pay*. As Marco has expressed the wish of paying with his city-card, the last provided fragment is the *payTransportMeansTicket* of the CityCard Service, which is necessary, finally, to execute the on-line ticket payment. Through five steps of refinement, the final protocol for the whole service execution has been provided in a dynamic and context-aware manner. As concern Paolo, instead, the service composition is almost equal to the one made for Marco but there are two important differences, exactly in the third and the fifth steps of the process of refinement. At the third phase, the provided fragment is the one exposed by the *Train Service* DO, namely the *trainBooking*, as shown in Figure 5(a), since Paolo prefers to go by train. At the fifth step, instead, the selected fragment for the payment protocol is the *onLinePayment* exposed by the *Bank Service* DO and depicted in Figure 5(b), to meet the wish of Paolo of paying with his bank account.

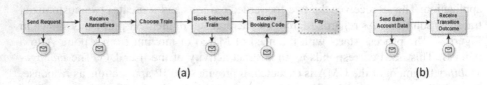

(a)                                                                    (b)

**Fig. 5.** trainBooking and onLinePayment Fragments

## 4 Formal Framework

In this Section we introduce the formal definitions of the elements of our approach and we show how the incremental service composition technique is defined and how it can be automatically resolved by using planning techniques. A system, such as that shown in Section 2, is modeled through a set of entities, each of which is represented by a *domain object* that is formalized as following:

**Definition 1.** *(Domain Object) A Domain Object is a tuple* $o = \langle \mathcal{CL}, \mathcal{F} \rangle$, *where:*

- $\mathcal{CL}$, *the core layer, represents the behavior of an entity;*
- $\mathcal{F}$ *is a set of services (i.e., process fragments) that an entity exposes and that can be used by other entities.*

In Figure 1, the *FlexiBus Manager* is an example of a DO with its two layers, namely the *Core layer* and the *Fragments layer*. The core layer models all the basic ingredients that make the domain object an independent unit. It essentially represents a set of processes, which configure the behaviors that the entity can execute. As we said, the processes can be not defined in a total and static way. The abstract activities are used to let processes have *opening points* to the outside.

**Definition 2.** *(Core Layer) The* Core Layer $\mathcal{CL}$ *of a Domain Object o is a tuple* $\mathcal{CL} = \langle L, L_0, E_{IN}, E_{OUT}, T \rangle$, *where:*

- *L is the state of a domain object. It is defined through a set of couple $(V, v)$ where:*
  - *V is the name of a variable describing a particular aspect of the domain object (e.g., current location of a user, bus delay, availability of a Flexi Bus);*
  - *v is the current value of the variable V at a specific execution time.*
  - *$L_0 \subseteq L$ is the initial state;*
- *$E_{IN}$ is a set of events (the "input" events to the object);*
- *$E_{OUT}$ is a set of events (the "output" events from the object), such that $E_{IN} \cap E_{OUT} = \emptyset$;*
- *$T \subseteq L \times E_{IN} \times L \times 2^{E_{OUT}}$ is a transition relation.*

We use the same model for both processes and process fragments (later in this section we call both 'fragments'). We remark that processes represent the behaviors of entities. Differently, fragments are pieces of process knowledge provided by entities to advertise their services to other entities around. For example, the *FlexiBus Manager* domain object provides a fragment, namely the *BookFlexiBus*, specifying how to perform the booking of a Flexibus. Now, any other process can perform the Flexibus booking by embedding and executing this fragment, following a specific refinement process. Formally, fragments are state transition systems, where each transition corresponds to a particular fragment activity. In particular, we distinguish four kinds of activities: input and output activities model communications between processes; concrete activities model internal elaborations; and abstract activities correspond to abstract tasks in the process. Abstract activity is what makes process structure dynamic. A process fragment is defined as follows:

**Definition 3.** *(Process Fragment) Process fragment is a tuple $p = \langle S, S_0, A, T, Goal \rangle$, where:*

- *S is a set of states and $S_0 \subseteq S$ is a set of initial states;*
- *$A = A_{in} \cup A_{out} \cup A_{con} \cup A_{abs}$ is a set of activities, where $A_{in}$ is a set of input activities, $A_{out}$ is a set of output activities, $A_{con}$ is a set of concrete activities, and $A_{abs}$ is a set of abstract activities. $A_{in}$, $A_{out}$, $A_{con}$, and $A_{abs}$ are disjoint sets;*
- *$T \subseteq S \times A \times S$ is a transition relation;*
- *$Goal : A_{abs} \rightarrow 2^L$ is the goal labeling function.*

On the basis of the previous definitions, a service-based application simply consists in a directed acyclic graph of DOs connected in a proper way, i.e., where the events produced by a DO are fully captured by all DOs monitoring it. This graph constructs a conceptual network of DO organized in a hierarchic way, as shown in Figure 2.

**Definition 4.** *(Service-based Application) A Service-based Application (SBA) is a pair $\Delta = \langle O, H \rangle$, where:*

- *O is a set of domain objects representing the entities of the system;*
- *$H \subseteq O \times O$ is a hierarchical direct relationship such that:*
  - *(a) it must be acyclic, i.e., there must exist no sequence $o_1, o_2, \ldots, o_n$ of domain objects in O such that $o_1 = o_n$ and $\forall i : \langle o_i, o_{i+1} \rangle \in H$, and*
  - *(b) $\forall \langle o_1, o_2 \rangle \in H : E_{OUT}(o_1) \subseteq E_{IN}(o_2)$.*

In the previous definition we have formalized how domain objects can be organized to configure a SBA. In the following, we formalize the execution of a single domain object, the execution of the entire SBA and, the activity refinement process. The execution of a domain object consists in the execution of its fragments, when they are invoked and/or in the execution of its internal processes, when they are triggered. In both cases, executing a fragment/process means to execute the sequence of activities from which they are composed.

**Definition 5.** *(Domain Object Configuration) We define a domain object configuration as a non-empty list of tuples $E_o = (p_1, a_1), (p_2, a_2) \ldots (p_n, a_n)$, where:*

- *$p_i$ are process fragments or internal processes;*
- *$a_i \in A(p_i)$ are activities in the corresponding process fragments, with $a_i \in A_{abs}(p_i)$ for $i \geq 2$ (i.e., all activities that are refined are abstract);*

Examples of tuples are those depicted in the levels of Figure 4. If, during the execution, an abstract activity is meet, this has to be refined by replacing it with a composition of other fragments. The refinement will modify the state of the domain object stating that the goal of the abstract activity has been reached. The advantage of performing the composition at run-time is twofold: (i) available fragments are not always known at design time (e.g., a new parking payment procedure may be activated and the corresponding fragment added to the system), and the composition strongly depends on the current state of an entity (e.g., the end-user change his preferences or some features in his profile). Composed fragments may also contain abstract activities which requires further refinements during the process execution. The execution of the whole service-based application $\Delta$ is defined by the current state of each domain objects, by the domain objects executions in the system, and by the set of available fragments provided by the different domain objects.

**Definition 6.** *(Service-based Application Configuration) Given a set $O$ of domain objects, we define a service-based application configuration for $O$ as a triple $S = \langle \mathcal{I}, \Gamma, \mathcal{F} \rangle$, where:*

- *$\mathcal{I} \in L(o_1) \times \ldots \times L(o_n), o_i \in O$ represents the set of current states of the domain objects;*
- *$\Gamma \in E_{p_1} \times \ldots \times E_{p_n}$ represents the configurations of the domain objects;*
- *$\mathcal{F}$ is the set of available fragments provided by all domain objects.*

For lack of space, we do not give a formal definition of the evolution of a SBA configuration. Intuitively, a SBA evolves in three different ways. First, through the execution of the behaviors of domain objects: this happens according to the standard rules of business process execution. Second, through the entrance (and exit) of new entities into the system: each new entity cause the introduction of a new domain object in $\Gamma$ and the instantiation of the corresponding relations; moreover, since entities can bring new fragments, it also corresponds to the extension of the set $\mathcal{F}$. Third, through the refinement of abstract activities, which will be discussed in detail in the following.

**Definition 7.** *(Abstract Activity Refinement) An abstract activity refinement is a tuple $\xi = \langle S, \mathcal{G} \rangle$, where $S$ is the current SBA configuration and $\mathcal{G}$ is a goal over the state of the domain object $o$ to which the abstract activity belongs.*

An abstract activity refinement $\xi$ is a process $R$ that is obtained as the composition of a set of fragments in $\mathcal{F}(\mathcal{S})$. When executed from the current domain object configuration $E_o$, $R$ ensures that the resulting domain object configuration satisfies the goal $\mathcal{G}(\xi)$. This means that the composition is obtained by chaining the new fragment in the configuration of the domain object $o$: $E'_o = (R, a_0) \cdot E_o$. For example, looking at the steps 3 and 4 of the Figure 4 we can see the current configuration of the FBM, representing $E_o$, at the step 3. The *Pay* abstract activity is $a_0$, the input for the refinement process. When executed, the refinement process $R$ leds to place the fragment shown at the step 4 in substitution of the abstract activity, bringing to a new configuration, exactly $E'_o$.

# 5   Implementation

In this Section we discuss the implementation of a *prototype* corresponding to the SBA described in Section 3 using our approach. The implementation language that we have used is Java. The aim of the prototype is to show an object-oriented representation of domain objects and their relations. The incremental service composition, instead, is dynamically realized by exploiting existing dynamic composition techniques such as those exposed in [4]. We primarily focused on the main ingredients of the model presented in this paper. The integration with the adaptation engine and the embedding of fragment compositions in replacing abstract activities are out of the scope of this paper and they are considered as future work. In the following paragraph we discuss the core layer implementation of a DO and an example of a fragment implementation.

**Core Layer Implementation.** In this Section we take the FBM code (see Figure 1) as an example of a core layer implementation. We present some chunk of java code implementing the three main parts of the FBM core layer introduced in Section 3, namely the structure, the interface and the behavior. The structure is made of variables and relations, such as those shown in Figure 6(a). The FBM maintains in its state information about the *routes*, the *flexiBuses* data and the *ticketStatus* for each seat of each flexi-bus (lines from 14 to 18). The relation *fbInstances* in lines 21-22, instead, is used by the FBM to manage the flexi-bus instances representing the real flexi-buses around in the city. The Figure 1 shows that the FBM has three main processes, namely the *paymentRequestManagement*, the *routePlanner* and the *flexiBusBooking*. They can be implemented as class methods, as depicted in Figure 6(b). Finally, in Figure 6(c) and 6(d), the interface implementation of the core layer is exposed. The Figure 6(c) reports the ports on which the domain object publishes its events or forwards some notification. They are identified by the *@Port* annotation and by the empty implementation. An example of a publication of an event on a port is reported in Figure 6(d), at line 83, where the *flexiBusServiceUnavailable* port is called. The Figure 6(d) displays both a *Service Notification* example, from line 78 to line 84, and a *Subscription Definition* example, from line 86 to line 90. The service notification is represented by the *@ServiceNotification* annotation and it is triggered by a notification from the service specified by the annotation parameters. The service subscription, instead, consists in a method labeled with the *@Subscribe* annotation whose parameters *event* and *type* say which is the monitored event and to which domain object it belongs (lines 86-87).

```
13    //VARIABLES                                    45    //PROCESSES
14    List<Route> routes = new ArrayList<Route>();  46    protected void paymentRequestManagement
15    List<FlexiBusData> flexiBuses =                47        (TicketPaymentRequest fragment, Data data){
16        new ArrayList<FlexiBusData>();             48        fragment.receiveReply(this.validateData(data));
17    Map<FlexiBus, Seat> ticketStatus =             49    }
18        new HashMap<FlexiBus, Seat>();             50
19                                                    51    protected void routePlanner
20    //RELATIONS                                     52        (BookFlexiBus fragment, Data data){
21    List<FlexiBus> fbInstances =                    53    //process implementation
22        new ArrayList<FlexiBus>();                  54    }
                                                      55
                                                      56    protected void flexiBusBooking
                                                      57        (BookFlexiBus fragment, Data data){
                                                      58    //process implementation
                                                      59    }
```

(a)                                                (b)

```
27    //PORTS                                        78    @ServiceNotification(serviceId = "FlexiBusService",
28    @Port                                          79        serviceMethodName = "GetFlexiBusServiceStatus",
29    public void flexiBusServiceUnavailable         80        subscriptionId = "this.subscriptionId")
30        (Status status) {                          81    public void serviceArrived(Status status) {
31    }                                              82        //some code
32                                                   83        flexiBusServiceUnavailable(status);
33    @Port                                          84    }
34    public void routesUpdate                       85
35        (List<Route> routes) {                     86    @Subscribe(type = TrafficManagementService.class,
36    }                                              87        event = "trafficJamNotification")
                                                      88    private void manageTrafficInfo(Info info) {
                                                      89        //some code
                                                      90    }
```

(c)                                                (d)

**Fig. 6.** Core Layer implementation

**Fragments Layer Implementation.** The fragments layer models the set of services that the domain object externally exposes. A fragment can be seen as a *class* whose methods implement the activities making the fragment. In Figure 7 we shown a basic implementation of the fragment *TicketPaymentRequest* of ther FBM. It is important to notice the following aspects. The fragment holds a reference to the core layer of the domain object to which it belongs, namely the *FlexiBusManagerCore* reference, at line 6, that is used to interact with the core layer processes. Lines from 15 to 20 implement the method *execute*, which is used in a service composition containing the current fragment to start its execution. Lines 30 and 31, instead, show how the abstract activity *pay* is defined. An abstract activity is essentially a method with no implementation. It is annotated with a specific annotation, *@abstractActivity* (line 30), stating that the method

```
3    @Fragment
4    public class TicketPaymentRequest implements FragmentsSet{
5
6        private FlexiBusManagerCore manager;
7        private Response response;
8        private Status ticketStatus = Status.NOT_PAID;
9
10       public TicketPaymentRequest(FlexiBusManagerCore manager) {
11           super();
12           this.manager = manager;
13       }
14
15       public void execute(Data data) {
16           this.sendBookingCodeAndUserData(data);
17           if (this.response == Response.ACK) {
18               this.pay();
19           }
20       }
21
22       private void sendBookingCodeAndUserData(Data data) {
23           this.manager.paymentRequestManagement(this, data);
24       }
25
26       protected void receiveReply(Response response){
27           this.response = response;
28       }
29
30       @abstractActivity(Goal = "manager.ticketStatus = paid")
31       private void pay(){}
32
33   }
```

**Fig. 7.** Fragment implementation

maps an abstract activity defined by the *goal* parameter of the annotation. In line 18, the abstract activity *pay* is called inside the 'execute' method. Being abstract it will not be executed but the adaptation engine is called and notified that an abstract activity needs to be refined, on the basis of its goal. At this point the engine will provide the fragments composition for replacing the abstract activity.

## 6 Related Work

In last years, different approaches have been proposed to provide relevant techniques for the modeling of services in a suitable way for making efficient dynamic service composition. From the scenario discussed above, the need of being able to define services in a way that they can dynamically adapt to the context, when this is discovered or when it changes, is emerged.

An approach is presented by Hull et al. [11] in their work about *Business Artifacts*. It consists in the definition of a formal/theoretical framework for defining conceptual entities, the artifacts, related to the execution of services whose operations influence the entities evolution, as they move through the business's operations. However, this approach deal not with dynamic service composition needs but it focuses only on service modeling aspects. Yu et al. propose MoDAR [24], an approach on how to design dynamically adaptive service-based systems. Essentially they propose a method to simplify business processes by using rules to abstract their complex structure and to capture their variable behavior. However, in dynamic context, to rethink rules every time is to expensive to manage continuous and unpredictable changes. In [12], the authors tackled the problem of the unpredictable execution of service-based applications. In particular, they focused on how to evolve a running service composition. To deal with this purpose they propose a way for modeling artifacts corresponding to composite services that can change at runtime. However, the software engineer intervention is needed to manipulate the runtime model of services. Moreover, the adaptation and application logics are mixed making the model not so flexible. In [7] the authors present DAMASCo, a framework managing the discover, composition, adaptation and monitor of services in a context-aware fashion by taking into account semantic information rather than only the syntactic one. Since they address the problem of making the reuse of software entities more agile and easy to model, they focus especially on the adaptation of pre-existing software entities that are used during the developing of SBA. Also the approach presented in [16] focuses on the need of explicitly manage the context in the composition of web services, to address the problem of semantic heterogeneities between services. The authors present a context-based mediation approach that allows services both to share a common meaning of exchanged data and to automatically resolve conflicts related to the semantic of the data, by using context-based annotations which offer an optimized handling of the data flow. It would be interesting to use the approaches [7] and [16] in the management of the composition of fragments coming from the different DOs and the definition of the data flow between them. In [10] the concepts of goals and plans are introduced in the business processes modeling with the purpose of extending the standard BPMN to make the BPM more flexible and responsive to change. However, even if plans are selected and executed at runtime, they are defined at design time together with the relations with the goals they can satisfy. [9] is a framework for, among other things, the management of the integration of services in the business processes implementation's process to speed the implementation and deployment phases. Services' integration is realized in a plug-and-play manner in which activities are selected from a repository and then dropped into a process. However, as regards the runtime adaptation of processes, in this approach only ad-hoc modifications are managed.

The approaches related to the automation of service composition processes can essentially be grouped into two main categories, *service orchestration* and *service choreography*. The most important in the first category is BPEL [6], which besides composing services, expresses relationships between multiple invocation and it employs a distributed concurrent computation model. WS-CDL [17] is targeted at composing interoperable, long-running, peer-to-peer collaborations between service participants with different roles, as defined by a choreography description. Nonetheless, these approaches refer essentially only to the syntactic aspects of services modeling, thus they provide a set of rigid services that cannot adapt to a changing environment without the human intervention. The vision underlying WSs [15] is to describe the various aspects of services by using explicit, machine-understandable semantics, and, as such, to automate all the stages of the WS lifecycle. OWL-S [14] is an attempt to define an ontology for the semantic markup of services intended to enable the automation of WS discovery, invocation, composition, interoperation and execution monitoring by providing appropriate semantic descriptions of WSs. The WS Modeling Ontology (WSMO) [23] is an attempt to create an ontology of aspects related to semantic WSs aiming to solve the integration problem. WSCI [2], literally *Web Services Choreography Interface*, is devoted to the description of the messages exchanged between the web services in a choreography and external services. This means that WSCI mainly focuses on the observable behavior of services without deal their internal process. The *Business Process Management Language* (BPML) [1] is also a standard within the service choreography category. To the contrary to WSCI, BPML is a language for the modeling of the internal processes of services in a way which can be supported and executed by business process management systems. It is possible a combined use of WSCI and BPML to design the interface and the business process of a service, respectively. The *Unified Service Description Language* (USDL) [22] has been developed to offer a language for the description of services independently from their belonging domain. The authors' purpose is to allow the definition of all kinds of services from the *Internet of Services* (IoS) perspective.

**Discussion.** We conclude this section with a discussion in which we try to point out the advantages of the proposed approach. As regards the standard approaches of service composition, such as those of orchestration and choreography, they have have some crucial limitations. A major problem of these approaches is that most of them are based on the assumption that during the composition requirements specification, the application designer knows the services to be composed. Besides, some of them, such as [17], [6], remain focused on the syntax level without consider the semantic aspects of composition, which are, instead, necessary in context-based applications. Others approaches like [15], [14], [23], [2] and [1], have introduced the management of semantic knowledge in their models to drive the services' composition and interoperation but, despite this, they do not allow processes to be defined at runtime, through dynamic service composition. [7], [16] and [10] allow for very efficient management of data and control flows, with their methodologies for the sharing of the common domain and context of services which have to be composed, by overcoming implicit discrepancies existing between heterogeneous services. However, the adaptation's strategies applied in these approaches are defined at design-time.

The DO approach, instead, offers a lightweight-model, with respect to the existing languages for service composition. It can be implemented with every object-oriented languages and it is more flexible and able to define both orchestrations and choreographies thanks to its hierarchical organization of DOs. Moreover, the model explicitly handle the context by managing the dynamicity of services, which can enter or leave the system in any moment, with a flexible connection strategy between DOs that exploit the *publish-subscribe paradigm*. Unlike specifications of traditional systems, where the behaviors are static descriptions of the expected run-time operation, our approach allows the application to define dynamic behaviors. This is made through the use of *abstract activities* representing opening points in the definition of processes, which allow the services to be refined when the context is known or discovered. The *bottom-up approach* for the activities' refinement allows *fragments*, once they are selected for the composition, to climb the DO's hierarchy to be embedded in the running process. Besides, the adaptation strategies are defined at runtime, so that exactly the available services are considered for the composition.

## 7 Conclusion

In this paper we have introduced an approach to enable a dynamic and incremental service composition, in highly dynamic environments. As future work, we plan to extend the model with the other techniques for the adaptation of SBAs exposed in [4] and to integrate it with our adaptation engine of [21]. We also plan to implement a process for the embedding of fragment compositions in replacing abstract activities in a dynamic and optimized manner. As concern the prototype, our intention is to implement a complete final version and to perform evaluations to assess the approach applicability. Finally, we are also reasoning on the possibility of realizing a design tool for the automation of SBAs design and implementation using DO.

**Acknowledgment.** This work is partially funded by the 7th Framework EU-FET project 600792 ALLOW Ensembles.

## References

[1] Bpml.org. business process modeling language, bpml (2002), http://www.bpmi.org

[2] Arkin, A., Askary, S., Fordin, S., Jekeli, W., Kawaguchi, K., Orchard, D., et al.: Web service choreography interface, wsci (2002), http://www.w3.org/TR/wsci

[3] Bartalos, P., Bieliková, M.: Automatic dynamic web service composition: A survey and problem formalization. Computing and Informatics 30(4), 793–827 (2011)

[4] Bucchiarone, A., Marconi, A., Pistore, M., Raik, H.: Dynamic adaptation of fragment-based and context-aware business processes. In: ICWS, pp. 33–41 (2012)

[5] Bucchiarone, A., Marconi, A., Pistore, M., Traverso, P., Bertoli, P., Kazhamiakin, R.: Domain objects for continuous context-aware adaptation of service-based systems. In: ICWS, pp. 571–578 (2013)

[6] OASIS WSBPEL Tecnical Committee. Web services business process execution language, version 2.0. (2007),
http://docs.oasis-open.org/wsbpel/2.0/wsbpel-v2.0,2007

[7] Cubo, J., Pimentel, E.: DAMASCo: A framework for the automatic composition of component-based and service-oriented architectures. In: Crnkovic, I., Gruhn, V., Book, M. (eds.) ECSA 2011. LNCS, vol. 6903, pp. 388–404. Springer, Heidelberg (2011)

[8] Eberle, H., Unger, T., Leymann, F.: Process fragments. In: Meersman, R., Dillon, T., Herrero, P. (eds.) OTM 2009, Part I. LNCS, vol. 5870, pp. 398–405. Springer, Heidelberg (2009)

[9] Göser, K., Jurisch, M., Acker, H., Kreher, U., Lauer, M., Rinderle, S., Reichert, M., Dadam, P.: Next-generation process management with adept2. In: BPM, Demos (2007)

[10] Greenwood, D.A.P.: Goal-oriented autonomic business process modeling and execution: Engineering change management demonstration. In: Dumas, M., Reichert, M., Shan, M.-C. (eds.) BPM 2008. LNCS, vol. 5240, pp. 390–393. Springer, Heidelberg (2008)

[11] Hull, R., Damaggio, E., De Masellis, R., Fournier, F., Gupta, M., Terry Heath, F., Hobson, S., Linehan, M.H., Maradugu, S., Nigam, A., Noi Sukaviriya, P., Vaculín, R.: Business artifacts with guard-stage-milestone lifecycles: managing artifact interactions with conditions and events. In: DEBS, pp. 51–62 (2011)

[12] Hussein, M., Han, J., Yu, Y., Colman, A.: Enabling runtime evolution of context-aware adaptive services. In: IEEE International Conference on Services Computing (2013)

[13] Laws, S., Combellack, M., Feng, R., Mahbod, H., Nash, S.: Tuscany SCA in Action. Manning Publications (2011)

[14] McGuinness, D.L., van Harmelen, F.: Owl web ontology language overview (2004),
http://www.w3.org/TR/owl-features/

[15] McIlraith, S.A., Son, T., Zeng, H.: Semantic web services. IEEE Intelligent Systems 16(2), 46–53 (2001)

[16] Mrissa, M., Ghedira, C., Benslimane, D., Maamar, Z., Rosenberg, F., Dustdar, S.: A context-based mediation approach to compose semantic web services. ACM Trans. Internet Techn. 8(1) (2007)

[17] Burdett, D., Kavantzas, N., Ritzinger, G.: Wscdl v1.0 (2004),
http://www.w3.org/TR/2004/WD-ws-cdl-10-20040427/

[18] OpenSOA. Service component architecture specifications (2007),
http://www.oasis-opencsa.org

[19] Peltz, C.: Web services orchestration and choreography. IEEE Computer 36(10), 46–52 (2003)

[20] Pistore, M., Traverso, P., Paolucci, M., Wagner, M.: From software services to a future internet of services. In: Future Internet Assembly, pp. 183–192 (2009)

[21] Raik, H., Bucchiarone, A., Khurshid, N., Marconi, A., Pistore, M.: Astro-captevo: Dynamic context-aware adaptation for service-based systems. In: SERVICES, pp. 385–392 (2012)

[22] Srividya, S., Bansal, A., Simon, L., Hite, T.: Usdl: A service-semantics description language for automatic service discovery and composition (2009)

[23] WSMO. Wsmo working group, http://www.wsmo.org

[24] Yu, J., Sheng, Q.Z., Swee, J.K.Y.: Model-driven development of adaptive service-based systems with aspects and rules. In: Chen, L., Triantafillou, P., Suel, T. (eds.) WISE 2010. LNCS, vol. 6488, pp. 548–563. Springer, Heidelberg (2010)

# SOA-Readiness of REST

Peter Leo Gorski, Luigi Lo Iacono,
Hoai Viet Nguyen, and Daniel Behnam Torkian

Cologne University of Applied Sciences, Germany
{peter.gorski,luigi.lo_iacono,viet.nguyen,daniel.torkian}@fh-koeln.de

**Abstract.** SOA is a core concept for designing distributed applications based on the abstraction of software services. The main strength lies in the ability to discover services and loosely-couple them with service consumers across platform-boundaries. The evolved service protocol SOAP and its accompanying standards provide a stable, rich and wide-spread technology stack for implementing SOA-based systems.

As an alternative approach to design and implement distributed systems based on services, the architectural style REST gains traction, due to its more light-weight and data format independent nature. Whether REST is also suited for acting as a basis for implementing SOA-based systems is still an open issue, however. This paper focuses on this question and provides an analysis on the SOA-readiness of REST. Both, a theoretical analysis and an empirical study of REST frameworks have been conducted in order to obtain a comprehensive understanding on this matter. The results show a lack of core SOA principles mainly related to the discoverability and the loose coupling of services.

**Keywords:** SOA, REST, Service Discovery, Service Coupling.

## 1 Introduction

The SOA (service-oriented architecture) [1] concept has become a prerequisite when it comes to the design of adaptable distributed software systems. Based on the notion of loosely-coupled services, functionality encapsulated in software services can be discovered and consumed by service clients at runtime. SOAP (simple object access protocol) [2] and its ambient standards have been for a notable period the only technology stack for implementing SOA-based systems. In recent years, the architectural style REST (representational state transfer) [3] has emerged as an alternative concept for designing distributed service-based applications. The most common technological basis for implementing REST-based services is the plain HTTP, what makes REST more lightweight and efficient than SOAP and keeps it data format independent.

Although REST has advantages in simple service invocation scenarios, the question remains whether it can still compete in settings in which an ad hoc discovery and coupling of services deployed in heterogeneous environments during system runtime is required. This paper investigates on this by examining the SOA-readiness of REST. First of all, an accurate understanding about the

M. Villari et al. (Eds.) : ESOCC 2014, LNCS 8745, pp. 81–92, 2014.

fundamental conditions which arise when applying REST to SOA is necessary for a well-founded conclusion on the SOA-readiness of REST. Since besides the dissertation of Roy Fielding [3] no further specifications are available at this point which can be used as a foundation, Section 2 lays the ground by recalling essential properties of REST. The main components of a SOA, i.e. service consumer, service provider and service registry, are the subject of a theoretical analysis in Section 3. Evolved technologies are available to implement these basic elements in SOAP-based environments. Along these lines, the availability and suitability of comparable approaches for REST are investigated and discussed. In addition to these theoretical considerations, an empirical study of distinct REST frameworks has been conducted to explore on the current state of implementation interoperability especially in the light of automatic service coupling. The methodology of the analysis is introduced in Section 4 and the gathered results are presented and discussed in Section 5. The paper concludes with a summary on the findings and gives an outlook on further research, development and standardisation demands in Section 6.

## 2   REST

REST has been introduced by Roy Fielding as an architectural style for designing distributed hypermedia systems. REST targets the scalability of application interaction, uniformity of interfaces and independent evolvement of components and intermediates with the intention to reduce latency, enable security and provide long-lived services. The uniform interface serves as the transfer protocol for identifying, accessing and manipulating resources. Furthermore, resources have different representations in terms of data formats which can vary according to the needs of the clients. Thus, services are able to deliver content for human-driven applications such as web browsers which use the data to render a web page. In turn, a machine-driven application would rather consume machine-readable representations from the same service. Data formats must be hypertext such that humans as well as autonomous processes are able to traverse hyperlinks in order to deduce the next state transition and action. Moreover, control data is used to define the semantic of the response by specifying—amongst others—resource states, error conditions and cache behaviour.

As being an architectural style, REST does not rely on any particular technology stack. REST does especially not depend on HTTP and URI as taking for granted in many publications. Still, HTTP and URI are the most common and widely used technologies for implementing REST-based architectures. HTTP is stateless in nature and it supports metadata (headers) to define various control and status information. It is intended to transfer resource representations marked up by MIME types. HTTP includes status codes to describe the semantic of a response and uses URIs to identify resources as well as a set of methods to determine actions, which makes up the unified interface.

Unfortunately, REST suffers from poor standardisation. Consequently, REST services are largely misunderstood and often assigned to simple web applications. This is for instance reflected by RMM (Richardson maturity model) [4], which defines four levels to categorise the "REST-fullness" of web services and applications. Due to this lacking clarity of the term and its meaning it is also questionable whether the maturity of REST has reached an acceptable level for being SOA-ready.

# 3    SOA-Readiness of REST

As depicted in Figure 1 a SOA consist of three parties. The service provider offers its services $\{S_1, ..., S_n\}$ to service consumers. To discover offered services a service registry maintains a database of services' descriptions. The providers attached to a particular service registry publish their services by supplying a so-called service contract, which contains all necessary information on the functionality of that service, its interface and other constraints demanded from a service consumer in order to make use of the service.

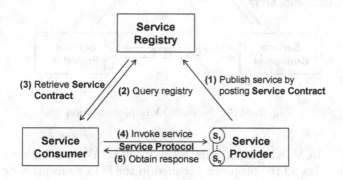

**Fig. 1.** Components of a SOA

Besides the discoverability of services, the service registry in conjunction with the service contract plays an important role in enabling the loose-coupling of service consumers and services. This means that service consumers are able to discover required services during runtime and to invoke such services without the need of adapting and recompiling the consumer code manually. This is accomplished by automatic code generation capabilities which rely on the rules and definitions specified in the service contract to generate the required code. Enriched with a platform-independent service protocol, the whole concept allows for the loose-coupling of even heterogeneous systems running on distinct platforms.

## 3.1    SOAP-Implemented SOA

A SOA is described in a technology-independent manner and henceforth can be implemented with any suitable set of technologies as long as the mentioned properties can be fulfilled. The most commonly used technology set is the service stack based on SOAP, where SOAP takes the role of the platform-independent service protocol (see Figure 2). The platform-independence of SOAP is achieved by it being based on XML. Due to this prerequisite, the stack further consists of other XML applications including WSDL (web service definition language) [5] as the standard for specifying a service contract and UDDI (universal description, discovery and integration) [6] as the standard for implementing the service registry.

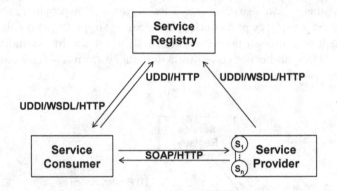

**Fig. 2.** SOAP-based SOA implementation

Thus, an SOA-based system implemented on SOAP and its accompanying standards contains all the properties defined in the SOA concept. Note, that the main protocol for transferring the service protocol messages is most commonly HTTP. This raises the question whether SOAP-based services can already be considered as REST-ful. In fact, most of the REST principles are also met by SOAP-based services, including the client-server, stateless, cache and layered system constraints. Still, the important constraint of a uniform interface cannot be fulfilled. This lies in the fact that SOAP-based services are operation-oriented which means that the interface is unique for each operation. REST instead is resource-oriented and defines the same four verbs for operating on each resource. The question arises, how a REST-implemented SOA then looks like and whether REST and its available implementation choices are already mature and comprehensive enough to implement SOA-based systems.

### 3.2   REST-Implemented SOA

To ground a SOA on the REST architecture style, according standards and technologies are required for implementing the various SOA components. As further demand, these standards and technologies need to adhere to the specifics of REST. Figure 3 illustrates a common instantiation of the SOA infrastructure when implementing REST on HTTP.

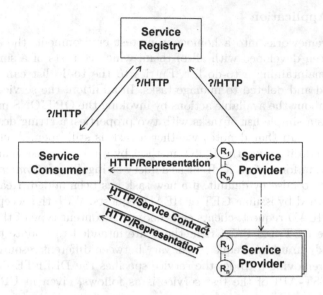

**Fig. 3.** REST-based SOA implementation

Instead of making solely use of a centralized service registry to discover services with REST this SOA principle can be extended to support decentralized discovery approaches, since REST services have the ability to refer to other services by providing hyperlinks [7]. Hence, a client is able to start at an initial (registry) service and henceforth discover a decentralized network of service referrals in order to find the looked for service. Figure 3 makes apparent, that for some of the SOA parts no standardised technological deployment choice exist yet. Especially the service registry and the service contract miss relevant standards and technologies in the REST universe, although a multitude of proposals exist to describe a REST service in a machine-readable manner [8–11]. Still, these approaches are yet in their infancy or not in conformance with the REST constraints, so that further work is required in order to distil the best fitting approach which may finally lead to a candidate for standardisation.

## 4   Empirical Analysis of REST Frameworks

In order to understand how the aforementioned shortcomings and especially the missing standardisation impact on concrete REST service development frameworks, an empirical analysis has been developed and conducted focusing on popular frameworks in distinct server-side programming environments, including Jersey (Java/JAX-RS), Play Framework (Java), ASP.NET (C#), restify (Javascript/Node.js), Ruby on Rails (Ruby) and Laravel (PHP). The goal of the study is to investigate on the processing of correct and intentionally flawed requests amongst the frameworks.

## 4.1   Test Application

To put all frameworks into a homogeneous test environment, the same application has been developed with all of them, which consists of a simple service that allows maintaining a to-do list. Entries to the to-do list can be created, read, updated and deleted to manage tasks. In addition, the service also offers information about the available actions by invoking the OPTIONS method. The data model is a simple list of tasks with two properties: a string describing the task and a boolean that denotes whether a task is still open. A client is able to create a to-do item via the POST method by sending a task name either in JSON format, in form of an XML or as a query string. The *isComplete* property is initially set to false by default, if a new task has been added. Reading to-dos can be performed by issuing GET or HEAD requests. With the accept header in a GET and HEAD request, clients can choose the content type of the requested resource. The PUT and PATCH methods are intended to update to-dos. Also the entity body in update requests can vary between different resource representations. For removing a to-do, the service specifies the DELETE method. The complete REST-API of the test service is as follows, given in URI Template notation [12]:

```
OPTIONS  /todos
OPTIONS  /todos/{id}
POST     /todos
HEAD     /todos
HEAD     /todos/{id}
GET      /todos
GET      /todos/{id}
PUT      /todos/{id}
PATCH    /todos/{id}
DELETE   /todos/{id}
```

## 4.2   Service Invocations

The test scenario assumes that the service provider and service consumer know each other and that no discovery step is required. The client is furthermore aware of the resource path and the data schema as introduced in the previous section. These prerequisites stem mainly from the fact that none of the considered frameworks include any form of service discovery or service exploration.

The analysis methodology is implemented in a specific client that executes the following test flow. First, the client adds a new task to the to-do list through the POST method. Afterwards, it checks the availability of a certain to-do item via the HEAD method. By usage of OPTIONS, the client gathers further information about available actions. Based on the gathered knowledge obtained from the OPTIONS method and HEAD request the client inquires to-dos via a sequence of GET requests. In order to mark an open task as completed, the PUT and PATCH methods are used. Once a task is completed the client takes it off the to-do list by invoking the DELETE action.

The whole test scenario consists of multiple test cases which can be grouped by the HTTP methods and one non-existing method EVIL as defined hereafter. Each test of a corresponding method owns a set of test cases denoted with a unique ID that starts with the first two characters of the method and a sequence number. The ID serves as a reference for the test case. The whole analysis encompasses the following test cases:

## POST Test Cases

**PO.1 Regular creation:** This action adds a resource via a supported data format (here XML and JSON) with semantically and syntactically correct content.

**PO.2 Unsupported content type:** This test creates a resource represented by an unsupported media type.

**PO.3 Content type and payload mismatch:** This test issues a request containing a mismatch between the specified content type and the actual data format of the payload, such as a request containing, for instance, a content type header with the value *application/json* while the body is XML-formatted. In further test variations the content type is completely absent.

**PO.4 Flawed content length:** This test case observes the service behaviour in case the value of the content length header differs from the actual size of the body. Test variations assign the content length value a alphanumerical string or remove the header entirely.

**PO.5 Flawed resource identifier:** This test examines the service response on wrong URIs including e.g. typing errors and URIs including IDs.

**PO.6 Malformed data:** Requests generated within this test class contain malformed payload data in their bodies such as a missing quotation mark in an JSON object or an absent greater-than sign in an XML document.

**PO.7 Unprocessible content:** The requests issued by this test category contain flawless headers and well formed data in the body, but encloses an unprocessible data schema that is not in conformance with the service's data model.

**PO.8 Unknown protocol version:** This test case invokes the service with a not existing HTTP version specified in the request line.

## HEAD and GET Test Cases

**HE.1/GE.1 Regular reading:** These test runs perform regular GET and HEAD requests with supported media types (here XML and JSON) specified within the accept header.

**HE.2/GE.2 Unsupported media types:** Requests unsupported resource representations form the service.

**HE.3/GE.3 Flawed resource identifier:** This test checks invocations on misspelled URIs and non-existing resources.

**HE.4/GE.4 Containing content:** This test issues HEAD and GET requests that contain content type headers and corresponding bodies which is actually not in conformance with the HTTP standard.

**HE.5/GE.5 Missing accept header:** This test constructs requests without an accept header.

**HE.6/GE.6 Unknown protocol version:** This test case invokes the service with a not existing HTTP version specified in the request line.

## OPTIONS Test Cases

**OP.1 Ping \*:** The HTTP specification defines a ping functionality by including an asterisk (\*) to the URI of an OPTIONS request. This test figures out whether this feature is supported.

**OP.2 Regular invocation:** The requests in this test case invokes regular OPTIONS actions.

**OP.3 Supported media types in accept header:** The goal of this test is to execute regular OPTIONS requests including supported media types (here XML and JSON) in the accept header.

**OP.4 Unsupported media types in accept header:** This test issues requests with unsupported media types specified in the accept header.

**OP.5 Flawed resource identifier:** Requests generated by this test class contain mis-spelled or missing resource identifiers.

**OP.6 Containing content:** The requests issued by this tests contain entity bodies, although the HTTP specification does not define any usage of payloads inside OPTIONS requests.

**OP.7 Unknown protocol version:** This test case invokes the service with a not existing HTTP version specified in the request line.

## PUT and PATCH Test Cases

**PU.1/PA.1 Regular update:** This test executes regular updates via the PATCH and PUT methods including supported content types (here XML and JSON) with semantically and syntactically correct content.

**PU.2/PA.2 Unsupported content type:** This test sends resource updates with unsupported resource representations.

**PU.3 Partial update / PA.3 Complete update:** This test issues partial updates via the PUT method and entire updates via PATCH with supported media types which are also semantically and syntactically correct.

**PU.4/PA.4 Content-Type and payload mismatch:** Requests generated by this test class contain a mismatch between the specified content type and the actual payload format.

**PU.5/PA.5 Flawed content length:** Intentional corruption of the length header value.

**PU.6/PA.6 Flawed resource identifier:** These tests perform updates specifying mis-spelled and non-existing URIs.

**PU.7/PA.7 Malformed data:** This test modifies resource representations so that they become syntactical and semantical incorrect.

**PU.8/PA.8 Unprocessible content:** Requests that contain well-formed and supported data, but it is not in conformance with the service's data schema.

**PU.9/PA.9 Unknown protocol version:** This test case invokes the service with a not existing HTTP version specified in the request line.

**DELETE Test Cases**

**DE.1 Regular deletion:** This test launches a deletion process of a single resource.

**DE.2 Non-erasable resource:** This test deletes a resource which must not be deleted according the business logic (here an uncompleted to-do task).

**DE.3 All resources:** The intention of this test run is to remove all the resources in one single request.

**DE.4 Flawed resource identifier:** Requests issued by this test class include mis-spelled and on non-existing URIs.

**DE.5 Containing content:** The DELETE request generated by this test case contains an entity body and a corresponding content type header.

**DE.6 Unknown protocol version:** This test case invokes the service with a not existing HTTP version specified in the request line.

**EVIL Test Cases**

**EV.1 Regular accept header:** This scenario tests a non-existing EVIL request with supported media types (here XML and JSON) in the accept header.

**EV.2 Unsupported media types:** This test generates EVIL requests with unsupported resource representations specified in in the accept header.

**EV.3 Flawed resource identifier:** The EVIL requests contain mis-spelled or non-existing URIs.

**EV.4 Containing content:** This test generates an EVIL request with a supported content type and a well-formed entity body.

**EV.5 Unknown protocol version:** This test case invokes the service with a not existing HTTP version specified in the request line.

## 5   Results

The results gathered from the empirical studies with six distinct REST frameworks based on the methodology introduced in the previous section are manifold. In general, they underline the need for a more stringent standardization of technologies suited to enrich REST-based services with service properties known from the SOA domain. By analysing the REST frameworks it became visible, that the missing standardisation leads to quite diverse implementations, causing incompatibilities, especially between system components deployed on heterogeneous platforms. This in turn means that such incompatibilities need to be resolved manually, which requires the involvement of an experience REST developer. In complex settings this might even not be feasible at all, yielding to constraints in respect to implementation choices.

The test runs show that when implementing the application scenario introduced in Section 4.1 with the examined frameworks, the main discrepancies appear in the usage of HTTP headers and the contained meta data therein as well as the status codes selected to signal the request processing state back to the service consumer (see Figure 4). As can be observed, the received status codes

| | Consolidated View | PHP | Play | Node | Jersey | RoR | ASP |
|---|---|---|---|---|---|---|---|
| **POST** | | | | | | | |
| PO.1 application/x-www-form-urlencoded | 201 | 201 | 201 | 201 | 201 | 400 | No Response |
| PO.1 application/json | 201 | 201 | 201 | 201 | 201 | 406 | 201 |
| PO.1 application/xml | 201 | 201 | 201 | 201 | 201 | 406 | 400 |
| PO.2 Unsupported content type | 415 | 415 | 415 | 415 | 415 | 400 | 500 |
| PO.3 Content type and payload mismatch | 400 | 500 | 400 | 400 | 400 | 400 | 400 |
| PO.3 No content type but with payload | 400 | 415 | 500 | 415 | 500 | 400 | 500 |
| PO.4 Wrong content length | 400 | No Response | No Response | No Response | No Response | No Response | No Response |
| PO.4 Content length as String | 400 | No Response | No Response | No Response | 400 | 400 | 400 |
| PO.4 No content length | 411 | No Response | 400 | No Response | 400 | 411 | 411 |
| PO.5 Wrong action on resource | 405 | 404 | 404 | 405 | 405 | 404 | 400 |
| PO.5 Wrong resource identifier | 404 | 404 | 404 | 404 | 404 | 404 | 404 |
| PO.6 Malformed XML | 400 | 500 | 400 | 400 | 400 | 400 | 400 |
| PO.6 Malformed JSON | 400 | 500 | 400 | 400 | 400 | 400 | 400 |
| PO.7 Wellformed JSON, unprocessible content | 400 | 500 | 400 | 400 | 400 | 400 | 400 |
| PO.7 Wellformed XML, unprocessible content | 400 | 500 | 400 | 400 | 400 | 400 | 400 |
| PO.8 Unknown protocol version | 505 | 201 | 201 | 201 | 505 | 406 | 201 |
| **HEAD** | | | | | | | |
| HE.1 application/json | 200 | 200 | 200 | 200 | 200 | 200 | 405 |
| HE.1 application/xml | 200 | 200 | 200 | 200 | 200 | 200 | 405 |
| HE.2 Unsupported media type | 406 | 200 | 406 | 406 | 500 | 406 | 405 |
| HE.3 Wrong resource identifier | 404 | 404 | 404 | 404 | 404 | 404 | 404 |
| HE.3 Not existing resource | 404 | 200 | 400 | 404 | 404 | 404 | 405 |
| HE.4 Containing content | 400 | 200 | 200 | 200 | 200 | 400 | 405 |
| HE.5 No accept header | 200 | 200 | 200 | 200 | 200 | 200 | 405 |
| HE.6 Unknown protocol version | 505 | 200 | 200 | 200 | 505 | 200 | 405 |
| **OPTIONS** | | | | | | | |
| OP.1 Ping * | 200 | 200 | 400 | 404 | 200 | 404 | 400 |
| OP.2 Regular | 200 | 200 | 200 | 405 | 200 | 404 | 405 |
| OP.2 Regular with resource id | 200 | 200 | 200 | 405 | 200 | 404 | 405 |
| OP.3 application/json | 200 | 200 | 200 | 405 | 200 | 404 | 405 |
| OP.3 application/xml | 200 | 200 | 200 | 405 | 200 | 404 | 405 |
| OP.4 Unsupported media type in accept header | 406 | 200 | 400 | 406 | 200 | 404 | 405 |
| OP.5 Wrong resource identifier | 404 | 404 | 404 | 404 | 404 | 404 | 404 |
| OP.5 Not existing resource | 404 | 200 | 400 | 405 | 200 | 404 | 405 |
| OP.6 Containing content | 400 | 200 | 400 | 405 | 200 | 400 | 405 |
| OP.7 Unknown protocol version | 505 | 200 | 200 | 405 | 505 | 404 | 405 |
| **GET** | | | | | | | |
| GE.1 application/json | 200 | 200 | 200 | 200 | 200 | 200 | 200 |
| GE.1 application/xml | 200 | 200 | 200 | 200 | 200 | 200 | 200 |
| GE.2 Unsupported media type | 406 | 200 | 415 | 406 | 500 | 406 | 200 |
| GE.3 Wrong resource identifier | 404 | 404 | 404 | 404 | 404 | 404 | 404 |
| GE.3 Not existing resource | 404 | 200 | 400 | 404 | 404 | 404 | 200 |
| GE.4 Containing content | 400 | 200 | 200 | 200 | 200 | 400 | 200 |
| GE.5 No accept header | 200 | 200 | 200 | No Response | 200 | 200 | 200 |
| GE.6 Unknown protocol version | 505 | 200 | 200 | No Response | 505 | 200 | 200 |
| **PUT** | | | | | | | |
| PU.1 application/x-www-form-urlencoded | 204 | 204 | 204 | 204 | 204 | 400 | 500 |
| PU.1 application/json | 204 | 200 | 204 | 204 | 204 | 204 | 500 |
| PU.1 application/xml | 204 | 204 | 204 | 204 | 415 | 204 | 500 |
| PU.2 Unsupported content type | 415 | 415 | 415 | 415 | 415 | 400 | 500 |
| PU.3 Partial update | 400 | 500 | 204 | 204 | 406 | 204 | 500 |
| PU.4 Content type and payload mismatch | 400 | 500 | 400 | 400 | 400 | 400 | 500 |
| PU.4 No content type but with payload | 400 | 415 | 500 | 415 | 415 | 400 | 500 |
| PU.5 Wrong content length | 400 | No Response | No Response | No Response | No Response | No Response | No Response |
| PU.5 Content length as String | 400 | No Response | No Response | No Response | 400 | 400 | 400 |
| PU.5 No content length | 411 | No Response | 400 | No Response | 400 | 411 | 411 |
| PU.6 Wrong action on resource | 404 | 404 | 404 | 404 | 404 | 404 | 404 |
| PU.6 Not existing resource | 404 | 500 | 400 | 500 | 415 | 404 | 500 |
| PU.7 Malformed XML | 400 | 500 | 400 | 400 | 400 | 400 | 500 |
| PU.7 Malformed XML isComplete=EVIL | 400 | 500 | 400 | 500 | 415 | 404 | 500 |
| PU.7 Malformed JSON | 400 | 500 | 400 | 400 | 400 | 400 | 500 |
| PU.7 Malformed JSON isComplete=EVIL | 400 | 500 | 400 | 400 | 400 | 400 | 500 |
| PU.8 Wellformed JSON, unprocessible content | 400 | 500 | 400 | 400 | 400 | 400 | 500 |
| PU.8 Wellformed XML, unprocessible content | 400 | 500 | 400 | 400 | 415 | 400 | 500 |
| PU.9 Unknown protocol version | 505 | 500 | 400 | 500 | 505 | 404 | 500 |
| **PATCH** | | | | | | | |
| PA.1 application/x-www-form-urlencoded | 204 | 500 | 204 | 204 | 204 | 400 | 204 |
| PA.1 application/json | 204 | 500 | 204 | 204 | 204 | 204 | 204 |
| PA.1 application/xml | 204 | 204 | 204 | 204 | 415 | 204 | 500 |
| PA.2 Unsupported content type | 415 | 415 | 415 | 415 | 415 | 400 | 500 |
| PA.3 Complete update | 204 | 200 | 204 | 204 | 204 | 204 | 204 |
| PA.4 Content type mismatch and payload | 400 | 500 | 400 | 400 | 400 | 400 | 500 |
| PA.4 No content type but with payload | 400 | 415 | 500 | 415 | 415 | 400 | 500 |
| PA.5 Wrong content length | 400 | No Response | No Response | No Response | No Response | No Response | No Response |
| PA.5 Content length as String | 400 | No Response | No Response | No Response | 400 | 400 | 400 |
| PA.5 No content length | 411 | No Response | 400 | No Response | 400 | 400 | 500 |
| PA.6 Wrong action on resource | 404 | 404 | 404 | 404 | 404 | 404 | 404 |
| PA.6 Not existing resource | 404 | 500 | 400 | 404 | 415 | 404 | 500 |
| PA.7 Malformed XML | 400 | 500 | 400 | 400 | 400 | 415 | 400 |
| PA.7 Malformed XML isComplete=Evil | 400 | 500 | 400 | 404 | 415 | 404 | 500 |
| PA.7 Malformed JSON | 400 | 500 | 400 | 400 | 400 | 400 | 204 |
| PA.7 Malformed JSON isComplete=Evil | 400 | 500 | 400 | 404 | 406 | 404 | 204 |
| PA.8 Wellformed JSON, unprocessible content | 400 | 500 | 400 | 404 | 404 | 404 | 204 |
| PA.8 Wellformed XML, unprocessible content | 400 | 500 | 400 | 404 | 415 | 404 | 500 |
| PA.9 Unknown protocol version | 505 | 500 | 400 | 404 | 505 | 404 | 204 |
| **DELETE** | | | | | | | |
| DE.1 Regular | 204 | 204 | 204 | 204 | 204 | 204 | 204 |
| DE.2 Regular isComplete=false | 403 | 204 | 403 | 403 | 403 | 204 | 403 |
| DE.3 all | 405 | 404 | 404 | 405 | 405 | 404 | 404 |
| DE.4 Not existing resource | 404 | 500 | 400 | 404 | 404 | 404 | 500 |
| DE.5 Containing content | 400 | 204 | 204 | 204 | 204 | 204 | 403 |
| DE.6 Unknown protocol version | 505 | 204 | 204 | 204 | 505 | 204 | 403 |
| **EVIL** | | | | | | | |
| EV.1 application/json | 501 | 501 | 404 | No Response | 405 | 500 | 404 |
| EV.1 application/xml | 501 | 501 | 404 | No Response | 405 | 500 | 404 |
| EV.2 Unsupported media type | 501 | 501 | 404 | No Response | 405 | 500 | 404 |
| EV.3 Wrong resource identifier | 501 | 501 | 404 | No Response | 404 | 500 | 404 |
| EV.4 Containing content | 501 | 501 | 404 | No Response | 405 | 500 | 404 |
| EV.5 Unknown protocol version | 501 | 501 | 404 | No Response | 505 | 500 | 404 |

**Fig. 4.** Status codes received by the frameworks for the test cases

differ amongst the frameworks for identical requests. This hinders the implementation of automatic code generation tools and loose coupling, due to the absence of an uniform behaviour. Especially a state transition based on the control data provided with the status codes is not feasible in an automatic manner across heterogeneous platforms.

An interesting and at the same time important result is the fact that the frameworks even when returning identical response codes sometime still are very different in other respect. One example can be noted in ASP.NET when a resource is created. The response code 201 created is returned as expected, but in addition to the URI of the freshly generated resource contained in the location header, the response carries the created object as its payload as well. This does not influence on the focussed SOA-readiness, but might raise other issues in terms of data volume to be transmitted.

Some of the tests even brought vulnerabilities to light which might get exploited in DoS (denial of service) attacks. The requests for which no responses have been received from the service are the potential attack targets. For the ones listed in Figure 4 the communication channel remains open. Thus, an attacker can occupy and block networking resource easily, by issuing such requests.

## 6 Conclusions and Outlook

REST is an established architecture style for designing distributed systems based on services and offers in conjunction with HTTP a wide-spread and well-understood implementation ground. It is less comprehensive as the SOA concept, though. Crucial service properties such as the discoverability and loose coupling are lacking for REST, including the related components and artefacts such as a service registry and a service contract. Still, such properties are required in order to enable the ad hoc usage of services during service consumer runtime. In this paper the need for such technologies has been motivated and initial contributions on REST-ful embodiments of a service registry and a service contract have been introduced. Still, there is a bunch of research and development challenge to solve in order to enrich REST with SOA service properties. According standardisation efforts need to be initiated and aligned with these developments as well.

The lack of standardisation in the REST domain got also apparent in another more elementary context. When conducting the study of REST frameworks one observation has been that the distinct frameworks construct and process service requests and responses very differently. This reveals that currently a heterogeneous system environment needs to be manually programmed and deployed by experienced REST developers in order to assimilate the system components. A stringent specification and mapping of the REST ingredients to HTTP is henceforth required, to lay the ground for a higher compatibility of REST implementations with less manual code interventions which finally forms the required foundation for automated code generation and the loose-coupling of REST services. Also, service security approaches require a REST/HTTP specification as a stable and reliable ground [13].

**Acknowledgment.** This work has been funded by the European Union within the European Regional Development Fund program.

# References

1. Erl, T.: SOA Principles of Service Design (The Prentice Hall Service-Oriented Computing Series from Thomas Erl). Prentice Hall PTR, Upper Saddle River (2007)
2. Gudgin, M., Hadley, M., Mendelsohn, N., Moreau, J.-J., Nielsen, H.F., Karmarkar, A., Lafon, Y.: SOAP Version 1.2 Part 1: Messaging Framework, 2nd edn. W3C Recommendation, W3C (2007)
3. Fielding, R.: Architectural Styles and the Design of Network-based Software Architectures. PhD thesis, University of California, Irvine (2000)
4. Wilde, E., Pautasso, C. (eds.): REST: From Research to Practice. Springer (2011)
5. Chinnici, R., Moreau, J.-J., Ryman, A., Weerawarana, S.: Web Services Description Language (WSDL) Version 2.0 Part 1: Core Language. W3C Recommendation, W3C (2007)
6. Clement, L., Hately, A., von Riegen, C., Rogers, T.: UDDI Version 3.0.2. Organization for the Advancement of Structured Information Standards, UDDI Spec Technical Committee Draft (2004)
7. Pautasso, C., Wilde, E.: Why is the web loosely coupled?: A multi-faceted metric for service design. In: Proceedings of the 18th International Conference on World Wide Web (WWW). ACM (2009)
8. Amundsen, M.: Hold Your Nose vs. Follow Your Nose, Observations on the state of service description on the Web. In: 5th International Workshop on Web APIs and RESTful Design, WS-REST (2014)
9. MuleSoft, Inc., RAML Version 0.8: RESTful API Modeling Language. Tech. rep. (2013)
10. Bennara, M., Mrissa, M., Amghar, Y.: An Approach for Composing RESTful Linked Services on the Web. In: 5th International Workshop on Web APIs and RESTful Design, WS-REST (2014)
11. Verborgh, R., Steiner, T., Van Deursen, D., De Roo, J., Van de Walle, R., Gabarró Vallés, J.: Description and Interaction of RESTful Services for Automatic Discovery and Execution. In: Proceedings of the FTRA 2011 International Workshop on Advanced Future Multimedia Services, AFMS (2011)
12. Gregorio, J., Fielding, R., Hadley, M., Nottingham, M., Orchard, D.: URI Template. RFC 6570, IETF (2012)
13. Gorski, P., Lo Iacono, L., Nguyen, H.V., Torkian, D.B.: Service Security Revisited. In: 11th IEEE International Conference on Services Computing, SCC (2014)

# QUELLE – A Framework for Accelerating the Development of Elastic Systems*

Daniel Moldovan, Georgiana Copil, Hong-Linh Truong, and Schahram Dustdar

Distributed Systems Group, Vienna University of Technology
{d.moldovan,e.copil,truong,dustdar}@dsg.tuwien.ac.at

**Abstract.** A large number of cloud providers offer diverse types of cloud services for constructing complex "cloud-native" software. However, there is a lack of supporting tools and mechanisms for accelerating the development of cloud-native software-defined elastic systems (SESs) based on elasticity capabilities of cloud services. In this paper we introduce QUELLE – a framework for evaluating and recommending SES deployment configurations. QUELLE presents models for describing the elasticity capabilities of cloud services and capturing elasticity requirements of SESs. Based on that QUELLE introduces novel functions and algorithms for quantifying the elasticity capabilities of cloud services. QUELLE's algorithms can recommend SES deployment configurations from cloud services that both provide the required elasticity, and fulfill cost, quality, and resource requirements, and thus can be incorporated into different phases of the development of SESs. We present several experiments based on real-world cloud services for the development of an elastic machine-to-machine data-as-a-service system.

**Keywords:** cloud service, software-defined, elasticity capability, elasticity quantification.

## 1 Introduction

Rapid development in cloud computing has introduced diverse types of cloud services offered by a large number of cloud software providers. This lead to increasing effort in investigating and developing native cloud systems by leveraging such cloud services in a multi-cloud environment [15,1,14]. In our work, we are interested in the development of cloud-native software-defined elastic systems (SESs), designed, developed and constructed directly in cloud, from functionality collectively provided by cloud services. Elastic cloud systems scale up/out if the workload is high, and scale back in/down when possible. In general, elasticity has three dimensions: resource, cost, and quality [5]. To achieve such elasticity, software-defined systems have their structure, requirements, and elasticity capabilities described and managed from software. Thus, their elasticity can be controlled via software-defined APIs by intelligent controllers [12]. While individual

---

* This work was partially supported by the European Commission in terms of the CELAR FP7 project (FP7-ICT-2011-8 #317790).

M. Villari et al. (Eds.) : ESOCC 2014, LNCS 8745, pp. 93–107, 2014.

cloud services might not be software-defined elastic – might not have elasticity capabilities controllable via APIs – when combined, we expect the resulting SES to be elastic. This triggers a challenging question on how to quantify the elasticity of these services and the SES to ensure that they meet the user's elasticity requirements. Although elasticity appears at run-time, through dynamic system reconfiguration with respect to certain requirements, selecting services providing the necessary elasticity capabilities when constructing SESs is crucial for answering the above-mentioned question. For example, we should avoided selecting a service which must be reserved for 1 year, when service instances are to be created/destroyed hourly. Although several frameworks allow a developer to model such systems, they are often limited to the exact specification of the required cloud services [8,9], without considering their elasticity. Currently, a SES developer has to manually search through cloud providers, and select services for the system s/he needs to construct, without support in evaluating if their elasticity capabilities support the required SES elasticity.

We believe that, to accelerate the development of SESs, we must quantify elasticity capabilities of cloud services and provide suitable functions for recommending services based on their elasticity, that can be incorporated in different phases of cloud-native system development. In this paper, we introduce novel functions and algorithms for recommending SES deployment configurations using cloud services providing the necessary elasticity capabilities, and which fulfill resources, quality, and cost requirements. We define an *Elasticity Quantification* function for quantifying the elasticity of cloud services. Based on the quantification function and algorithms, and multi-level SES requirements over cost, quality, and resources, we provide a framework for accelerating the construction of SESs by recommending SES deployment configurations using existing cloud services, which can be integrated in existing cloud provisioning frameworks [4] or recommender systems [10]. This paper presents the following contributions: (i) models for capturing elasticity capabilities of cloud services and multi-level elasticity requirements of SESs, and (ii) a set of customizable quantification functions and algorithms for evaluating the elasticity of cloud services. The contributions are provided as a set of models, functions and algorithms under the QUELLE (QUantifying ELasticity utiLity Engine) framework, which can be used by developers, automatic cloud composition tools, or elasticity controllers, in determining suitable SES deployment configurations w.r.t. elasticity requirements.

The rest of this paper is structured as follows. Section 2 presents the motivation and approach. Section 3 discusses elasticity quantification of cloud services. Section 4 introduces our algorithms for recommending SES deployment configurations. Section 5 presents our prototype and experiments. We discuss related work in Section 6. Section 7 concludes the paper and outlines the future work.

## 2    Motivation and Approach

To understand the challenges in constructing *cloud-native, software-defined elastic systems (SES)*, let us consider the development of a cloud-native

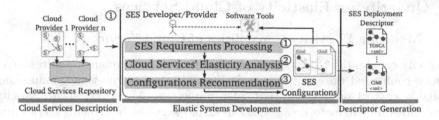

**Fig. 1.** Constructing software-defined elastic systems

Data-as-a-Service (DaaS)[1], which provides data storage and exchange services for Machine-to-Machine (M2M) platforms, such as smart cities. The system would be built from several cloud services, from basic IaaS VM services, to PaaS complex event processing for sensor data, data storage, and a message oriented middleware for events notifications. A core requirement for this elastic DaaS is that it should be able to be reconfigured at run-time to maintain a performance/cost balance. The development of DaaS is completely based on existing cloud offered services from IaaS to SaaS, and the elasticity capabilities they provide.

To develop the DaaS, in current approaches [10,7], the developer has to manually investigate all services offered by various cloud providers, and evaluate if their elasticity capabilities provide the required elasticity control options. Then, s/he can use existing design and modeling tools such as Winery [8] or MODA-Clouds [9] to design and deploy the DaaS on cloud infrastructures. Manually selecting each service needed for constructing the DaaS is laborious, complex, and error prone. These problems can be reduced and the development can be accelerated if we could provide features, shown in (Fig. 1), for:

- capturing and modeling elasticity capabilities of services from different cloud providers and multi-level SES requirements (indicated by ①),
- providing service elasticity quantification functions for software development tools (indicated by ②),
- recommending SES configurations, which can later on be mapped to software-interpretable deployment descriptor (indicated by ③).

Due to the complexity of existent services, their components dependencies, and heterogeneity of cloud providers, it is very challenging to develop functions and algorithms for quantifying elasticity of cloud services from multiple service providers. Such functions and algorithms have currently not been developed, thus hindering the automation of the software development for SESs. In this paper, we focus on providing a set of customizable functions and algorithms for quantifying the elasticity of cloud services, under the form of an elasticity quantification framework which can be integrated in semi or fully automated third party SES development and/or provisioning tools.

---

[1] A non cloud-native version of DaaS - (although designed for and running in the cloud) is available at https://github.com/tuwiendsg/DaaSM2M.

# 3   Quantifying Elasticity of Cloud Services

## 3.1   Modeling Elasticity Capabilities of Cloud Services

Elasticity capabilities of a service can affect how its cost, quality, and resources can be configured during its life-cycle (instantiation or run-time), influencing available control options for particular properties. Moreover, such elasticity capabilities also characterize associations among services, influencing service run-time behavior. Therefore, the elasticity capabilities of both individual and associations of services are crucial in providing a base for evaluating which services are suitable for a particular SES's elasticity. Therefore, we must understand and model the elasticity capabilities of cloud services and their dependencies, and quantify the elasticity of cloud services to support the development of SESs.

Following the multi-dimensional principle of elasticity [5], we define elasticity capabilities of a service as *configuration possibilities with respect to cost, quality, resources, and associations with other services, and the dependencies among them.* Thus, an elasticity capability defines what resource, cost, quality or associations among services can be created, when (instantiation or run time), and how often the services can be reconfigured. By studying main cloud providers, such as Amazon EC2[2], Rackspace[3], HPCloud[4], and Windows Azure[5], and through other studies [11], we found that elasticity capabilities of cloud services indicate which types of configurations are available and in which phases of the service's life-cycle. While some providers give hints about the capabilities of their services, (e.g., Amazon EC2 spot instances can be replaced faster than reserved instances), existing tools do not capture and evaluate such capabilities.

SESs are reconfigured dynamically during run-time by elasticity controllers, according to certain requirements. To evaluate if a cloud service provides the necessary elasticity capabilities for such run-time elasticity control, we need to capture when we can use an elasticity capability (elasticity phase), how often can we change it (volatility), and if it can be used standalone or not (dependency type). As most existing cloud services representation models capture resources and quality properties [6],[13], we focus on capturing elasticity capabilities (Fig. 2). An `Elasticity Capability` has an `elasticityPhase`, specifying if the capability is available during the service's `Instantiation-Time`, `Run-Time`, or `Both`. The elasticity dimension associated to the capability is defined by the `elasticityDim` property, and is one of `Cost`, `Quality`, `Resource`, or `Service Associations`. As one capability might indicate multiple configuration possibilities, the elasticity capability has a set of `Elasticity Dependency` instances. An `ElasticityDependency` specifies to which `Cost`, `Quality`, `Resource`, or `Service` a cloud service can be associated using the `to` property. `Volatility` is the most important dependency property, defining its minimum "usage" time, determining the frequency at which the dependency can be allocated/deallocated for the

---

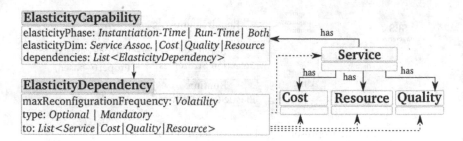

**Fig. 2.** Representing elasticity capabilities of cloud services

service (e.g., hourly, or monthly), and thus influencing the service's elasticity. For example, a service having dependencies which can be allocated/deallocated hourly is more elastic than one with dependencies which can be reconfigured only on a monthly basis. We describe if a dependency is `Mandatory`, or `Optional` using the `type` property. Mandatory dependencies decrease the elasticity of a service by requiring for the dependency to be always allocated with the service, reducing its usage flexibility. This model provides a base for evaluating if services' configuration options are appropriate for particular SES's elasticity control.

## 3.2 Representing Elasticity Requirements for SES

Using the previous elasticity capabilities model, towards accelerating the development of SESs, we provide customizable functions quantifying the elasticity of cloud services, to be used in recommending services best suited to the expected SES run-time elasticity control. For this we must understand and model requirements, run-time properties, and service selection strategies of SESs.

Different stakeholders might have different perspectives over a SES. Using our framework, requirements can be specified at different SES levels, according to the model defined in [2]. An SES is composed of units, logically grouped in topologies (Fig. 3). Elasticity of a SES appears at run-time, through dynamic reconfiguration with respect to SES requirements. Thus, describing and analyzing the expected run-time properties of the SES is crucial in discovering services that support the expected behavior. Through `Runtime Elasticity Properties`, we capture the expected run-time behavior of a SES using `Volatility` and `Dynamism`. Volatility is applied in recommending services with suitable capabilities for the expected unit usage time. Dynamism describes the number of units expected to be allocated/deallocated within a time period in a time interval. For example, we can describe a SES unit which uses its instances on average one hour (volatility), and allocates/deallocates 10 instances within 5 minutes every hour (dynamism).

A SES might require different elasticity control strategies over its units, topologies, or whole SES, such as maximize performance for a unit, and quality for another. Thus, for selecting services which support the required control, we use `Services Selection Strategies`. We first define `Elasticity`-based selection strategies, which recommend services based on their elasticity capabilities,

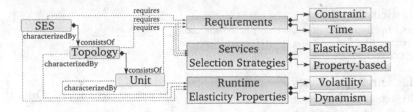

**Fig. 3.** Representing elasticity requirements for SES

relying on a set of elasticity quantification functions defined in the next section. These strategies are crucial in considering the elasticity capabilities of cloud services when building SESs. We define 5 `Elasticity-based` strategies: `Max {Overall, Cost, Quality, Resource, Service Association} Elasticity`. To also cover property-based user requirements, we support `Property-based` strategies: `Max {Fulfilled Requirements, Quality, Resources}`, and `Min Cost`. Multiple different strategies can be specified for each SES unit, topology, or whole SES, covering all potential SES requirements.

In turn, `Requirements` specify the cost, quality and resources required by the SES, and are represented as functions of form $f_{elReq}(constraint, g(time))$, where the `constraint` is a function depending on the cost, quality or resource metric on which the requirement is made, the type of constraint (e.g., greater than) and the required values ($h_{constraint}(metric, operator, value)$). A `time` parameter enables the specification of time-varying requirements.

### 3.3 Functions for Quantifying Elasticity of Cloud Services

Different SESs have different elasticity requirements, depending on SES requirements, and designed elasticity control mechanisms. For example, one SES might require more cost control options, and thus cost elasticity would be more important than quality elasticity. Thus, we provide a set of customizable coefficients for quantifying the elasticity of services, which can be tailored to suit particular SES requirements. Quantifying elasticity enables a numerical ordering of services after their elasticity, crucial in recommending services for SES configurations.

One important factor in evaluating elasticity of cloud services is the phase during the service's lifetime when elasticity capabilities are active: instantiation-time, run-time, or both. Let $v_i$, $v_r$, and $v_{ir}$ be user-defined values representing the importance of `Instantiation-Time`, `Run-Time`, and `Both` phases, respectively, for a particular SES; $v_i, v_r, v_{ir} \in [0, 1]$. Thus, we define an `ElPhaseQ` coefficient for quantifying the *phase* in which a service can exhibit elasticity, as follows:

$$ElPhaseQ(phase) = \begin{cases} v_i & \text{if } phase = \texttt{Instantiation-Time} \\ v_r & \text{if } phase = \texttt{Run-Time} \\ v_{ir} & \text{if } phase = \texttt{Both} \end{cases} \qquad (1)$$

Typically, to obtain SES configurations with maximum elasticity, $v_r$ should be at least twice as $v_i$, and $v_{ir}$ their sum (e.g., $v_i = 0.33$, $v_r = 0.67$, and $v_{ir} = 1$).

Dependencies between services increase (optional dependencies) or decrease (mandatory dependencies) the service's elasticity. Let $v_o$, $v_m$ be user-defined values representing the "importance" of Optional and Mandatory dependencies, respectively, for a particular SES; $v_o, v_m \in [-1, 1]$. We define an ElDepQ for quantifying the elasticity dependencies between services as follows:

$$ElDepQ(dependency) = \begin{cases} v_o \text{ if } dependency.type = \text{Optional} \\ v_m \text{ if } dependency.type = \text{Mandatory} \end{cases} \quad (2)$$

Typically, to obtain SES configurations with maximum elasticity, $v_o$ and $v_m$ should have the same value but opposite signs, with $v_m < 0$ as mandatory dependencies decrease elasticity (e.g., $v_o = 1$, and $v_m = -1$).

The Volatility of a cloud service heavily influences the service's elasticity, and might have different importance for different SESs. Thus, we consider a custom VolatilityQ coefficient for quantifying volatility, supplied as to suit particular SES requirements. Typically, VolatilityQ would have the form $numberOfAllowedReconfigurations/timeInterval$.

Based on the above coefficients, we quantify a single elasticity capability of a cloud service as $ECQ$:

$$ECQ(C) = ElPhaseQ(C.phase)$$
$$* \Sigma_{dep \in C.dependencies} \, VolatilityQ(dep) * ElDepQ(dep) \quad (3)$$

where $C$ is an elasticity capability, $C.phase$ its elasticity phase, $C.dependencies$ its elasticity dependencies, and $dep$ a single elasticity dependency.

For evaluating the overall elasticity of a cloud service $S$ over all elasticity dimensions (Cost, Quality, Resource, and Services Associations) we define an Elasticity Quantification (EQ) function as:

$$EQ(S) = \Sigma_{D \in cost,quality,res,servicesAssoc} \, W_D * \Sigma_{C \in D.capabilities} \, ECQ(C) \quad (4)$$

where $D$ is an elasticity dimension, $W_D \in [0, 1]$ is its weight, and $C$ is an elasticity capability of $S$ on dimension $D$. Different $W_D$ coefficients for each dimension $D$ can be set to suit particular SES requirements. For example, a SES interested only in cost elasticity would set $W_{cost}$ to 1, and the other $W_D$ coefficients to 0.

## 4    Algorithms for Recommending SES Configurations

In this section we introduce algorithms for recommendations SES deployment configurations based on the elasticity capabilities of existing cloud services. As one service could be instantiated under different configurations depending on its elasticity capabilities, Algorithm 1 evaluates an entity (service, quality, cost, or resource) with respect to a SES unit requirements, obtaining a set of potential configurations for the entity's elasticity dependencies (entityCfgs), depending

---

**Algorithm 1.** Evaluating cloud service against SES unit requirements

---

**Input:** *entity,requirements*; **Output:** *entityCfgs*

```
 1: function GETENTITYCFGS(entity, requirements)
 2:     fulfilledReqs = EvalRequirements(entity, requirements)
 3:     for d in entity.elasticityCapabilities.mandatoryDependencies do
 4:         capabilityCfgs = GetEntityCfgs(d,requirements)
 5:         entityCfgs.addCapabilityCfgs(d, capabilityCfgs)
 6:     end for
 7:     for d in entity.elasticityCapabilities.optionalDependencies do
 8:         capabilityCfgs = GetEntityCfgs(d,requirements)
 9:         entityCfgs.addCapabilityCfgs(d, capabilityCfgs)
10:     end for
11:     return entityCfgs
12: end function
```

---

on the requirements they fulfill. One cloud service might have different mandatory and optional elasticity dependencies on other entities with different properties (e.g., different cost). Thus, after the algorithm evaluates the static properties of the cloud service in Line 2 (`EvalRequirements` function), it continues by applying the `GetEntityCfgs` function recursively over its *mandatory* dependencies (must be used). Lines 3-6 determines the unit requirements fulfilled by the dependencies' configuration options, and adds these options to the `entityCfgs`. Next, the potential configurations of the entity's optional dependencies are evaluated against requirements (Lines 7-10), and their configurations added to the `entityCfgs`, obtaining the complete set of possible configurations for the entity.

---

**Algorithm 2.** Elasticity-driven SES configurations generation

---

**Input:** *SES*, *services*, *cfgsCount*

**Output:** *cfgs* - set of possible SES configurations

```
 1: function RECOMMENDSESCFGS(SES, services, cfgsCount)
 2:     unitsRequirements = MapRequirements(SES.requirements)
 3:     for unit in unitsRequirements do
 4:         EQ = SES.eqFunction(unit)
 5:         potentialCfgs = []
 6:         for s in services do
 7:             entityCfgs = GetEntityCfgs(s,unit.reqs)
 8:             if entityCfgs != empty then
 9:                 potentialCfgs.add(entityCfgs, EQ(entityCfgs))
10:             end if
11:         end for
12:         cfgs.add(unit, potentialCfgs.getBest(cfgsCount, SES.strategies(unit)))
13:     end for
14:     return cfgs
15: end function
```

---

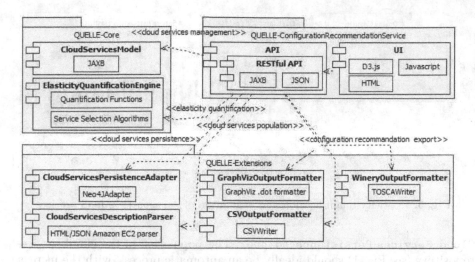

**Fig. 4.** QUELLE framework

Algorithm 2 applies elasticity quantification functions to generate a user-specified number of decreasingly elastic SES deployment configurations. Input SES description contains requirements, run-time properties, service selection strategies, and custom EQ functions defined at any SES level, from the whole SES, to topologies and units, which are mapped to SES units (Line 2). If conflicts are detected between levels, the lower level is applied. For each unit, its elasticity quantification function EQ is retrieved from the supplied SES description (Line 4). Then, for each cloud service, GetEntityCfgs (Algorithm 1) is called, obtaining a set of potential service configurations entityCfgs (Lines 6-11). The EQ function for the SES unit is used to quantify the elasticity of the potential service configurations from entityCfgs (Line 9). Finally, supplied unit strategies SES.strategies(unit) are applied sequentially in recommending from potentialCfgs the best cfgsCount decreasingly elastic configurations, according to their elasticity quantification (Line 12).

Quantifying elasticity towards selecting cloud services ensures that during the SES execution, an elasticity controller has the appropriate control options to be enforced depending on SES requirements and run-time behavior.

# 5  Prototype and Experiments

## 5.1  Prototype

We provide the QUELLE framework[6](Figure 4), exposing the functions, algorithms and models described in Sections 3 and 4, using RESTful services. For managing the Cloud Services Model, we implemented a graph-based Neo4j[7]

---

[6] Prototype and supplement materials: http://tuwiendsg.github.io/QUELLE/
[7] http://www.neo4j.org/

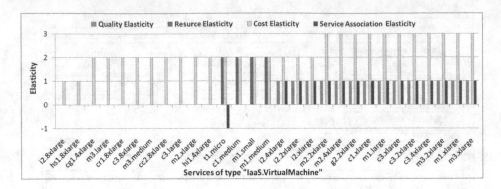

**Fig. 5.** Elasticity quantification and evaluation of Amazon EC2 IaaS services

**Cloud Services Persistence Adapter.** The population of the cloud services' repository (see Fig. 1) should ideally be an automatic process, with the increase in cloud providers' description APIs. However, currently we rely on available custom description services and HTML parsing to populate our model. For integrating QUELLE in existing software engineering processes, SES requirements constructed by third party tools are submitted as XML, and configuration recommendations returned as XML for easy processing. Finally, a TOSCA[8]-based output is generated using QUELLE's output formatter for Winery[8].

### 5.2   Evaluating Elasticity of Amazon Cloud Services

Most cloud providers still offer only basic cloud services, with reduced configuration and combination options, and implicitly, reduced elasticity. This limits our options of using real cloud services in our experiments. Thus, we focus on a single real cloud provider, Amazon EC2, providing 29 IaaS VM cloud services, each with various elasticity capabilities, generating a total of 253 possible service configurations, sufficient for showcasing our elasticity quantification functions. Additionally, EBS storage, Monitoring and Messaging services are provided, each with individual elasticity capabilities, sufficient for building our DaaS (Section 2).

As the desired elasticity might vary depending on the stakeholder, our framework provides a customizable elasticity quantification function relying on user-defined `VolatilityQ, ElDepQ`, and `ElPhaseQ` coefficients. As the user is interested in building an elastic system, s/he expects services to be allocated/deallocated often. As Amazon bills its services minimum on a hourly basis, the supplied volatility quantification coefficient is `VolatilityQ = 1/minLifetime (Hours)`, generating a volatility of 1 for hourly reserved services, and 1 / (365 * 24) for yearly reserved services. As the user wants to use services which have as few dependencies on other services, s/he supplies an elasticity dependency quantification coefficient `ElDepQ = {1 if Optional`, and `-1 if Mandatory}`. Finally, the supplied elasticity phase quantification coefficient is `ElPhaseQ = {0.33 if Instantiation-Time,`

---

[8] https://www.oasis-open.org/committees/tosca

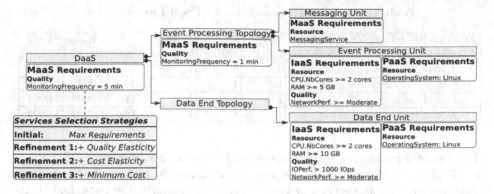

**Fig. 6.** Multi-level DaaS elasticity requirements

0.67 if Run-Time, 1 if Both}, and all elasticity dimensions have same weight coefficient $W_d$=1.

The result of quantifying the elasticity of Amazon EC2[9] services over cost, quality, resources, and services associations is depicted in Fig. 5. As the defined VolatilityQ function quantifies close to zero all options of reserving a service for 1 or 3 years, the cost elasticity of most services, such as m3.large is quantified close to 2. Amazon EC2 services which have optional dependencies have additional cost and quality control options. Thus, Amazon EC2 IaaS services with can be associated with an EBS service have their service association elasticity quantified to $\geq$ 1, and cost elasticity quantified to $\simeq$ 3.

## 5.3   Recommending SES Configurations

We aim to accelerate the development of SESs by recommending deployment configurations using cloud services providing the required elasticity capabilities. Thus, we define a four phase recommendation process: (i) processing SES requirements, (ii) quantifying elasticity of cloud services, (iii) recommending elasticity-driven SES configurations, and (iv) exporting SES configurations as cloud deployment descriptor.

As a user might not initially know the complete SES requirements, we apply an iterative approach, in which recommended configurations are analyzed by a user, the SES requirements refined accordingly, and resubmitted. First, mixed SES requirements w.r.t. cost, resource and quality, are described by the user in a top-down fashion, from the entire SES to individual units. At the SES level, a requirement for a Management as a Service (MaaS) service with a monitoring frequency of 5 minutes is specified, which will be applied to all SES's units. As the units belonging to the Event Processing Topology level perform sensitive computation, a MaaS requirement for a service with 1 minute monitoring frequency is specified, overriding the 5 minutes frequency SES level requirement.

---

[9] Services' description accurate at time of writing.

Table 1. Iterative services selection for Event Processing unit

| Service Selection Strategies | Recommended IaaS Services | Quality Elasticity | | | Cost Elasticity | | |
|---|---|---|---|---|---|---|---|
| | | Avg. | Min. | Max. | Avg. | Min. | Max. |
| Max Requirements | 23 | 0.6 | 0 | 1 | 2.39 | 1.0004 | 3.0004 |
| + Quality Elasticity | 14 | 1 | 1 | 1 | 2.78 | 2.004 | 3.0004 |
| + Cost Elasticity | 11 | 1 | 1 | 1 | 3.0004 | 3.0004 | 3.0004 |
| + Minimum Cost | 1 | 1 | 1 | 1 | 3.0004 | 3.0004 | 3.0004 |

The Event Processing Unit requires an IaaS service with over 2 CPU cores and 5 GB of RAM, and a Moderate network performance. In turn, the Messaging Unit requires a PaaS service of type messaging. Similarly, the Data End Unit requires an IaaS service providing at least 10 GB of RAM, I/O Performance of at least 1000 IOps together with at least a Moderate network performance.

While in the following we focus on IaaS services as they are most abundant and exhibit most elasticity in current cloud computing, we can apply the same approach for PaaS and MaaS requirements, as shown at the end of this section.

**First iteration:** The user submits to QUELLE SES requirements, without elasticity-based selection strategies. Focusing on the Event Processing Unit, the user sees that 23 IaaS services were recommended (Table 1), with varying quality and cost elasticity. **Second iteration:** The user adds a Quality Elasticity strategy, maximizing the quality options available at run-time. In turn, 14 services are recommended, with quality elasticity equal to 1, as the only modeled quality elasticity capability is an EBS Optimized storage option. **Third iteration:** The user adds a Cost Elasticity strategy, ensuring the SES can switch between as many pricing schemes as possible during run-time. Thus, 11 services are recommended, with cost elasticity of $\simeq 3$, due to supplied VolatilityQ function evaluating yearly cost schemes $\simeq 0$, and hourly pricing schemes (e.g., Spot) to 1. **Fourth iteration:** The user also wants Minimum Cost, reducing the recommended services to 1, fulfilling most resource requirements, having maximum quality and cost elasticity, and minimum cost.

In Table 2 we showcase the importance of quantifying elasticity capabilities of cloud services in SES construction, by comparing the usage of Elasticity-based service selection strategies with only using the Property-based strategies Minimum Cost and Max Requirements. With the later strategies, requirements are matched and services with minimum cost selected in a traditional fashion, recommending 3 service with varying quality and cost elasticity. Applying Elasticity-based strategies, the SES'e elasticity is increased, recommending a m1.xlarge service with more control options over its quality and cost elasticity dimensions.

Processing all IaaS, PaaS, and MaaS requirements refined above, our prototype generates a TOSCA descriptor containing the recommended SES configuration. For the Event Processing Topology, the recommendation is visualized in (Fig. 7) using Winery[8], a TOSCA modeling and visualization tool. The recommendation contains an m1.large IaaS service fulfilling the resource and network performance quality requirements with associated SpotCost, due the

**Table 2.** Elasticity versus property-based service selection for Event Processing unit

| Service Selection Strategies | Recommended IaaS Services | Avg. Quality Elasticity | Avg. Cost Elasticity |
|---|---|---|---|
| Max Requirements + Minimum Cost | m3.large, m1.large m2.xlarge | 0.33 | 2.33 |
| Max Requirements + Quality Elasticity + Cost Elasticity + Minimum Cost | m1.xlarge | 1 | 3.0004 |

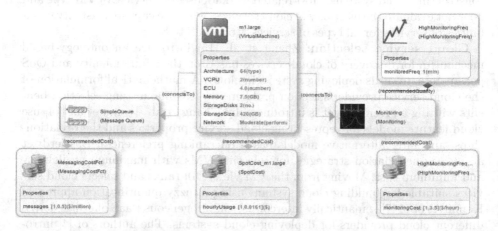

**Fig. 7.** Complete configuration recommendation for Event Processing topology

Minimum Cost strategy. A PaaS Monitoring Service with a High Monitoring Frequency is recommended for the monitoring frequency requirement, and a MaaS SimpleQueue service for the message oriented middleware requirements. In a similar fashion, recommendations are provided for the Data End Topology.

In these experiments we highlighted that, using our framework, a SES developer does not have to search trough all cloud providers for services providing necessary elasticity, and thus, accelerates the SES's time to deployment.

## 6   Related Work

**SES design and cloud provisioning:** Tools, such as Winery[8], Slipstream[10], Azure's Octopus Deploy[11] or ModaClouds [9], support construction of cloud services. Such tools require from the user a completely specified SES configuration, and the selected cloud provider. We differ, as we provide recommendations for SES deployment configurations, considering required elasticity capabilities, aiding in the process of choosing cloud services which provide the required run-time elasticity control.

---

[10] http://sixsq.com/products/slipstream.html
[11] http://octopusdeploy.com

**Cloud provider modeling:** Several approaches focus on modeling cloud providers towards cloud services provisioning. Goncalves et al. [6] define CloudML, a cloud modeling language, describing the resources and functional capabilities of cloud services. Villegas et al. [13] analyze provisioning and allocation policies in IaaS clouds by associating cost of services with their run-time. Wittern et al. [14] capture properties of cloud services and requirements using variability modeling, and integrate human decision-makers, towards filtering cloud services for constructing cloud systems. Most related work focuses on services of VM type and does not evaluate the elasticity of cloud services, while we capture elasticity capabilities of services for all types of services, from IaaS to SaaS.

**Cloud service selection:** Zhang et al. [15] introduce an ontology-based mechanism for discovery of cloud services based on their functionality and QoS parameters, towards deploying systems in cloud. A mathematical formulation of the cloud service provider selection problem towards maximizing selection benefits withing a given budget is introduced by Chang et al. [1]. Liu et al. [14] use cloud feature models for representing cloud service properties and their relationships, and filter alternative models based on ranking preferences. Dastjerdi et al. [3] use negotiation strategies for selecting VMs with maximum availability and minimum cost. Moving from the VM view, [10] ranks and selects cloud services suitable for building cloud systems using a fuzzy quantification approach. Kamateri et al [7] semantically interconnect heterogeneous PaaS offerings across different cloud providers for deploying cloud systems. The authors of [4] introduce GEMBus, an automated services composition platform providing federated network access to distributed applications and resources towards creating service oriented architectures. We differ as we do not focus only on initial system construction and deployment. Instead, we analyze the elasticity capabilities of selected services, recommending SES configurations which provide the required elasticity capabilities for controlling the SES's elasticity during run-time.

## 7    Conclusions and Future Work

In this paper we have presented a novel approach for accelerating the development of software-defined elastic systems (SES) by introducing the QUELLE framework which supports the quantification of elasticity capabilities and dependencies among cloud services. We demonstrated that QUELLE can be useful for many situations via the evaluation of elasticity of individual cloud services, and integration of QUELLE into software development phases of elastic systems.

We believe that the introduced models, functions and algorithms will simplify and reduce development effort in complex, diverse cloud service providers. Currently, we are focusing on modeling and evaluating the elasticity dependencies between service units and topologies, and use these dependencies in new functions for the SES development tools. We are also working on the integration of QUELLE into an integrated SES development environment.

## References

1. Chang, C.W., Liu, P., Wu, J.J.: Probability-based cloud storage providers selection algorithms with maximum availability. In: 2012 41st International Conference on Parallel Processing (ICPP), pp. 199–208 (2012)

2. Copil, G., Moldovan, D., Truong, H.-L., Dustdar, S.: Multi-level Elasticity Control of Cloud Services. In: Basu, S., Pautasso, C., Zhang, L., Fu, X. (eds.) ICSOC 2013. LNCS, vol. 8274, pp. 429–436. Springer, Heidelberg (2013)

3. Dastjerdi, A., Buyya, R.: An autonomous reliability-aware negotiation strategy for cloud computing environments. In: International Symposium on Cluster, Cloud and Grid Computing (CCGRID), pp. 284–291. IEEE/ACM (2012)

4. Demchenko, Y., et al.: Gembus based services composition platform for cloud paas. In: De Paoli, F., Pimentel, E., Zavattaro, G. (eds.) ESOCC 2012. LNCS, vol. 7592, pp. 32–47. Springer, Heidelberg (2012)

5. Dustdar, S., Guo, Y., Satzger, B., Truong, H.L.: Principles of elastic processes. IEEE Computing (5), 66–71 (2011)

6. Goncalves, G., Endo, P., Santos, M., Sadok, D., Kelner, J., Melander, B., Mangs, J.E.: Cloudml: An integrated language for resource, service and request description for d-clouds. In: International Conference on Cloud Computing Technology and Science (CloudCom), pp. 399–406. IEEE (2011)

7. Kamateri, E., et al.: Cloud4SOA: A semantic-interoperability paaS solution for multi-cloud platform management and portability. In: Lau, K.-K., Lamersdorf, W., Pimentel, E. (eds.) ESOCC 2013. LNCS, vol. 8135, pp. 64–78. Springer, Heidelberg (2013)

8. Kopp, O., Binz, T., Breitenbücher, U., Leymann, F.: Winery – A modeling tool for TOSCA-based cloud applications. In: Basu, S., Pautasso, C., Zhang, L., Fu, X. (eds.) ICSOC 2013. LNCS, vol. 8274, pp. 700–704. Springer, Heidelberg (2013)

9. Nitto, E.D.: Supporting the development and operation of multi-cloud applications: The modaclouds approach. In: International Symposium on Symbolic and Numeric Algorithms for Scientific Computing (SYNASC). IEEE (2013)

10. Patiniotakis, I., Rizou, S., Verginadis, Y., Mentzas, G.: Managing imprecise criteria in cloud service ranking with a fuzzy multi-criteria decision making method. In: Lau, K.-K., Lamersdorf, W., Pimentel, E. (eds.) ESOCC 2013. LNCS, vol. 8135, pp. 34–48. Springer, Heidelberg (2013)

11. Suleiman, B., Sakr, S., Jeffery, R., Liu, A.: On understanding the economics and elasticity challenges of deploying business applications on public cloud infrastructure. Journal of Internet Services and Applications, 173–193 (2011)

12. Truong, H.L., Dustdar, S., Copil, G., Gambi, A., Hummer, W., Le, D.H., Moldovan, D.: CoMoT - A Platform-as-a-Service for Elasticity in the Cloud. In: International Workshop on the Future of PaaS. IEEE (2014)

13. Villegas, D., Antoniou, A., Sadjadi, S., Iosup, A.: An analysis of provisioning and allocation policies for infrastructure-as-a-service clouds. In: International Symposium on Cluster, Cloud and Grid Computing (CCGRID), pp. 612–619. IEEE/ACM (2012)

14. Wittern, E., Kuhlenkamp, J., Menzel, M.: Cloud service selection based on variability modeling. In: Liu, C., Ludwig, H., Toumani, F., Yu, Q. (eds.) ICSOC 2012. LNCS, vol. 7636, pp. 127–141. Springer, Heidelberg (2012)

15. Zhang, M., Ranjan, R., Nepal, S., Menzel, M., Haller, A.: A declarative recommender system for cloud infrastructure services selection. In: Vanmechelen, K., Altmann, J., Rana, O.F. (eds.) GECON 2012. LNCS, vol. 7714, pp. 102–113. Springer, Heidelberg (2012)

# DevOpSlang – Bridging the Gap between Development and Operations

Johannes Wettinger, Uwe Breitenbücher, and Frank Leymann

Institute of Architecture of Application Systems, University of Stuttgart
{wettinger,breitenbuecher,leymann}@iaas.uni-stuttgart.de

**Abstract** DevOps is an emerging paradigm to eliminate the split and barrier between developers and operations personnel that traditionally exists in many enterprises today. The main promise of DevOps is to enable continuous delivery of software in order to enable fast and frequent releases. This enables quick responses to changing requirements of customers and thus may be a critical competitive advantage. In this work we propose a language called *DevOpSlang* in conjunction with a methodology to implement DevOps as an efficient means for collaboration and automation purposes. Efficient collaboration and automation are the key enablers to implement continuous delivery and thus to react to changing customer requirements quickly.

**Keywords:** DevOps, DevOps Specification, Devopsfile, Deployment Automation, Application Evolution, Cloud Computing.

## 1 Introduction

Today, many enterprises face a common, major challenge in terms of software delivery: customers and users expect fast responses to their constantly changing requirements, concerning both functional and non-functional properties of a software [6]. Frequent releases are vital to satisfy such expectations, which is indeed a crucial competitive advantage. However, technical and non-technical challenges have to be addressed in order to implement short release cycles. Cloud computing [10,2] introduced key enablers such as on-demand provisioning of resources (virtual machines, storage, network, platform-level services, etc.) and the pay-per-use model to tackle some of the major technical challenges. With these properties Cloud computing provides a means to support different service models such as infrastructure as a service (IaaS) and platform as a service (PaaS) combined with different deployment models (public, private, or hybrid Cloud) [10]. Beside these technical enablers, further conditions are required to enable fast and continuous delivery of software. The DevOps paradigm [6,7,17] addresses another major challenge, namely the split and barrier between developers and operations personnel. To overcome such a split that is predominant in many organizations today, organizational changes, cultural changes, and technical frameworks are required. In terms of organizational changes teams consisting

M. Villari et al. (Eds.) : ESOCC 2014, LNCS 8745, pp. 108–122, 2014.

of both developers and operations people may be established. Moreover, 'DevOps' may be introduced as a new role for people mainly working on coordinating the collaboration between both. Major companies such as Facebook[1], Yahoo[2], and others[3] are seriously implementing DevOps.

The DevOps paradigm is not bound to Cloud computing. Although combining these two makes a lot of sense as outlined before, DevOps could also be implemented in conjunction with other computing paradigms. In this work we mainly focus on enabling DevOps in combination with Cloud computing to reveal the full potential of DevOps. Our major contributions in this context are:

- We define a methodology to implement the DevOps paradigm in practice with a high degree of automation.
- We propose a language to be used to support the aforementioned methodology for collaboration and automation purposes.
- Based on the requirements stated in the motivating scenario we implement and evaluate DevOps-centric artifacts to deploy and operate an application, following our methodology and using the language we introduce.

The remaining of this paper is structured as follows: Section 2 refines the problem statement based on the introduction presented here. Moreover, a motivating scenario is introduced. Derived from this scenario and the problem statement in general, Sect. 3 defines a DevOps-centric methodology to deploy and operate applications in an automated manner. Section 4 introduces a language to practically support our proposed methodology. The evaluation of both the methodology and the language is described in Sect. 5. Finally, Sect. 6 and Sect. 7 present related work, conclusions, and future work.

## 2    Problem Statement and Motivating Scenario

In the previous Sect. 1 we briefly introduced the DevOps paradigm, aiming to eliminate the traditional split and barrier between developers and operations personnel. This split causes long release cycles for applications in many enterprises, very often several months. However, most users and customers today expect much faster responses to their changing and growing requirements. Thus, it becomes a critical competitive advantage to deliver software continuously [6], incorporating users' feedback and requirements as fast as possible. One major precondition to implement continuous delivery of software is to automate the whole deployment process in a repeatable way [6], including steps such as:

- Retrieve sources from version control
- Build binaries using build scripts
- Verify correctness of built binaries and run unit tests

---

[1] Facebook uses Chef (DevOps tool): http://www.getchef.com/customers/facebook
[2] DevOps at Flickr (Yahoo): http://goo.gl/XBKq
[3] Companies moving to DevOps: http://www.getchef.com/solutions/devops

- Provision infrastructure resources using provisioning scripts
- Deploy middleware and application components using deployment scripts

Ideally, the implementation of such an overarching automated process takes place in parallel to the development of the application itself, always taking into account changing and growing requirements of the application. The necessary constant collaboration between developers and operations is enabled by implementing the DevOps paradigm. Optionally, the automation of the deployment process can also be implemented afterwards, e.g., for legacy applications that still need to be maintained. In this paper we consider applications that are continuously delivered based on a fully automated deployment process. We assume that an application always consists of two major building blocks:

1. Business functionality such as the business logic, user interfaces, APIs, etc.
2. Supporting functionality such as the *operations logic,* tests, etc.

The *operations logic* is the fundamental enabler to implement a fully automated deployment process because it provides the necessary artifacts such as build scripts to create the application's binaries and deployment scripts to repeatable deploy the application to different environments (development, test, production, etc.). Most of today's enterprises and Web applications that aim for fast and frequent releases fall into this category of applications[4]. However, there are other kinds of applications such as legacy applications running in production that are maintained using highly manual processes without any means to deploy or re-deploy the application in an automated and repeatable manner. Our research does not focus on such applications without full deployment automation.

We put emphasis on creating and operating applications that have an evolutionary emerging and changing architecture, mostly by following agile software development practices [1]. This is a common way to create new applications in these days because a huge variety of IaaS and PaaS [10] offerings such as Amazon Web Services[5], Google Cloud Platform[6], and Heroku[7] with many add-on services[8] are easy to use and fast to integrate with each other. Thus, application developers start with some basic offerings such as a simple virtual machine (VM) or a Ruby runtime for an initial version of their application and add or remove additional services such as data stores, caching, queues, and monitoring services as they require it. This results in an evolutionary emerging and changing application architecture according to the requirements of the application's stakeholders.

Figure 1 shows an example for the architecture evolution of a simple chat application. Initially, the application is simply running in a Node.js runtime environment. Then, a database based on MongoDB is added to store some chat

---

[4] DevOps at Flickr (Yahoo): http://goo.gl/XBKq
[5] Amazon Web Services: http://aws.amazon.com
[6] Google Cloud Platform: http://cloud.google.com
[7] Heroku: http://www.heroku.com
[8] Heroku add-ons: http://addons.heroku.com

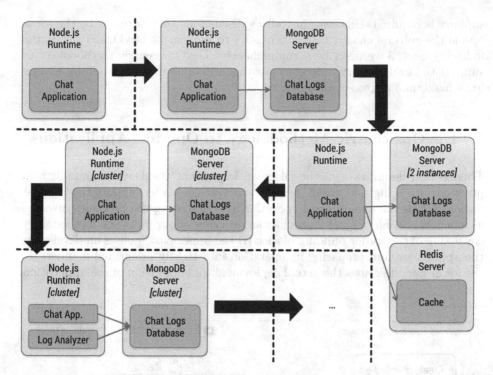

**Fig. 1.** Evolution of chat application architecture

logs. As the application needs to get more scalable, two instance of MongoDB are run. Moreover, a Redis server is used for caching purposes. However, this architecture does not seem to scale. Thus, the MongoDB server and the Node.js runtime environment are both run as clusters. The Redis server gets removed. In the next iteration, a log analyzer gets introduced as another application component to extract valuable information from the chat logs. The evolution may continue in this fashion including further aspects such as changing the underlying infrastructure. Whereas the first iterations may be hosted on local VMs or VMs provided by an IaaS provider such as Amazon, later versions of the applications might be hosted on PaaS offerings such as Heroku and MongoHQ[9] to address scalability issues.

In a conventional setup with development and operations split across different departments it would be hard or even impossible to catch up with such constantly changing operations requirements of an application. The DevOps paradigm aims to improve the situation for such scenarios by moving together development and operations. However, repeatable and fast processes can only be achieved with comprehensive automation, reducing manual intervention as much as possible. Manual processes to deploy and operate applications are error-prone, slow, and costly [14]. To implement such automated processes not only integrated tool

---

[9] MongoHQ: http://www.mongohq.com

support is required. However, in today's discussions this seems to be the focus beside the cultural change that is necessary to implement DevOps. Thus, in the following Sect. 3 we describe a comprehensive DevOps-centric methodology to support the evolutionary process of creating and operating applications, aiming for a maximum degree of automation.

## 3  DevOps-centric Methodology to Operate Applications

This section describes a methodology to implement the DevOps paradigm in practice with a high degree of automation. Our goal is to support DevOps scenarios such as the one outlined in Sect. 2 by automating the processes involved as much as possible. Figure 2 provides an overview of our proposed methodology, consisting of two major building blocks: (i) the upper part focuses on developing the application and preparing its operation in a tightly integrated manner; (ii) the lower part describes the actual deployment and operation of the application.

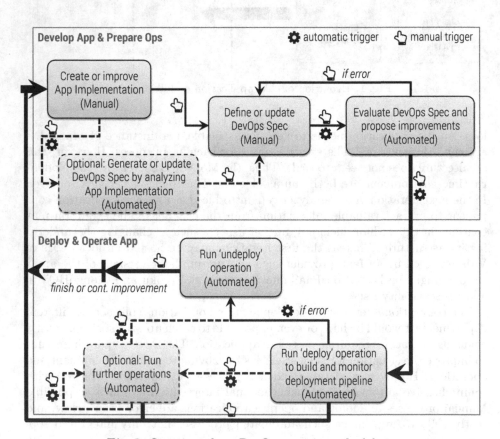

**Fig. 2.** Overview of our DevOps-centric methodology

Syntactically, Fig. 2 describes our methodology as a cyclic, directed graph. Each node represents a step of the methodology; the edges define the order of the steps. Dashed lines denote optional steps and paths. An edge can be seen as a trigger of the step to which it points. Depending on the annotation of the edge, the following step may be triggered automatically or manually. The entry point of the whole methodology is the *creation of the application implementation.* Obviously, we consider this step as a mainly manual process. As implied in Sect. 2 it does not only cover the implementation of the business functionality such as the business logic and the user interfaces; supporting functionality such as the operations logic are part of the implementation, too. Then, a central artifact in our methodology comes into play, namely the *DevOps Spec,* i.e., the DevOps specification:

**Definition 1 (DevOps Spec).** *A DevOps Spec specifies all developer- and operations-related aspects of a particular application to deploy it fully automated. For this purpose, an executable 'deploy' operation is defined in the DevOps Spec. This operation may utilize developer-centric operations such as 'build', 'test', and 'start' defined in the DevOps Spec, too. Moreover, operations to manage the application (e.g., 'scale', 'backup-database', 'undeploy', etc.) are specified to be triggered either automatically or manually after a successful deployment.*

Developers and operations people work closely together when maintaining the DevOps Spec, so the DevOps Spec serves as an important means to enable efficient collaboration between the two parties. As shown in Fig. 2 the *DevOps Spec* for an application may be *created* manually, either after a first iteration of the application implementation has been created or in parallel to creating the implementation. Optionally, an initial version or a skeleton of the *DevOps Spec* can be *generated* by analyzing the application implementation to find out some initial deployment requirements of the application. Such an analysis may be based on common conventions for application components such as the existence and the content of certain descriptor files [18]. For instance, a Node.js application typically owns a `package.json` file specifying its dependencies and the command to start the application.

The next step, triggered automatically or manually, is the automated *evaluation of the DevOps Spec.* The goal of this step is to use a set of rules to find possible conflicts, errors, missing parts, or weaknesses. Based on these findings, improvements are proposed to refine the DevOps Spec. As an example, a set of platform-bound commands to deploy a particular middleware component may be better replaced by a portable, tested, open-source artifact such as a Chef cookbook[10] maintained by the DevOps community. Based on these improvement suggestions the DevOps Spec may be updated accordingly.

Once the DevOps Spec is declared to be in a condition to be ready for deployment (by addressing the reported issues or by ignoring them), we switch to the second part of our methodology to deploy and operate the application. The *'deploy' operation* is run to *build the deployment pipeline:*

---

[10] Chef cookbooks: `http://community.opscode.com/cookbooks`

**Definition 2 (Deployment Pipeline).** *A deployment pipeline is an automated manifestation of the process for getting software from its sources (e.g., from version control) to be deployed to the target environment (e.g., development, test, production, etc.) [6]. The 'deploy' operation defined in the DevOps Spec prescribes how to build the deployment pipeline.*

The *deployment pipeline,* i.e., the execution of the 'deploy' operation is *monitored.* If an error occurs, the *'undeploy' operation is run* automatically. All error logs are stored for later analysis. Optionally, further operations such as 'scale' or 'backup-database' may run to manage the application. These runs may be triggered manually or automatically. In any case after the 'undeploy' operation has been run, it depends on a manual decision to go back to the first part to continuously improve the application implementation, update the DevOps Spec, and eventually re-deploy the application. Alternatively, the application is not targeted for re-deployment, e.g., in case the application is decommissioned completely. In this case, running the 'undeploy' operation is the final step. Moreover, we may also go back to the first part improving the application implementation and updating the DevOps Spec while the application is already deployed and operated. We could, for instance, deploy an updated version of the application in parallel and decommission older versions once the updated version is considered to run correctly. In the context of this paper we focus on the first part of our methodology *(Develop App & Prepare Ops),* especially on the automated and manual steps to define, generate, update, and evaluate the DevOps Spec. For this purpose, the next Sect. 4 proposes a language to be used to create and maintain a DevOps Spec.

## 4   DevOpSlang – A Language to Bridge the Gap

Based on the need to implement DevOps in practice (Sect. 1 and Sect. 2) we introduced a DevOps-centric methodology to deploy and operate applications (Sect. 3). We defined the notion of a *DevOps Spec* (Definition 1) as a key artifact to enable the implementation of our methodology. However, in the methodology's context we do not define how such a DevOps Spec is structured technically. This is absolutely necessary to implement the methodology in practice and to implement automated processes in particular. In this section we propose *DevOpSlang,* a new domain-specific language to be used for implementing DevOps Specs. The most important goal of DevOpSlang in conjunction with our methodology (Sect. 3) is to enable and support efficient collaboration between developers and operations, leading to automated processes as much as possible. Technically, DevOpSlang is a domain-specific language based on JavaScript Object Notation (JSON) [4]. We use JSON Schema [8] to define a formal schema for DevOpSlang that may be used for validation purposes. `Devopsfiles` are the technical artifacts rendered using DevOpSlang:

**Definition 3 (`Devopsfile`).** *A `Devopsfile` is the technical implementation of a DevOps Spec using DevOpSlang. A `Devopsfile` orchestrates arbitrary artifacts (Unix shell commands, Chef scripts, etc.) to implement operations.*

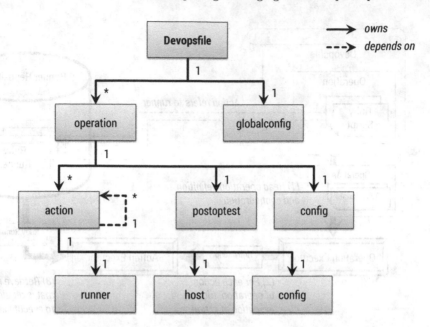

**Fig. 3.** Structure of a `Devopsfile` based on DevOpSlang

Figure 3 shows the structure of a `Devopsfile` based on DevOpSlang. The complete JSON schema definition of DevOpSlang is publicly available on GitHub[11]. An arbitrary number of operations can be defined. A single operation is implemented by a collection of actions that may depend on each other. Each action may implement an individual step of an operation. To make an action executable a *runner* is used. For instance, an operation may consist of two actions. The first one may be a Ruby script, using a *Ruby runner* to execute the script. The second one may be a single Unix shell command, using a command runner to execute the command. This makes the runners to be the actual workers to execute operations defined in a `Devopsfile`.

**Definition 4 (Runner).** *A* runner *is an executable enabler in the context of a* runner *framework (Fig. 4). It enables the execution of a certain action defined in a* `Devopsfile`.

An architecture overview of a runner framework that may be used to run such operations is shown in Fig. 4. Runners that are stored in the *runner repository* are reusable by different actions implementing operations in different `Devopsfiles`. However, highly application-specific runners can be implemented and stored inside the runner repository, too. An operation is run by the *operation executor*. Each action of the operation is executed by the *action executor*, considering the dependencies among actions. To actually execute an action, the action executor retrieves

---

[11] GitHub project *DevOpSlang:* `http://github.com/jojow/devopslang`

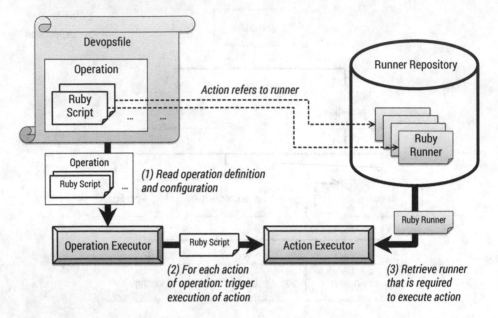

**Fig. 4.** Architecture overview of runner framework

the corresponding runner from the runner repository. [19] presents a similar architecture that may serve as a foundation for such a runner framework. Hosts such as VMs, containers, or platforms may be defined as a means to run different actions on different hosts. If no host is defined for an action, the invoker of the Devopsfile or the operation in particular determines where to run the action (e.g., localhost or a sandbox). In terms of configuration there is a global configuration at the top. Operations may have individual configurations that are merged with the the global configuration and may override parts of the global one. The same is true for configurations on the action level: they are merged with the operation's configuration and then with the global configuration, possibly overriding parts of them.

The following Sect. 5 presents the validation and evaluation of DevOpSlang in conjunction with our methodology (Sect. 3). We stick to the motivating scenario (Sect. 2) to create and refine Devopsfiles in an evolutionary manner as proposed by our methodology. This is enabled by the evolution of Devopsfiles and related runners.

## 5    Validation and Evaluation

The evaluation of our methodology in conjunction with DevOpSlang is twofold: the first part shows how Devopsfiles can evolve based on the changing architecture of an application and based on the collaboration between developers and operations personnel. The second part outlines the possibility to orchestrate multiple Devopsfiles recursively, so Devopsfiles remain maintainable even for large applications. Beside the `Devopsfile` schema all `Devopsfiles` discussed in this section are completely and publicly available on GitHub[12]. We validated all `Devopsfiles` against the `Devopsfile` schema using the JSON Schema Validator[13].

## 5.1  Devopsfile Evolution

Based on the evolutionary developed chat application described in Sect. 2 the following listing shows an initial version of a `Devopsfile` for the application:

```
 1 {
 2    "name": "chat−app",
 3    "version": "0.1",
 4    "author": "Johannes <wettinger@iaas.uni−stuttgart.org>",
 5    "description": "Automated deployment and operations for chat app
         ",
 6
 7    "operations": {
 8        "build": {
 9            "actions": {
10                "install−deps": {
11                    "runner": "command−runner",
12                    "comment": "Node.js 0.10+ must be installed",
13                    "config": { "command": "npm install" }
14                }
15            }
16        },
17        "start": {
18            "actions": {
19                "chatapp": {
20                    "runner": "command−runner",
21                    "comment": "Node.js 0.10+ must be installed",
22                    "config": { "command": "node app.js" }
23                }
24            }
25        },
26        "deploy": {
27            "actions": {
28                "build−app": {
29                    "runner": "operation−runner",
30                    "config": { "operation": "build" }
31                },
32                "start−app": {
33                    "runner": "operation−runner",
34                    "config": { "operation": "start" }
35                }
36            },
37            "dependencies": [
38                [ "start−app", "build−app" ]
39            ]
40        }
41    }
42 }
```

Beside some meta data such as 'version' and 'author' this `Devopsfile` defines a 'start' operation consisting of a single action entitled 'chatapp'. This is a minimalist definition specifying the command to run the Node.js-based application. Similarly, a 'build' operation is defined to install the dependencies required to

---

[12] `Devopsfile` schema and sample `Devopsfiles`:
   http://github.com/jojow/devopslang
[13] JSON Schema Validator: http://github.com/fge/json-schema-validator

run the application. The 'deploy' operation in its initial version points to the operations 'build' and 'start'. Such initial definitions may be automatically derived from existing application descriptor files such as the `package.json`[14] file for Node.js-based applications. For the next iteration of the chat application the Node.js runtime solely is not enough. A database is used to store chat logs. Thus, we need to start MongoDB as an additional component before running the application ('chatapp' action depends on 'mongodb' action):

```
1  "start": {
2      "actions": {
3          "chatapp": { ... },
4          "mongodb": {
5              "runner": "command-runner",
6              "comment": "MongoDB 2.6+ must be installed",
7              "config": { "command": "mongod" }
8          }
9      },
10     "dependencies": [
11         [ "chatapp", "mongodb" ]
12     ]
13 }
```

Up to now, we assume the middleware components such as the Node.js runtime and the MongoDB server are available already when running the 'deploy' operation. This might be true for some developer machines. However, on a freshly provisioned VM, for instance, these components need to be installed, too. Thus, the operation definition may be extended as follows to retrieve and install all components that are involved:

```
1  "deploy": {
2      "actions": {
3          "deploy-nodejs": {
4              "runner": "command-runner",
5              "config": {
6                  "command": "... && sudo apt-get install nodejs"
7              }
8          },
9          "deploy-mongodb": {
10             "runner": "command-runner",
11             "config": {
12                 "command": "... && sudo apt-get install mongodb-org"
13             }
14         },
15         "build-app": { ... },
16         "start-app": { ... }
17     },
18     ...
19 }
```

Defining actions on the level of commands might be a good starting point because this is what developers typically use for creating the first prototypes and iterations of an application. However, the DevOps community publicly shares and maintains reusable artifacts such as Chef cookbooks to deploy middleware and application components. To increase the portability and reliability of operations it may make sense to reuse these artifacts instead of putting together a few platform-specific commands. The following listing shows how this can be done using a different runner for the 'mongodb' action:

---

[14] `Package.json` description: http://www.npmjs.org/doc/json.html

```
1  "deploy": {
2      "actions": {
3          ...
4          "deploy-mongodb": {
5              "runner": "chef-solo-runner",
6              "config": {
7                  "files": { "mongodb.tgz": "http://.../mongodb.tgz" },
8                  "runlist": [ "recipe[mongodb::default]" ]
9              }
10         }
11     },
12     ...
13     "postoptest": {
14         "runner": "command-runner",
15         "config": {
16             "command": "export RESCODE=$(curl -sL -w \"%{http_code}\\
                   n\" \"http://localhost:3000\" -o /dev/null) && [[ \"
                   $RESCODE\" == \"200\" ]] && true || false"
17         }
18     }
19 }
```

Moreover, a 'postoptest' is defined. It implements a test case that is executed directly after the operation execution finished. This is to check whether the operation was executed successfully. In this example we simply send an HTTP request to our application and check if the response code is 200 (OK).

All **Devopsfile** iterations discussed so far assume that the whole application is deployed to a single host such as a VM. To address scalability and performance issues the application needs to be deployed in a distributed manner. As a first step, the Node.js runtime and the MongoDB server are running on two distinct VMs. Moreover, additional actions need to be included in the operation definition to cover the provisioning of these VMs. This further improves the completeness of the **Devopsfile**. The following listing provides a small extract of a more advanced iteration of the **Devopsfile**[15] to provision a new VM:

```
1  "deploy": {
2      "actions": {
3          "provision-app-vm": {
4              "runner": "js-sandbox-runner",
5              "config": {
6                  "hostname": "app-vm",
7                  "files": { "ec2-provision.js": "http://ops-artifact-
                       store/aws-management/ec2-provision.js" },
8                  "include": [ "ec2-provision.js" ]
9              }
10         },
11         ...
12         "deploy-nodejs": {
13             "host": "app-vm",
14             ...
15         },
16         ...
17     },
18     ...
19 }
```

In this iteration of the **Devopsfile** we assume that the application is always deployed to VMs at Amazon's EC2 platform. However, this could be changed

---

[15] Devopsfile v8: http://goo.gl/mda8c4

easily by using provider abstraction libraries such as fog[16] to implement more generic provisioning scripts or corresponding runners. In any case, actions of an operation need to be annotated with a host for a distributed deployment, so it is clear where the action should run. Further iterations of the `Devopsfile`[17] may define additional management operations such as an 'expose' operation to explicitly make the application available to the outside world. Technically, this could be a script to configure a security group of an Amazon EC2 VM, opening port 80 for inbound traffic to retrieve HTTP requests.

We have seen that DevOpSlang provides an efficient means to change the level of abstraction implementing operations seamlessly. Moreover, different abstraction levels may be combined consistently such as a 'deploy' operation consisting of actions on the level of Unix shell commands and actions using portable Chef cookbooks.

### 5.2   Recursive Orchestration of `Devopsfiles`

As an application grows, the `Devopsfile` may get huge and thus more difficult to maintain. To avoid such issues the application may be split into different components that own their individual `Devopsfiles`. The 'operation-runner' may be utilized to transparently invoke operations defined in other `Devopsfiles` as shown in the following listing. This approach enables the recursive orchestration of `Devopsfiles` to keep them maintainable in size and thus enabling separation of concerns.

```
1  "deploy": {
2      "actions": {
3          ...
4          "deploy-app-core": {
5              "runner": "operation-runner",
6              "config": {
7                  "Devopsfile": "./core/Devopsfile",
8                  "operation": "deploy"
9              }
10         },
11         ...
12     },
13     ...
14 }
```

## 6   Related Work

Our work is related to similar approaches in the field of Cloud computing that introduce a domain-specific language to deploy and operate applications in an automated manner. On the IaaS level approaches such as Amazon CloudFormation[18] or OpenStack Heat[19] are used to orchestrate infrastructure resources (VMs, storage, network, etc.). Moreover, middleware and application components can be

---

[16] fog library: http://fog.io
[17] Devopsfile v9: http://goo.gl/b6FuOf
[18] Amazon CloudFormation: http://aws.amazon.com/cloudformation
[19] OpenStack Heat: http://wiki.openstack.org/wiki/Heat

stacked and orchestrated using application topologies based on Ubuntu Juju[20], Amazon OpsWorks [16], Blueprints [15], or enterprise topology graphs [3]. The Topology and Orchestration Specification for Cloud Applications (TOSCA) [12] is an emerging standard to define portable application topologies. However, some of these approaches are bound to specific providers or tools (CloudFormation, OpsWorks, Juju, etc.); some are focused on defining the higher-level structure of an application (TOSCA, Blueprints, etc.), so implementing automation requires additional imperative logic such as build plans, or conventions for declarative processing have to be defined. Others focus on prescribing fine-grained technical mechanisms how to implement automation, mainly considering operations-related aspects. Thus, they can hardly be used as a means of collaboration to fill the DevOps gap. Furthermore, there are modeling languages such as UML deployment diagrams [13] that may be a nice fit for collaboration purposes, but corresponding models are not executable.

DevOpSlang aims to fill this gap as a language to improve DevOps collaboration and to enable comprehensive automation based on the fact that operations defined in Devopsfiles are executable. However, to implement a framework to process Devopsfiles, the aforementioned and other existing approaches [19,5] may be used and combined to enable the automated run of operations. Furthermore, the DevOps community proposes several domain-specific languages centered around tools such as Puppet [9], CFEngine [20], and Chef [11]. However, these languages focus on the configuration of lower-level resources such as middleware and application components installed on VMs. Moreover, they are bound to a specific tool such as Chef or Puppet. Consequently, they are less appropriate as a holistic means of collaboration and can hardly be used to automate deployment and operations of applications based on an arbitrary combination of tools and artifacts. However, they may perfectly complement DevOpSlang to implement actions using these lower-level domain-specific languages.

## 7   Conclusions

In this paper we introduced a new domain-specific language called *DevOpSlang* in conjunction with a methodology to enable the implementation of DevOps. The language serves as an efficient means of collaboration and provides the foundation to automate deployment and operations of an application. We evaluated both DevOpSlang and the methodology based on an evolutionary emerging application described in our motivating scenario. In terms of future work we plan to implement a runner framework to process Devopsfiles based on DevOpSlang. We further plan to implement mechanisms to generate Devopsfile skeletons based on existing descriptor files, evaluate Devopsfiles automatically, and make suggestions how to improve a given Devopsfile. Moreover, our goal is to provide alternative renderings of Devopsfiles based on XML and YAML.

---

[20] Ubuntu Juju: http://juju.ubuntu.com

**Acknowledgments.** This work was partially funded by the BMWi project CloudCycle (01MD11023).

# References

1. Manifesto for Agile Software Development (2001), http://agilemanifesto.org
2. Armbrust, M., Fox, A., Griffith, R., Joseph, A.D., Katz, R., Konwinski, A., Lee, G., Patterson, D., Rabkin, A., Stoica, I., Zaharia, M.: A View of Cloud Computing. Communications of the ACM 53(4), 50–58 (2010)
3. Binz, T., Fehling, C., Leymann, F., Nowak, A., Schumm, D.: Formalizing the Cloud through Enterprise Topology Graphs. In: Proceedings of 2012 IEEE International Conference on Cloud Computing. IEEE Computer Society Conference Publishing Services (2012)
4. Ecma International: The JSON Data Interchange Format (2013), http://json.org
5. Fischer, J., Majumdar, R., Esmaeilsabzali, S.: Engage: A Deployment Management System. SIGPLAN Not. 47(6), 263–274 (2012)
6. Humble, J., Farley, D.: Continuous Delivery: Reliable Software Releases Through Build, Test, and Deployment Automation. Addison-Wesley Professional (2010)
7. Humble, J., Molesky, J.: Why Enterprises Must Adopt Devops to Enable Continuous Delivery. Cutter IT Journal 24 (2011)
8. Internet Engineering Task Force: JSON Schema, http://json-schema.org
9. Loope, J.: Managing Infrastructure with Puppet. O'Reilly Media, Inc. (2011)
10. Mell, P., Grance, T.: The NIST Definition of Cloud Computing. National Institute of Standards and Technology (2011)
11. Nelson-Smith, S.: Test-Driven Infrastructure with Chef. O'Reilly Media, Inc. (2013)
12. OASIS: Topology and Orchestration Specification for Cloud Applications (TOSCA) Version 1.0, Committee Specification 01 (2013), http://docs.oasis-open.org/tosca/TOSCA/v1.0/cs01/TOSCA-v1.0-cs01.html
13. OMG: Unified Modeling Language (UML), Version 2.4.1 (2011)
14. Oppenheimer, D., Ganapathi, A., Patterson, D.A.: Why do internet services fail, and what can be done about it? In: USENIX Symposium on Internet Technologies and Systems, Seattle, WA, vol. 67 (2003)
15. Papazoglou, M., van den Heuvel, W.: Blueprinting the Cloud. IEEE Internet Computing 15(6), 74–79 (2011)
16. Rosner, T.: Learning AWS OpsWorks. Packt Publishing Ltd. (2013)
17. Shamow, E.: Devops at Advance Internet: How We Got in the Door. IT Journal, 14 (2011)
18. Wettinger, J., Andrikopoulos, V., Strauch, S., Leymann, F.: Characterizing and Evaluating Different Deployment Approaches for Cloud Applications. In: Proceedings of the IEEE International Conference on Cloud Engineering (IEEE IC2E 2014), Boston, Massachusetts, USA, March 10-14. IEEE Computer Society (2014)
19. Wettinger, J., Binz, T., Breitenbücher, U., Kopp, O., Leymann, F., Zimmermann, M.: Unified Invocation of Scripts and Services for Provisioning, Deployment, and Management of Cloud Applications Based on TOSCA. In: Proceedings of the 4th International Conference on Cloud Computing and Services Science. SciTePress (2014)
20. Zamboni, D.: Learning CFEngine 3: Automated System Administration for Sites of Any Size. O'Reilly Media, Inc. (2012)

# A Procurement Market to Allocate Cloud Providers' Residual Computing Capacity

Paolo Bonacquisto, Giuseppe Di Modica,
Giuseppe Petralia, and Orazio Tomarchio

Department of Electrical, Electronic and Computer Engineering,
University of Catania,
Catania, Italy
`firstname.lastname@dieei.unict.it`

**Abstract.** Commercial cloud providers are used to allocate computing resources to requesting customers according to the well known direct-sell, fixed-price mechanism. This mechanism is proved to be economically inefficient, as it does not account for the market's supply-demand rate. Nevertheless, providers will unlikely abandon a pricing mechanism which is very easy and cheap to implement in favour of alternative schemes. On the other end, none of the commercial providers adopting the fixed-price mechanism is able to allocate their overall computing capacity. Not selling a single virtual machine within a predefined time slot means a profit loss to the provider. Alternative mechanisms are therefore needed to sell what we call the "residual" computing capacity, i.e., the capacity which the provider is not able to allocate through direct-sell. We argue that auction-based sells may meet this need. In this paper the design of a procurement market for computing resources is proposed. Also, an adaptive bidding strategy has been devised to help providers to maximize the revenue in the context of procurement auctions. Simulations have been run to test the responsiveness of the strategy to the provider's business objective.

## 1 Introduction

Cloud computing has emerged as a key technology for the realization of scalable on-demand computing infrastructures, where resources are provided to remote customers on the basis of Service Level Agreements (SLAs). Several features, such as virtualization of hardware, scalability, elasticity enable Clouds to adapt resource provisioning to the dynamic demands of Internet users. Resources are thus provided to customers as other public utilities like water or electricity, following a commodity market model [3].

In such a market commercial providers compete to offer their services, while customers compete to acquire resources on the basis of their Quality of Service (QoS) and pricing requirements [8]. Given the high dynamism of resources' availability and workloads, meeting the QoS constraints and maintaining an acceptable level of system performance and utilization are some of the primary

M. Villari et al. (Eds.) : ESOCC 2014, LNCS 8745, pp. 123–137, 2014.

problems to tackle. Effective resource allocation strategies must be devised that, besides the technical features, also take into account the business features. We claim that benefits for both the customers and the providers may be obtained from adopting resource allocation strategies based on market principles.

One factor that strongly influences a market-based resource allocation scheme is the **pricing model**. The pricing strategy mostly adopted by main commercial IaaS providers to allocate virtual machines to requesting customers is known as "On-Demand". According to this strategy, customers are charged for the time frame during which the resource is actually utilized[1]. Providers ask customers to pay a fixed price for accessing computing capacity by the hour. Though the "fixed-price" scheme is considered to be economically inefficient, it is easily applicable to the cloud paradigm. There is apparently no evident reason for providers to abandon the direct-sell, fixed-price scheme in favor of alternative schemes. Especially for long-term requests, direct-sell is profitable to providers.

It is a matter of fact, however, that providers are not able to allocate their full computing capacity. Taking a look at the one-hour time window, there is a variable portion of computing resources (which we are going to name *spare* resources) which remain unsold and therefore do not produce income. We argue that if direct-sell fails to allocate 100% of providers' nominal computing capacity, alternative (possibly supply-demand based) pricing schemes should be adopted to allocate the spare capacity. Provided that costs for running the spare machines are covered, providers may be willing to sell that capacity at lower prices. So, on the one end providers may be interested in allocating the spare capacity to short-term customers' requests at a supply-demand regulated price (for longer commitments the regular direct-sell is more convenient). On the other end customers needing computing capacity for very short periods might want to obtain it at (lower) market prices.

In this paper, we propose to employ a **procurement auction** mechanism to allocate spare computing resources. We analyze the factors that mainly impact the strategic choices of providers in the acquisition of the goods allocated through auctions. The purpose of this work is to define a bidding strategy which guides the providers in the choice of the right actions to take in the context of a procurement process in order to maximize their business objective. In the addressed market scenario, our attention is devoted to the optimization of the utilization rate of providers' data centers. The remainder of the paper is structured as follows. Section 2 proposes a review of the literature and discusses the rationale of the work. Section 3 introduces the proposed idea and delves into technical details about the procurement auctions. Section 4 describes the proposed adaptive strategy to be used by the provider when participating in procurement auctions. In Section 5 simulation results are presented and discussed. Finally, the work is concluded in Section 6.

---

[1] http://aws.amazon.com/ec2/,
http://www.microsoft.com/windowsazure/,
http://www.rackspace.com/

## 2   Motivation and Literature Review

Many IT researchers are very much concerned with the application of auction mechanisms to the problem of optimal allocation of computing resources [13,5]. For the majority of researchers, combinatorial auctions are the most appropriate sale mechanism for allocating virtual machines in the cloud. In combinatorial auctions the participants bid for bundles of items rather than individual items [6]. This mechanism seems to perfectly fit the Cloud context, as customers usually need to acquire not just one resource but a bunch of resources. In [17] authors address the scenario of multiple resource procurement in the realm of cloud computing. In the observed context, they pre-process the user requests, analyze the auction and declare a set of vendors bidding for the auction as winners based on the Combinatorial Auction Branch on Bids (CABOB) model. In [14] a combinatorial, double-auction, resource allocation model is instead proposed. The efficiency of the proposed economic model is proved in the paper, but to our advice that idea is not technically viable since a bundle allocated to a customer is composed of computing resources offered by different providers, thus forcing the customer to deploy their application on a geographically distributed cluster of machines.

The auction mechanisms proposed so far in the literature put the provider in a privileged position in the market: computing resources are seen as scarce and precious goods, whose allocation is carried out through competitions run among customers. We argue this viewpoint must be overturned. Spare resources are resources which providers do not manage to allocate through direct-sell. From the provider's perspective they must be regarded as perishable goods that need to be sold within a certain time frame otherwise they get wasted. Not selling a virtual machine in a given time slot means a profit loss to the provider, who is spending money anyway to keep the physical machines up and running. We then look at the trade of computing resources from a new perspective, in which providers, in the aim of maximizing their data center's utilization, may be willing to attract customers by lowering the offer price. On their turn, customers may get what they need, at the time they need it, at a price which is lower than the standard price at which they usually buy.

In the last few years, Amazon has been trying to allocate its spare resources through the *Spot Instance* model[2]. This model enables the customer to bid for what they call unused computing capacity. Though this model represents the very first attempt to build up a virtual market of computing resources regulated by market prices, it is still unclear and is not proved to be resistant to potential malicious behaviors of customers (dishonest customers can abuse the system and obtain short-term advantages by bidding large maximum price bid while being charged only at the lower spot price [18]). Furthermore in [1] authors prove that the Amazon's Spot Price is not market driven, rather is typically generated as a random value near to the hidden reserve price within a tight price interval.

---

[2] https://aws.amazon.com/ec2/purchasing-options/spot-instances/

We advocate that the market model best fitting the just described perspective is the one which provides for the sale of computing resources through **procurement auctions**. Procurement auctions [10] (also called *reverse auctions*) reverse the roles of sellers and buyers, in the sense that the bidders are those who have interest in selling a good (the providers), and therefore the competition for acquiring the right-to-sell the good is run among providers.

Smeltzer et al. [15] outlines potential advantages and drawbacks of adopting reverse auctions for goods allocation. Further, they point out the appropriate conditions which must apply for the reverse auction to be effective and convenient to both goods' suppliers and buyers. The most important are a clear specification of the commodity to be allocated and the fragmentation of the market. As for the first point, in the cloud community there is a common understanding of computing capacity's technical specification: information such as core numbers, CPU speed, RAM size, etc. are the only data needed to clearly and unequivocally state the product specification. With respect to the second point, we are proposing an open market of computing capacity where customers may look for spare resources to buy at lower prices, and that will naturally attract many providers interested in allocating spare resources and increasing their market share. Clear advantages for providers are that they may find customers in one single big market with no extra effort and that the market gives them the chance to maximize the occupancy rate of their data centers; on the other side, customers do not have to search for providers' offers and will get the requested computing capacity at a lower, supply-demand regulated price.

## 3    The Procurement Process

In this section we discuss the design of an open market of computing capacity to which any provider and any customer is admitted, and where computing resources can be sold through auction-based allocation schemes. The perspective is that of *procurement auctions*, where an initial price is called out on a good/service, and bidders iteratively have to call lower prices in order to gain the *right-to-serve*. The market mechanism is the following. Customers communicate their computing demand to the market. A *broker* will take care of demands. For each specific demand, the broker (auctioneer) will run a public auction in which any provider (bidder) can participate and compete for acquiring the right to serve the demand. The winning provider (who offered the lowest price) will eventually have to serve the customer's demand. Being the auctions open to the participation of multiple providers, the competition is granted. Providers will have to fight to gain the right-to-serve the demand. For a given demand, the determination of the final price is driven only by the evaluation that each provider has on the demand to be served. Advantages for customers are clear: they will get their demand served at the lowest price. Further, they will no longer have the burden to search for providers, as providers gather autonomously in the market.

Focus in this paper is on two different types of procurement auctions. The common part of the two auction mechanisms is the preparation phase: it provides

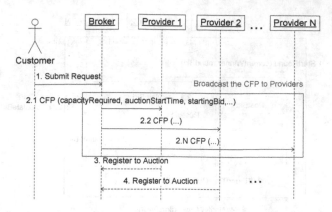

**Fig. 1.** Auction process: distribution of the CFP

that upon the arrival of a demand, the broker issues a public "call for proposal" (CFP) to invite providers. The CFP shall specify a minimum set of auction parameters including the start-provision time, the stop-provision time, the initial price (from which discount bids are expected), the bidding rules (who can bid and when, restrictions on bids) and the clearing policy (when to "terminate" the auction, who gets what, which price has to be paid). Figure 1 depicts the involved actors and the messages exchanged to carry out the auction preparation phase.

After collecting the willingness of providers to participate in the auction, the preparation phase ends up and the competition starts according to what is specified in the CFP. Basically, the broker will launch a number of competition rounds which depends on the type of auction advertised in the CFP. When the exit condition specified in the clearing policy holds true, the winner is appointed and is communicated to all participants along with the final price. Figure 2 depicts the just described steps.

What makes one auction mechanism different from another is the information specified in the bidding rules and the clearing policy respectively. For our purpose, in this paper the following auction types will be addressed: English Reverse (ER) and Second Price Sealed Bid (SPSB) [12]. The ER is a multi-round auction. The CFP specifies the initial price from which discounting bids (offers) are expected. The participating bidders may post their offers. Discounting offers are called out, so that every bidder is always aware of the reference price for which further discounts are to be proposed. If no offer arrives within a time-frame (publicly set in the CFP), the good will be assigned to the last best (i.e., the lowest priced) offer. This type of auction allows bidders to gather information of each other's evaluation of the good. The SPSB is a single round auction. All bidders have the chance to bid just once before the auction is cleared. When bidders receive the CFP, they check the initial price and decide to either bid or not to bid. After all participants have posted their bid, the broker clears the auction and allocates the "demand" to the second best bidder. The peculiarity of this auction is that bidders are not aware of each other's offer (only the

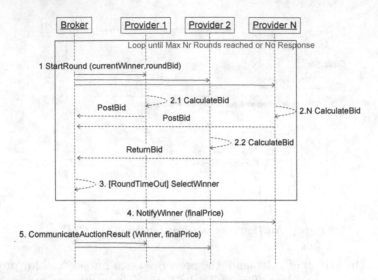

**Fig. 2.** Auction process: winner determination

winning bid will be broadcast at the end of the auction) and that the winner will be acknowledged a price which is higher than their own bid, thus increasing their overall utility.

As a basic market rule, a provider is admitted to participate in any CFP they like, with the obligation that if they win the auction, they are committed to serve the customer's demand, otherwise they will incur a penalty. The commitment rule mandates the provider to reserve resources for the CFPs they take part in. Those resources will remain "locked" until the auction is cleared, i.e., the resources may not be considered available to accommodate any new demand or to participate in a new auction. In a few words, the participation of a provider to an auction is subjected to the provider's availability of the amount of resources for which the auction has been called. If we consider that, on a statistical base, a provider will unlikely win the 100% of the auctions they take part to, there will always be an amount of resources which will remain not utilized because they are locked (i.e., awaiting for the respective auction to be cleared). In some previous works [7,2] we touched on the phenomenon of underutilization of data centers in procurement-based markets. In this work we will address that problem and propose to overcome it by applying the mechanism of **resource overbooking** [16] to the cloud market. In particular, our objective is to investigate the impact of such a mechanism on the utilization level of data centers. Section 5 provides interesting feedbacks on that study. The overbooking lets providers compete for more customers' demands than they are able to eventually serve. Providers may participate in a given auction even though, at the time of joining the auction, they have no resource available to serve the demand which is object of that auction. But, what happens if a provider is out of resources at the time they are appointed the auction's winner? If we want this mechanism to be fair and transparent to customers, some market rules must be enforced that grant the customer's right to receive the service on the one hand, and penalize providers that overuse the overbooking on the other one. One of the objectives of this work is to define the "reassignment" policy, i.e., the actions to be taken to grant the delivery of the service to the customer in the case that the provider(s) appointed as winner(s) can not provide it. This policy must state a) who among the remaining participants is assigned the right-to-serve, b) who is in charge of paying the penalty and c) how much is due. In this respect some proposals can be found in the literature. In [5] authors discuss some penalty functions which may be used in what they call "computational economies". Those functions may be classified into constant and dynamic ones. The former provide for an application of a constant penalty for those who win the auction but are not able to serve the demand (*defaulting providers*), the latter apply different penalties according to the impact of violation made by each party. We designed a reassignment scheme which tries to re-assign the right-to-serve among those who participate in the auction and applies dynamic penalties. The general rule is that if a winning provider is defaulting, the right-to-serve is passed to the next best-offering provider. This process may iterate until a provider is found which is able to serve the demand. In the case that all participants are defaulting, the CFP is re-issued (every defaulting participant is given a constant penalty). The general penalty rule is that every defaulting provider in the chain will have to pay a fee that is proportional to the difference between the final price (that called by the provider who will eventually serve the demand) and the price they had called out. The proportionality is implemented through the concept of price "distance" from the final price. Let $x_{final}$ be that price, and $x_{winner}$ the price called out by the provider who won the auction. Also, let $x_i$ be the price called by the generic provider $P_i$ in the chain of defaulting providers. Of course, $x_{winner} <= x_i < x_{final}$. We define the price distance of a given price $x_i$ as $d_i = x_{final} - x_i$. According to this definition, $d_{winner}$ is the highest among price distances, and will represent the *overall penalty* to be proportionally shared among defaulting providers. Also, let us define the penalty coefficient as:

$$c_i = \frac{d_i}{\sum_{i=1}^{n} d_i} \quad (1)$$

The reader may notice that the summation of coefficients is equal to 1. Finally, the portion of penalty each defaulting provider will have to pay is calculated as:

$$p_i = c_i \times d_{winner} \quad (2)$$

In the end, the provider who will serve the demand is also awarded the amount deriving from the overall penalty ($d_{winner}$), but the price for serving the demand (which is due by the customer) will be that called by the bidder who was appointed the auction's winner ($x_{winner}$).

Let us make an explanatory example. Suppose provider $P_1$ wins the auction calling a price $x_1 = 2$, but is defaulting. Then, the next best bidder $P_2$ will be selected, who called out the price $x_2 = 5$. Again, since $P_2$ is not able to honor, $P_3$ who called price $x_3 = 7$ is selected. The overall due penalty is $d_{winner} = x_{final} - x_{winner} = 5$, to be shared among defaulting providers $P_1$ and $P_2$ in the following way:

$$p_1 = c_1 \times d_{winner} = \frac{d_1}{d_1 + d_2} \times d_1 = 3.125$$

$$p_2 = c_2 \times d_{winner} = \frac{d_2}{d_1 + d_2} \times d_1 = 1.875$$

while the final price to which the request will be served is $x_1 = 2$. In conclusion, the described mechanism penalizes more the bidders that behaved more aggressively during the auction, preserves the customer by granting them the auction's official winning price and awards the bidder who eventually will serve the customer's demand.

## 4   An Adaptive Strategy for Cloud Providers

In this section we focus on the definition of an adaptive strategy that the provider may use when participating to procurement auctions. By strategy we mean a set of rules producing the decisions a provider must take to maximize its own business objective. According to the literature, the behavior of an auction's participant is mainly driven by the information the participant has on the value of the good being sold [10]. If we better analyze the context of cloud auctions, a computing resource can be seen as a good whose actual value (price) is common to all providers, but the estimate $E_{pi}$ of the i-th provider for a given good may differ from the the estimate $E_{pj}$ of the j-th provider according to the diverse needs each provider may have in pursuing their own business objective. The objective of a strategy is to suggest the provider the price to call for the next bid. In calling a price, a strategy may be more or less "aggressive", i.e., may propose higher or lower discounts. The strategy is adaptive, in the sense that is able to adapt the aggressiveness according to a list of *factors*. Providers may then tune their aggressiveness by adequately weighting factors according to their own business needs. Recalling a formula presented in [11], the adaptive strategy will suggest the next bid as:

$$bid = \frac{n - 1}{n - (1 - \alpha)} \times lastWinningBid \tag{3}$$

where $n$ is the number of bidders participating in the auction and $lastWinningBid$ is the price offered by the bid that won the last round. In case of single-round auctions, $lastWinningBid$ will be the auction's starting price. The parameter $\alpha$ is calculated as follows:

$$\alpha = w_1 \times \frac{P_a}{P_f} + w_2 \times \frac{T_{vm}}{T_{max}} + w_3 \times \frac{L}{L_{max}} + w_4 \times H(t) \tag{4}$$

Each parameter is weighted by a factor $(w_1, w_2, w_3, w_4)$, whose summation gives 1. The formula in 4 was presented in our previous work [7]. Here we briefly recall the meaning of the parameters. $\frac{P_a}{P_f}$ is the ratio between the resource's starting price in the auction and the corresponding price in the standard fixed-price market. $\frac{L}{L_{max}}$ represents the ratio between the time period for which the computing resource is requested and the maximum time period for which a resource can be requested. $\frac{T_{vm}}{T_{max}}$ is the ratio between the computing power demanded by the request and the computing power of the most powerful resource. Finally the $H(t)$ is the current utilization of the host on which the customer task to serve will be scheduled. Different combinations of weights lead to different strategies. When participating in an auction, providers will be guided by the strategy to:

- check the availability of resources required to serve the demand;
- check if the price called by the auctioneer is higher than than the lower bound price [3];
- calculate the bid;
- send the bid to the auctioneer.

In the case of multi rounds auctions, this mechanism is iteratively repeated. If no offer arrives within a round, the good will be assigned to the last round's best offer.

As stressed earlier in Section 3, this mechanism prevents the providers from committing their overall capacity. To face this issue, providers may decide to **overbook** resources, trying to acquire more requests than they are able to serve. The strategy and the formula to evaluate the bids have been rearranged in order to account for the overbooking. The formula for calculating the $\alpha$ parameters becomes:

$$\alpha = w_1 \times \frac{P_a}{P_f} + w_2 \times \frac{T_{vm}}{T_{max}} + w_3 \times \frac{L}{L_{max}} + w_4 \times O(t) \qquad (5)$$

where $O(t)$ is the ratio between the auctions lost by the provider while performing the overbooking, and the total number of the auctions in which they participated. According to this parameter, the provider is more aggressive when the won auctions decrease, while they will be more conservative when the won auctions increase. Further, to estimate the convenience of participating in an auction, the provider performing the overbooking will not have to check if resources are available, but will consider the amount of resources which remained unused in the past, and accordingly compute the number of concurrent auctions in which they may compete. As mentioned earlier, penalties must be carefully monitored. A provider may decide to inhibit the overbooking mechanism when the ratio between penalties and gains exceeds a customized threshold.

---

[3] The lower bound price is specific to the provider. It indicates the minimum price at which the provider is willing to sell the resource

# 5    Implementation and Testing

To assess the viability of the proposed approach a simulator of the designed market has been implemented. The objective was to define a tool capable of simulating a) the procurement auction processes, b) the behavior of the participating providers and c) the arrival of customers' demands of VMs. Tests conducted on simulator were aimed at monitoring the utilization level of providers' datacenters and the responsiveness of the providers' strategies to the declared business objective.

*Architectural details of the simulator.* The Cloudsim tool [4] has been used to implement the simulation environment where procurement auctions are run. In addition to the existing Cloudsim components, a new component called *Auctioneer* has been introduced. It cooperates with the Cloudsim *Broker* to manage auctions for cloud applications. The Cloudsim *Datacenter* component has been extended to add functions for a)reserving the resources needed to serve a request, b) estimating bids and b)implementing the overbooking mechanism. Also, the *AdaptiveStrategy* class has been implemented which models the strategy providers may adopt. Finally, the Cloudsim *Cloudlet* component, which represents the task submitted by a customer to Cloudsim, has been extended to include features such as the duration of the requested service, the submission time of the demand, the type of the requested VM, and all the necessary information needed to analyze the data extracted from the simulator for statistical purposes.

*Characterization of the customers' demand.* To characterize the customers' demand for computing capacity, the same pattern of requests reported in Google's cluster data trace [9] has been reproduced. The trace file stores usage information collected during a 29-day period in the month of May 2011 in one of Googles production cluster cell composed of about 12K machines. In particular, we have reproduced the same workload of Google's trace (in terms of jobs and tasks) and used it to simulate the customer's demand in the procurement market. The reason behind this choice is that the Google cluster's workload is characterized by machine requests which range from a few minutes to one-day usage. We believe such workload characterization may be a good candidate to model the customers' demand for short-term VMs, which providers may be willing to serve with their residual capacity (spare pool of VMs). Actually, the customers' demand to submit to the procurement market was obtained by filtering out all the Google workload's micro requests falling behind the hour usage.

The types of requests appearing in the trace have been mapped onto their equivalent Amazon's virtual machine types. In the following list the characteristics of those machines are reported along with the workload percentage of each VM type with respect to the overall daily workload:

- General purpose
  - m1.small - 32/64-bit architecture, 1 vCPU, 1 CU, 1.7GB RAM, 160GB Storage, Low Bandwidth (workload % = 0.6)

- m1.medium - 32/64-bit architecture, 1 vCPU, 2 CU, 3.75GB RAM, 410GB Storage, Moderate Bandwidth (workload % = 0.3)
- m1.large - 64-bit architecture, 2 vCPU, 4 CU, 7.5GB RAM, 820GB Storage, Moderate Bandwidth (workload % = 56)
- m1.xlarge - 64-bit architecture, 4 vCPU, 8 CU, 15GB RAM, 1.6TB Storage, High Bandwidth (workload % = 7)
- m3.xlarge - 64-bit architecture, 4 vCPU, 13 CU, 15GB RAM, 0 Storage, Moderate Bandwidth (workload % = 0.1)

– Compute optimized
  - c1.medium - 32/64-bit architecture, 2 vCPU, 5 CU, 1.7GB RAM, 350GB Storage, Moderate Bandwidth (workload % = 28.9)
– Memory optimized
  - m2.xlarge - 64-bit architecture, 2 vCPU, 6.5 CU, 17.1GB RAM, 420GB Storage, Moderate Bandwidth (workload % = 7.1 )

*Features of the datacenters.* To test the adaptive strategy, we created a set of 24 Datacenters, of which 22 adopt the proposed adaptive strategy and 2 adopt a *Random strategy*. The latters make bids like the formers, with the difference that for them the $\alpha$ parameter is assigned random values in the [0,1] range (they have no specific business objective to pursue). Each Datacenter is provided with 60 physical machines (hosts) equipped with 64 cores, 60 hosts equipped with 128 cores, 60 hosts equipped with 256 cores and 60 hosts equipped with 512 cores, for an overall computing power of 56K cores. Features of Datacenters have been chosen in such a way that all the Datacenters participating in the procurement market will be to sustain the earlier discussed workload.

**Table 1.** Weight Setting for the Datacenters' strategies

| Provider ID | Strategy | $w_1$ | $w_2$ | $w_3$ | $w_4$ | Overbooking | Provider ID | Strategy | $w_1$ | $w_2$ | $w_3$ | $w_4$ | Overbooking |
|---|---|---|---|---|---|---|---|---|---|---|---|---|---|
| PR1 | Adaptive | 0.7 | 0.1 | 0.1 | 0.1 | No | PR13 | Adaptive | 0.4 | 0.1 | 0.1 | 0.4 | No |
| PR2 | Adaptive | 0.7 | 0.1 | 0.1 | 0.1 | Yes | PR14 | Adaptive | 0.4 | 0.1 | 0.1 | 0.4 | Yes |
| PR3 | Adaptive | 0.1 | 0.7 | 0.1 | 0.1 | No | PR15 | Adaptive | 0.1 | 0.4 | 0.4 | 0.1 | No |
| PR4 | Adaptive | 0.1 | 0.7 | 0.1 | 0.1 | Yes | PR16 | Adaptive | 0.1 | 0.4 | 0.4 | 0.1 | Yes |
| PR5 | Adaptive | 0.1 | 0.1 | 0.7 | 0.1 | No | PR17 | Adaptive | 0.1 | 0.4 | 0.1 | 0.4 | No |
| PR6 | Adaptive | 0.1 | 0.1 | 0.7 | 0.1 | Yes | PR18 | Adaptive | 0.1 | 0.4 | 0.1 | 0.4 | Yes |
| PR7 | Adaptive | 0.1 | 0.1 | 0.1 | 0.7 | No | PR19 | Adaptive | 0.1 | 0.1 | 0.4 | 0.4 | No |
| PR8 | Adaptive | 0.1 | 0.1 | 0.1 | 0.7 | Yes | PR20 | Adaptive | 0.1 | 0.1 | 0.4 | 0.4 | Yes |
| PR9 | Adaptive | 0.4 | 0.4 | 0.1 | 0.1 | No | PR21 | Adaptive | 0.25 | 0.25 | 0.25 | 0.25 | No |
| PR10 | Adaptive | 0.4 | 0.4 | 0.1 | 0.1 | Yes | PR22 | Adaptive | 0.25 | 0.25 | 0.25 | 0.25 | Yes |
| PR11 | Adaptive | 0.4 | 0.1 | 0.4 | 0.1 | No | PR23 | Random | | | | | No |
| PR12 | Adaptive | 0.4 | 0.1 | 0.4 | 0.1 | Yes | PR24 | Random | | | | | Yes |

The 22 Datacenters have been split into two sets, of which only one makes use of overbooking. The weights characterizing the $\alpha$ parameter are shown in Table 1. As the reader may notice, strategies were expressly split in *unbalanced*, for which Datacenters point on just one or two factors, and *balanced*, for which all the weights are assigned the same value. The objective of the simulation is

to show that strategies actually guide Datacenters in the choice of the tasks to compete for.

In the tests, the spare resources which providers use to compete in auctions are 20% of their overall resources; the remaining 80% is sold in the traditional fixed-price market. In the context of the simulations we are going to interchangeably use the terms Providers and Datacenters.

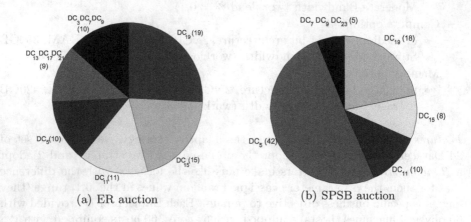

(a) ER auction          (b) SPSB auction

**Fig. 3.** Number of 23h-long VMs obtained by Datacenters

*Experiments.* We ran two different simulations where the workload defined above is submitted to the procurement market. In the first simulation the broker decided to use the ER mechanism to allocate the providers' computing capacity, while in the second the SPSB was used. In the following, results from the two simulations are shown.

The simulations demonstrate that each provider, by properly sizing the weights of their strategy, is able to achieve the chosen objective. In Figures 3(a) and 3(b) we report the number of VM instances having a duration of 23 hours obtained by each Datacenter, respectively in the simulation of the ER and SPSB auction.

Datacenters #5, #11, #15, #19 succeed in pursuing the objective of acquiring a high number of VMs; the reader may notice in Table 1 that those Datacenters have a strategy which points to win auctions where long-lasting VMs are sold. In Figures 4(a) and 4(b) we report the number of VM instances of the VM type *m2.xlarge* (which is the largest among VM types) obtained by Datacenters in the two simulations. It may be noticed in Table 1 that Datacenters #3, #9, #15 and #17 adopt a strategy pointing on large-sized VM, and in fact won a large number of *m2.xlarge* VMs.

One of the most interesting performance indexes is the **host utilization**. All providers aim to achieve the maximum utilization of their data centers. Providers will be willing to call lower bids in order to gain the right to sell the VMs needed to increase the occupancy of their data centers, since the marginal gain from these resources will be certainly high and so it is worth being more aggressive.

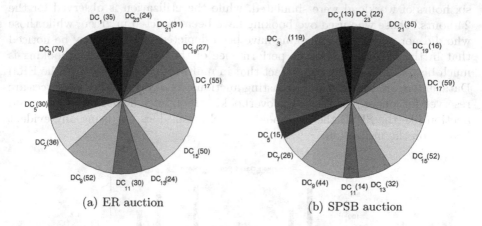

(a) ER auction

(b) SPSB auction

**Fig. 4.** Number of m2.large VMs obtained by Datacenters

One may argue that a higher monetary gain may be obtained by selling a few resources at a higher price than selling lots of resources at a very discounted price. But again, the capability of maximizing the gain is out of the scope of this work. Again, what we have proposed is a tool to define, customize and enforce a strategy.

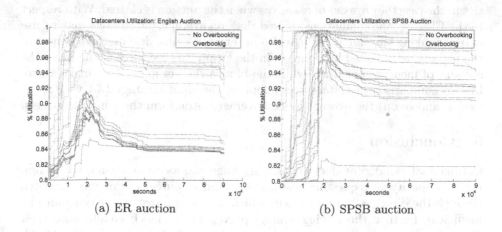

(a) ER auction

(b) SPSB auction

**Fig. 5.** Datacenters utilization

As mentioned above, depending on the roughness of competition, the goal of maximizing the data center's occupancy is roughly pursuable for providers. The overbooking strategy is then necessary to raise the utilization level. Figures 5(a) and 5(b) show the utilization of Datacenters in the ER and the SPSB simulations. The figure depicts the result of a simulation where only the first six hours of workload were simulated, while the utilization is observed for the 24 hours. Those who used overbooking have been depicted in green, while those who did not perform overbooking have been depicted in red. It may be noticed that in the ER simulation the performance of those who used overbooking is much better. This is due by the fact that in multi-round auctions (like the ERs) Datacenters are engaged in long lasting auctions; as a consequence resources are reserved for longer periods, so the overbooking if of much help. In a single-round auction like the SPSB the overbooking mechanism does not bring any evident benefit on the utilization.

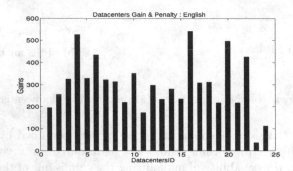

**Fig. 6.** Gains and penalties of Datacenters in ER auction

Datacenters calling on overbooking must also consider the exposition to penalties in the case they are out of resources when the auction is cleared. With respect to the ER case, the simulations showed that, on average, datacenters making use of overbooking have an advantage also in terms of gains, despite the payment of the penalty, as depicted in Figure 6. In the graph, the red piece of the bar is the amount of incurred penalties, while the blue is the net gain. If we make a two-by-two comparison of Datacenters adopting the same strategy (#1 vs #2, #3 vs #4, and so on) the overbookers on average outperform the non-overbookers.

## 6   Conclusion

Commercial cloud providers are making huge profits from leasing their computing capacity to requesting customers. Cloud resources are mainly allocated through the direct-sell pricing model which has been proved to be economically inefficient. Further, this pricing strategy prevents providers from allocating their full computing capacity, thus causing a residual capacity to remain unsold. Alternative pricing schemes should then be sought that might help Cloud providers to increment their profit. In this paper, we proposed the design of an open market of cloud resources, where the residual computing capacity of providers is allocated through procurement auctions. An adaptive strategy was also devised that, suitably tailored to the provider's business objective, helps them to maximize the revenue in the context of procurement auctions. Tests conducted on a simulator showed the viability of the proposal.

# References

1. Agmon Ben-Yehuda, O., Ben-Yehuda, M., Schuster, A., Tsafrir, D.: Deconstructing amazon ec2 spot instance pricing. In: 2011 IEEE Third International Conference on Cloud Computing Technology and Science (CloudCom), pp. 304–311 (2011)
2. Bonacquisto, P., Di Modica, G., Petralia, G., Tomarchio, O.: Procurement auctions to maximize players' utility in cloud markets. In: Proceedings of the 4th International Conference on Cloud Computing and Services Science, CLOSER 2014, Barcelona, Spain (April 2014)
3. Buyya, R., Yeo, C.S., Venugopal, S.: Market-oriented cloud computing: Vision, hype, and reality for delivering it services as computing utilities. In: 10th IEEE International Conference on High Performance Computing and Communications (HPCC 2008), pp. 5–13 (September 2008)
4. Calheiros, R., Ranjan, R., Beloglazov, A., De Rose, C.A., Buyya, R.: Cloudsim: A toolkit for modeling and simulation of cloud computing environments and evaluation of resource provisioning algorithms. In: Software: Practice and Experience (2011)
5. Chard, K., Bubendorfer, K.: High Performance Resource Allocation Strategies for Computational Economies. IEEE Trans. Parallel Distrib. Syst. 24(1), 72–84 (2013)
6. Cramton, P., Shoham, Y., Steinberg, R.: Combinatorial auctions. The MIT Press (2005)
7. Di Modica, G., Petralia, G., Tomarchio, O.: Procurement auctions to trade computing capacity in the Cloud. In: 8th Int. Conf. on P2P, Parallel, Grid, Cloud and Internet Computing (3PGCIC 2013), Compiegne, France (October 2013)
8. Di Modica, G., Tomarchio, O.: Matching the business perspectives of providers and customers in future cloud markets. Cluster Computing, 1–19 (2014)
9. Google: Traces of google workloads (2011), http://code.google.com/p/googleclusterdata/
10. Klemperer, P.: Auction Theory: A Guide to the Literature. Journal of Economic Surveys 13(3) (1999)
11. McAfee, R.P., McMillan, J.: Auctions and bidding. Journal of Economic Literature 15, 699–738 (1987)
12. Parsons, S., Rodriguez-Aguilar, J.A., Klein, M.: Auctions and bidding: A guide for computer scientists. ACM Computing Surveys 43(2) (February 2011)
13. Risch, M., Altmann, J., Guo, L., Fleming, A., Courcoubetis, C.: The GridEcon Platform: A Business Scenario Testbed for Commercial Cloud Services. In: Altmann, J., Buyya, R., Rana, O.F. (eds.) GECON 2009. LNCS, vol. 5745, pp. 46–59. Springer, Heidelberg (2009)
14. Samimi, P., Teimouri, Y., Mukhtar, M.: A combinatorial double auction resource allocation model in cloud computing. Information Sciences (in press, 2014)
15. Smeltzer, L.R., Carr, A.: Reverse auctions in industrial marketing and buying. Business Horizons 45(2), 47–52 (2002)
16. Sulistio, A., Kim, K.H., Buyya, R.: Managing Cancellations and No-Shows of Reservations with Overbooking to Increase Resource Revenue. In: 8th IEEE International Symposium on Cluster Computing and the Grid (CCGRID 2008), pp. 267–276 (May 2008)
17. Vinu Prasad, G., Rao, S., Prasad, A.: A Combinatorial Auction mechanism for multiple resource procurement in cloud computing. In: 2012 12th International Conference on Intelligent Systems Design and Applications, ISDA (2012)
18. Wang, Q., Ren, K., Meng, X.: When cloud meets ebay: Towards effective pricing for cloud computing. In: 2012 Proceedings IEEE INFOCOM, pp. 936–944 (2012)

# Event Pattern Discovery for Cross-Layer Adaptation of Multi-cloud Applications

Chrysostomos Zeginis, Kyriakos Kritikos, and Dimitris Plexousakis

ICS-FORTH
Heraklion GR-70013, Greece
{zegchris,kritikos,dp}@ics.forth.gr

**Abstract.** As Cloud computing becomes a widely accepted service delivery platform, developers usually resort in multi-cloud setups to optimize their application deployment. In such heterogeneous environments, during application execution, various events are produced by several layers (Cloud and SOA specific), leading to or indicating Service Level Objective (SLO) violations. To this end, this paper proposes a meta-model to describe the components of multi-cloud Service-based Applications (SBAs) and an event pattern discovery algorithm to discover valid event patterns causing specific SLO violations. The proposed approach is empirically evaluated based on a real-world application.

**Keywords:** Cloud computing, SOA, adaptation, modeling, pattern discovery.

## 1 Introduction

Cloud computing is a rapidly emerging paradigm offering virtualized resources for developing applications. Its adoption in the Service Oriented Architecture (SOA) world is increasing; enterprises acknowledge its flexibility and elasticity by choosing among various offerings at all Cloud layers (IaaS, PaaS and SaaS). In addition, as developers try to optimize their application deployment cost and performance, they may also deploy application parts on multiple VMs [1].

In this paper we focus on SBAs deployed on Clouds, which feature three main functional layers: the Business Process Management (BPM) layer, the Service Composition and Coordination (SCC) layer and the Service Infrastructure (SI) layer. In a Cloud environment, the SI layer maps to the PaaS and IaaS layers, while the SaaS layer includes the BPM and SCC layers. It is imperative that such distributed hosting environments, exhibit efficient cross-layer monitoring and adaptation mechanisms combining multi-layer monitored events and mapping them to suitable adaptation strategies. In [2] we have investigated the need for cross-layer adaptation, as current techniques are mainly fragmented by considering a single SBA layer, while the few cross-layer ones [3, 4] do not consider multi-cloud aspects. Concerning monitoring, in [5] we have presented a multi-cloud SBA framework. This paper goes a step further supporting multi-cloud SBA adaptation by focusing on an efficient method for processing the

M. Villari et al. (Eds.) : ESOCC 2014, LNCS 8745, pp. 138–147, 2014.

huge amount of monitored events and discovering frequent patterns leading to
SLO violations. As such, a pattern discovery algorithm is introduced, exploiting
a component meta-model whose instances describe SBA component dependencies. The discovered event patterns interrelate events leading to SLO violations
and can be further exploited to enrich the scalability rules defined by experts.

The rest of the paper is structured as follows. Section 2 provides a motivating
example, while Section 3 analyzes the multi-cloud monitoring and adaptation
framework. In Section 4 we describe the component meta-model, exploited by
the proposed pattern discovery algorithm (Section 5). Section 6 evaluates the
algorithm's accuracy and performance. Finally, Section 7 reviews the related
work, before Section 8 concludes and provides future work directions.

## 2   Motivating Example

A traffic management SBA deployed in a multi-cloud setup motivates our approach. In a normal traffic scanariq, four tasks occur: environmental variable
monitoring $(T_M)$, public event and high traffic hours checking $(T_C)$, current
condition assessment $(T_A)$ and device configuration $(T_D)$. Task $T_A$ requires high
computation and storage capabilities, while the other three tasks require moderate storage capacity and low computational power and must be deployed geographically close to the municipal infrastructure. Thus, these tasks can operate
on a private/municipal Cloud with their data periodically sent for processing to
a central Cloud, hosting $T_A$. As illustrated in Fig. 1, various events are detected
by the monitoring mechanisms in this multi-cloud setting, from lower level infrastructure events (e.g. low memory $((w)e_1)$, high CPU_load $((c)e_2)$, network
uptime $((c)e_4)$, to higher level events (e.g. service execution time $((w)e_3, (w)e_6$
or throughput $((w)e_5)$ violations. The main non-functional application goal is
to capture warning (identified by $we$) or critical events (identified by $ce$) and
interrelate them to discover event patterns leading to SLO violations.

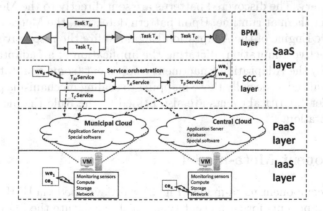

**Fig. 1.** Traffic management example

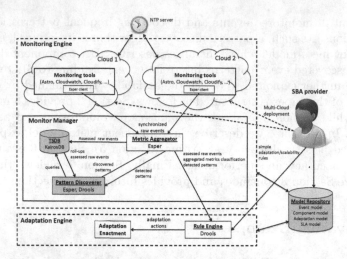

**Fig. 2.** Framework's architecture

# 3    Framework's Architecture

The architecture presented in our previous work [5] for cross-layer multi-cloud SBA monitoring is realized and enhanced with specific techniques and algorithms to support proactive adaptation. In this multi-cloud framework (Fig. 2 – the shadowed components indicate where this paper focuses), each of these Clouds exhibits monitoring components, which directly interact with the Monitor Manager, through a complex event processing (CEP) server-client mechanism. The *Metric Aggregator* component assesses and stores the monitored events to the time-series database (TSDB). The *Pattern Discoverer* component periodically queries the TSDB to get the assessed raw events for a specific time interval and identifies raw event patterns leading to SLO violations (mapping to specific aggregate metrics). The TSDB provides the aggregated metric values, necessary for pattern discovery. The discovered patterns are sent directly to the Metric Aggregator to detect them at runtime. Upon pattern detection, the Metric Aggregator urges the Rule Engine of the Adaptation Engine to fire the respective scalability rule (i.e. proactive adaptation) dictating the application of an adaptation strategy, realized by the Adaptation Enactment component (some adaptation actions are already realized, especially those mapping to scaling mechanisms provided by Cloud providers). Critical events are also passed to the Rule Engine to perform reactive adaptation.

# 4    Component Meta-model

A particular component meta-model (Fig. 3) was developed via UML to describe the source components for each event type which constitute the SBA system, as well as their dependencies. Its main benefits are that it is extensive to capture the most common multi-cloud SBA components, related to functional and non-functional violations, and extensible to meet any SBA provider's needs, which may incorporate other layer-specific components utilized by its applications. Any adaptation manager can also exploit it to carefully design scalability rules based on the components' properties to stimulate the mapping from events to specific adaptation actions. Through capturing the component dependencies in a multi-cloud system, a root cause analysis for system faults can be performed. The Pattern Discovery Algorithm also exploits such dependencies to detect valid event patterns leading to critical events, where validity lies on causality by selecting events in the stream that drive the occurrence of other events in the pattern. Model-driven technologies of the Eclipse Modeling Framework (EMF) are exploited to create models complying to this meta-model. The core meta-model is graphically produced in ecore and then used to generate the base domain code. Next, the Connected Data Objects (CDO) technology is used, offering a model repository and a run-time persistence framework, accessible via querying mechanisms (SQL, HQL). For instance, the following SQL query returns the total number of active components included in the VM hosting the Monitor and DeviceConfig services (componentID=7001) and having ID 7026 or 7027 (i.e., the components producing $e_1$ and $e_2$ events), in order to identify if both components reside in the same VM and thus affect each other when a violation occurs.

```
SELECT COUNT(*)
FROM (SELECT VM_COMPUTE_LIST
    FROM VM WHERE ComponentID=7001) as computeList
WHERE componentID IN (7026,7027) AND (state = active);
```

## 5    Pattern Discovery

This section presents an offline algorithm for discovering event patterns leading to specific SLO violations, based on propositional logic [6]. The algorithm exploits component dependencies and contingency tables (Fig. 4) to identify association rules between events. These tables display frequency distributions of candidate patterns and their negations as antecedents and the specified metric event, as well as its negation as consequences. It mainly focuses on discovering patterns by considering SOA and Cloud layers, but it can also be applied on a single layer, discovering layer-specific patterns.

The algorithm starts by filtering the event stream (*line 3*) from events coming from different Cloud providers than those used by the SBA. Then, the event stream is split based on the aggregate metric's time interval (*line 4*). Intervals are characterized as critical, if there is an aggregate metric violation, or non-critical, otherwise (*line 5*). For critical intervals, the temporal ordered sets of the raw events subset's powerset are calculated, from the first interval event to that before the last critical raw measurement. All the sets of the interval powersets are filtered to discard the ones not interrelated with each other, based on the component model (*lines 6–11*), but the single events that might map to

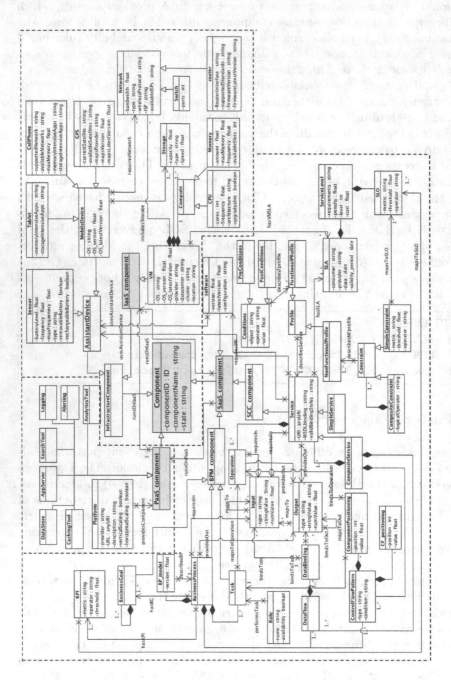

**Fig. 3.** The Cloud component meta-model

---

**Algorithm 1.**   Event pattern discovery algorithm

---

1: **Input:** event stream, application, metric, interval size, component model
2: **Output:** discovered patterns, patterns ranking, association rules, ambiguous rules
3: filter raw events (ignore success /other applications'/other Cloud provider events)
4: divide event stream in event time intervals
5: define critical and non-critical intervals
6: **while** not end of event stream **do**
7:     A = events before the last critical raw event in this interval
8:     $\mathbb{P}(A) \rightarrow$ powerset of set A
9:     filter sets of $\mathbb{P}(A)$ according to the component model
10:     update the powerset tree
11: **end while**
12: **for** $i \leftarrow 1, treelevels$ **do**
13:     **for** $j \leftarrow 1, treebranches$ **do**
14:         $\mathbf{B_{i,j}}$ = current branch
15:         **while** not end of event stream **do**
16:             A = events before the last critical raw event in this interval
17:             C = critical aggregate event for the specified metric
18:             compute $S(B_{i,j}, C)$, $S(B_{i,j}, \neg C)$, $S(\neg B_{i,j}, C)$, $S(\neg B_{i,j}, \neg C)$ in A
19:             update contingency table
20:         **end while**
21:         **if** $(S(B_{i,j}, C) + S(\neg B_{i,j}, \neg C)) > (S(\neg B_{i,j}, C) + S(B_{i,j}, \neg C))$ **then**
22:             create **association rule** $(B_{i,j} \rightarrow C)$
23:             store $B_{i,j}$ in pattern repository
24:         **else**
25:             discard $B_{i,j}$
26:         **end if**
27:     **end for**
28: **end for**

---

the critical violation are considered. Then, a level- and a branch-based traversal of the tree-based structure storing the candidate patterns are performed to calculate and store (*lines 15–20*) the frequencies for each considered set's contingency table. The powerset tree (Fig. 4) stores only unique sets and each node maps to a candidate pattern comprising all the events from the root to the current node. $B_{i,j}$ is the concerned sub-branch ($i$ indicates the tree level and $j$ the branch counter), $C$ represents the aggregate metric violation, while the pair $S(B_{i,j}, C)$ is the frequency of $B_{i,j}$ set in critical intervals. A candidate set's negation means that either of the included events does not appear. For instance, for the pattern $\{e_1, e_2, e_4\}$, the following negation definition exists: $\neg\{\mathbf{e_1, e_2, e_4}\} \equiv \neg\mathbf{e_1} \vee \neg\mathbf{e_2} \vee \neg\mathbf{e_4}$. A negated event means that another or no event appears in the specific pattern's position. Frequencies $S(B_{i,j}, C)$ and $S(\neg B_{i,j}, \neg C)$ are used to determine an association rule. The latter invigorates the association rule under consideration, as the concurrent absence of a pattern and the considered violation event also interrelates the root and cause of the association rule. Consequently, to determine such a rule, the sum of frequencies

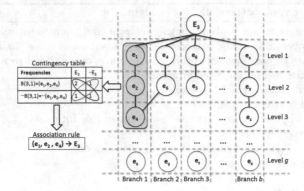

**Fig. 4.** Powerset tree

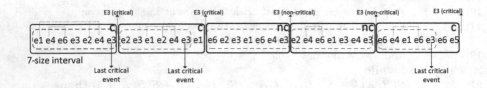

**Fig. 5.** Event stream split for pattern discovery algorithm

invigorating the association rule should be greater than the sum of frequencies weakening it (*lines 21–23*). The algorithm's time complexity depends on the event stream size $n$, the average tree level size $g$ and the tree branches $b$. Thus, as the algorithm requires $g*b$ (i.e., approximately the cardinality of the power-sets) iterations on the event stream, its complexity is $\mathcal{O}(n*b*g)$. This means that the powerset tree is extensively traversed to discover the association rules.

Fig. 5 clarifies the way intervals are processed to identify patterns for the average DeviceConfig average execution time violations (i.e., violation of $E_3$ event). The event stream comprises 35 events (after event filtering) of Section 2's 6 metrics. Each interval's powerset sets (figure's connected events) are processed to determine association rules. Thus, the event stream is split into 5 intervals: 3 critical ($c$ mark on interval's upper right corner) and 2 non-critical ($nc$ mark on interval's upper right corner). For critical intervals, the subset before the last raw critical DeviceConfig SaaS execution time event is considered, while for non-critical ones the whole interval. The algorithm discovers two patterns and extracts the association rules: (i) $\{e_1, e_2, e_4 \rightarrow E3\}$ and (ii) $\{e_4, e_6 \rightarrow E3\}$.

## 6    Evaluation

This section experimentally evaluates the algorithm's performance and accuracy, in order to optimize the definition of the aggregate metric (i.e., its optimal

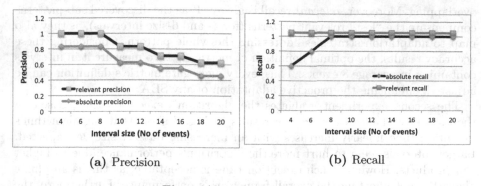

(a) Precision                    (b) Recall

**Fig. 6.** Algorithm's accuracy

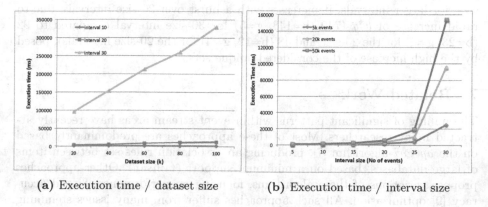

(a) Execution time / dataset size    (b) Execution time / interval size

**Fig. 7.** Algorithm's performance

interval). An event dataset comprising 100k events from the traffic management app is used. During a pre-processing of the event stream, five periodic patterns are identified (two 2-size patterns, one 3-size pattern and two 4-size patterns). The main task is to discover patterns causing DeviceConfig SaaS execution time violations (i.e., violations of $E_3$). The experiments were performed on a machine with quad-core CPU 2.6GhZ, 8GB RAM and Mac OS X operating system.

The first experiment evaluates the algorithm's raw *relevant and absolute accuracy*. The former considers only the five known patterns, while the latter additionally considers their sub-patterns, as they can also drive proactive adaptation. The algorithm's *precision* and *recall* is measured while fluctuating the interval size from 4 to 20 events. Fig. 6a shows that *relevant precision* is 1 for small intervals and falls while increasing the interval size, while *absolute precision* fluctuates similarly at lower levels (as more irrelevant sub-patterns are discovered). The precision starts to fall over 8-size intervals, i.e., above the double of the maximum pattern (4 events). Fig. 6b shows that the algorithm's *absolute* recall is 1 for all considered interval sizes, except for 4-size and 6-size intervals, where it fails to discover two and one 4-size patterns respectively, due to interval overlapping. Moreover, *relevant* recall is always 1, as the discovered sub-patterns compensate the "lost" relevant patterns (for 4- and 6-size intervals), as they also map to adaptation strategies addressing the whole pattern. Considering these accuracy results, the optimal definition of metric $E_3$ is to measure it in intervals containing in average 8 events. Thus, every aggregate metric's definition can be adjusted, enhancing the proactive adaptation of any SBA.

The second experiment evaluates the algorithm's execution time, based on the dataset and interval size. The results in Fig. 7 show that the algorithm's execution time linearly increases with an increasing dataset size, as expected. Larger intervals seem to hurt more the algorithm's performance, due to higher $b*g$ products. However, such execution time is acceptable, as this is an offline algorithm not affecting the overall framework's performance. Furthermore, the results in Fig. 7b reveal a changing relation between execution time and interval size; for larger intervals, it increases with a burst over 20-size intervals, due to rapid increase of $b*g$ (740 (b=148, g=5) for 30-size interval compared to 92 (b=23, g=4) for the 25-size and 48 (b=12, g=4) for the 20-size intervals), posed by the high increase of the considered unique sets.

# 7    Related Work

The mining of significant patterns within event stream areas have recently attracted many researchers. Most of these approaches are predominantly based on the *apriori* algorithm [7], producing an association rules set between items of large databases, based on a minimum support (*minsup*). Other approaches propose variations of these algorithms, focusing on performance [8] and accuracy [9] optimization. All such approaches suffer from many issues stemming from the difficulty in determining the optimal *minsup*. Contrarily, logic-based approaches exploit inferencing to discover patterns defining respective association rules. In [6] a pattern discovery approach is proposed mapping logical equivalences based on propositional logic. In particular, a rule mining framework is introduced, generating coherent rules for a given dataset that do not require setting an arbitrary *minsup*. [10] proposes an event calculus (EC) dialect for efficient run-time recognition that is scalable to large data streams.

Concerning IaaS modeling, some well-established approaches, such as the OASIS Cloud Application Management for Platforms (CAMP) specification (www.oasis-open.org), focus on modeling the most generic infrastructure components. At the PaaS layer, the mOSAIC EU Project's (www.mosaic-cloud.eu) entity ontology stands out as a solution for improving interoperability among existing Cloud solutions, platforms and services. Finally, SaaS layer modeling has been widely influenced by the service computing, such as the models introduced within the S-Cube EU project (www.s-cube-network.eu).

Compared to the related work, the main benefits of our approach are the following. First, we propose a component meta-model able to describe the components of multi-cloud SBA along with their interrelationships. The models complying to this meta-model assist in identifying correct event patterns by considering only events originating from interrelated components. Second, we propose a logic-based algorithm for discovering event patterns leading to critical events within a monitoring event stream, enabling injecting proactiveness in an SBA system via mapping event patterns to respective adaptation strategies.

## 8    Conclusions and Future Work

This paper has presented an approach towards efficiently discovering detrimental event patterns causing critical violations during multi-cloud SBA execution. In particular, a component model is presented, describing SBA components and their interrelationships, that is exploited by a logic-based algorithm discovering event patterns leading to specific metric violations and can be further exploited by any adaptation engine to trigger suitable proactive adaptation actions when detected. For future work, we plan to optimize the pattern discovery algorithm's accuracy and performance and develop a scalability rule mechanism that could semi-automatically map discovered event patterns to suitable adaptation strategies. Finally, we are going to employ new techniques to infer new component dependencies from the current irrelevant discovered patterns.

**Acknowledgements.** We thankfully acknowledge the support of the PaaSage (FP7-317715) EU project.

## References

1. Baryannis, G., Garefalakis, P., Kritikos, K., Magoutis, K., Papaioannou, A., Plexousakis, D., Zeginis, C.: Lifecycle Management of Service-based Applications on Multi-Clouds: A Research Roadmap. In: MultiCloud (2013)
2. Zeginis, C., Konsolaki, K., Kritikos, K., Plexousakis, D.: Towards proactive cross-layer service adaptation. In: Wang, X.S., Cruz, I., Delis, A., Huang, G. (eds.) WISE 2012. LNCS, vol. 7651, pp. 704–711. Springer, Heidelberg (2012)
3. Zengin, A., Marconi, A., Pistore, M.: CLAM: Cross-layer Adaptation Manager for Service-Based Applications. In: QASBA 2011, pp. 21–27. ACM (2011)
4. Popescu, R., Staikopoulos, A., Liu, P., Brogi, A., Clarke, S.: Taxonomy-driven Adaptation of Multi-Layer Applications using Templates. In: SASO (2010)
5. Zeginis, C., Kritikos, K., Garefalakis, P., Konsolaki, K., Magoutis, K., Plexousakis, D.: Towards cross-layer monitoring of multi-cloud service-based applications. In: Lau, K.-K., Lamersdorf, W., Pimentel, E. (eds.) ESOCC 2013. LNCS, vol. 8135, pp. 188–195. Springer, Heidelberg (2013)
6. Sim, A.T.H., Indrawan, M., Zutshi, S., Srinivasan, B.: Logic-based pattern discovery. IEEE Trans. Knowl. Data Eng. 22(6), 798–811 (2010)
7. Agrawal, R., Srikant, R.: Fast algorithms for mining association rules in large databases. In: VLDB, pp. 487–499 (1994)
8. Bettini, C., Wang, X.S., Jajodia, S., Lin, J.L.: Discovering frequent event patterns with multiple granularities in time sequences. IEEE Trans. Knowl. Data Eng. 10(2), 222–237 (1998)
9. Hellerstein, J.L., Ma, S., Perng, C.S.: Discovering actionable patterns in event data. IBM Systems Journal 41(3), 475–493 (2002)
10. Artikis, A., Sergot, M.J., Paliouras, G.: Run-time composite event recognition. In: DEBS, pp. 69–80. ACM (2012)

# A GENTL Approach for Cloud Application Topologies

Vasilios Andrikopoulos, Anja Reuter,
Santiago Gómez Sáez, and Frank Leymann

IAAS, University of Stuttgart
Universitätsstr. 38, 70569 Stuttgart, Germany
{andrikopoulos,gomez-saez,leymann}@iaas.uni-stuttgart.de,
anja@reutertv.de

**Abstract.** The availability of an increasing number of cloud offerings
allows for innovative solutions in designing applications for the cloud and
in adapting existing ones for this environment. An important ingredient
in identifying the optimal distribution of an application in the cloud,
potentially across offerings and providers, is a robust topology model
that can be used for the automated deployment and management of the
application. In order to support this process, in this work we present
an application topology language aimed for cloud applications that is
generic enough to allow the mapping from other existing languages and
comes with a powerful annotation mechanism already built-in. We discuss its supporting environment that we developed and show how it can
be used in practice to assist application designers.

**Keywords:** application topology language, annotation schemes, application distribution, cloud migration.

## 1 Introduction

Cloud computing offers a platform for innovative systems that are partially
or fully implemented and/or hosted using cloud offerings. Novel services like
Database as a Service (DBaaS) offerings, for example, can be used for designing
a new generation of applications, or for adapting existing ones in order to reap
the well documented benefits of virtually infinite cloud capacity [5] — of course
at a cost. Being able to distribute the application components across cloud offerings, potentially across cloud providers too, opens up the design space for cloud
applications significantly [1]. However, the plethora of existing offerings, and the
multitude of performance characteristics and pricing models attached to them
creates a multi-dimensional problem in identifying the optimal distribution of
an application in the cloud.

Toward this goal, in previous work [2], we introduced a design support process
and reference architecture that builds on two systems: a *knowledge base* which
aggregates information from cloud providers and allows for the identification of
appropriate cloud offerings, as well as cost calculation for a given usage profile,

M. Villari et al. (Eds.) : ESOCC 2014, LNCS 8745, pp. 148–159, 2014.

and an *application topology language* and its *supporting environment* which is used for identifying the optimal distribution of the application components across cloud offerings. In [2] we provide a brief introduction to both systems; in this work we focus on the latter, i.e. the topology language and its environment. More specifically, in the following we present the main concepts of the Generalized Topology Language (GENTL), its relationship to existing topology modeling languages, and the implementation of a supporting environment for the language. While the language can be used for different purposes, its main focus for this work is on providing design support capabilities, following the discussion in [2].

The contributions of this work can therefore be summarized by the following:

1. An investigation into existing application topology modeling languages and an identification of their common concepts.
2. The presentation of a generic topology language that allows for the mapping from these languages into a common model, and which supports different types of annotations for additional information to the topology model.
3. An in-depth discussion on the supporting environment for the proposed language.

The rest of this paper is structured as follows: Section 2 discusses some application topology language approaches for background purposes. Based on the identified commonalities between them, Section 3 introduces our proposal for a generalized application topology language. Section 4 enhances the language with a mechanism for annotations that are used for providing additional information to application designers. Section 5 discusses the tooling support for the language. Finally, Section 6 discusses related work, and Section 7 concludes with some future work.

## 2   Background

Cloud management tools like AWS CloudFormation[1], OpenStack[2], OpenNebula[3], and the Flexiant Cloud Orchestrator (FCO)[4] use representations of application topologies aiming at easy deployment and management of cloud resources. The application topology models used are expressed using various means like domain-specific languages (DSLs), visual templates, or graphical models. These models however are specific for each tool and are not portable across providers.

Addressing this deficiency, the Topology and Orchestration Specification for Cloud Applications (TOSCA) [6] is an OASIS standardized language for the portable description of service components, their relationships and management processes. TOSCA documents, or more precisely, Service Templates, contain *node types* defining the properties and interfaces of components, *node templates*

---

[1] AWS CloudFormation: https://aws.amazon.com/cloudformation/
[2] OpenStack: https://www.openstack.org/
[3] OpenNebula: http://opennebula.org/
[4] FCO: http://www.flexiant.com/flexiant-cloud-orchestrator/

representing specific components as a reference to a defined node type, *relationship types* between node types and *relationship templates* instantiating the relationship types, *topology templates* that bring together node and relationship templates, and *management plans* that define how to manage (deploy, provision, update etc.) the application. *Policies* can be attached to node or relationship templates by means of an external language like WS-Policy[5]. TOSCA also allows for the annotation of node types with requirement and capability definitions, as well as the composition of different service templates by e.g. substituting a node template with a service template having the same properties, management interfaces, requirements and capabilities.

A similar approach is Cloud Blueprinting [15] which defines the concepts of *blueprints* as abstract descriptions of cloud service offerings. Blueprints are meant to facilitate cloud service selection, customization and composition into service-based applications. *Blueprint templates* allow application developers to define their requirements in terms of functional capabilities, QoS characteristics, as well as deployment and provisioning resources as target blueprints. A Blueprint document consists of six parts: *general properties* describing the topology, the *offering(s)* described by the document, the *artifacts* necessary to implement these offerings, the *resources* required to deploy these artifacts, the virtual architecture formed by the *relations* between offerings, implementation artifacts and resources, and the *policies* that govern the elements of the document.

CloudML [8] is an approach built on model-driven engineering (MDE) principles with the intention of facilitating the provisioning, deployment, monitoring and adaptation of multi-cloud applications. It provides a DSL for topology modeling, and a runtime environment for the enactment, provisioning, modeling and adaptation of these models. Topology models define the *nodes* of the cloud infrastructure, as well as the *software artifacts* that are deployed on these nodes. Both nodes and artifacts are typed, which allows for reasoning on the topology models. Similarly, the Composite Application Framework (Cafe) [12] provides the means to describe composite service-oriented applications and deploy them automatically across different providers. A Cafe application template consists of an *application model*, a *variability model* containing variability points for the parametrization of the application, and *code artifacts and references*. Application models consist of typed components and implementation elements that allow for nested definition of topologies.

As it can be seen for the discussion above, the topology languages discussed rely on a set of common fundamental concepts with different representations in each language. They all fundamentally use a graph-based view of application topologies which consists of typed components (nodes) and connectors (edges), with the possibility of assembling components into groups, essentially forming subgraphs. Furthermore, components and connectors may have attributes that define them. The degree of granularity in these concepts across the languages however differs. This underlying similarity between these approaches is used for our definition of the GENTL language.

---

[5] Web Services Policy 1.5 - Framework: http://www.w3.org/TR/ws-policy/

# 3    The Generalized Topology Language

The key concepts to be addressed in developing a generic application topology language are *reusability* of existing models, *extensibility* to accommodate future developments, and *composability* of topology models of various granularity levels into larger, more complicated ones. Furthermore, and in order to facilitate the mapping from and to other languages, the topology language should also allow all model elements to capture information that is external to the language itself. In the following section we present our proposal for a language that satisfies these requirements.

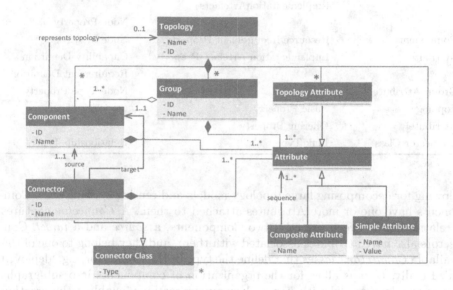

**Fig. 1.** The Metamodel of GENTL

## 3.1    The GENTL Language

The GEneralized Topology Language (GENTL) relies on a generic, but typed system. The metamodel of the language is illustrated in Fig. 1 using UML Class diagram notation. More specifically, GENTL models are built around a *Topology* element with a (unique) ID and a name which acts as a composer of the other elements in the model. Topology elements may have *Topology Attributes* that capture information about the topology model as a whole that cannot be reflected by the other elements. *Topology Attributes* are *Attributes*, either *Simple Attributes* (with a name and a value of string, integer, etc. type) or *Composite Attributes* that organize other Attributes in sequences and allow for nested attribute composition. *Components* have, in addition to a (unique) ID and a name, links to other GENTL Topology elements via the *representsTopology* association

**Table 1.** Mapping between GENTL, and Blueprints and TOSCA

| GENTL | Blueprints | TOSCA |
|---|---|---|
| Topology | Offering | Topology Template |
| Component | Resource Requirement<br>Implementation Artefact | Node Template |
| Connector | Vertical Link<br>Horizontal Link<br>Resource Link | Relationship Template |
| Group | (resourceRequirements)<br>(implementationArtefacts) | Node Type |
| Component<br>Attribute | Resource Requirement Property<br>Implementation Artefact Property | Node Property<br>Node Interface<br>Capability Definition<br>Requirement Definition |
| Group Attribute | | Node Type Property |
| Topology<br>Attribute | Basic Property<br>Offering Property | |
| Connector Class | Link Type | Relationship Type |

allowing for decomposing large topology models and reusing existing ones. Components have one or more Attributes attached to them. A *Connector* captures a relationship between (exactly) two Components, a *source* and a *target*. Connectors also have attributes associated with them, and they belong to one of the available *Connector Classes* that define the type of the Connector, e.g. 'deployed on'. Finally, *Groups* allow for the organization of components into sub-graphs of the topology model with non-exclusive memberships, enabling the creation of views on the topological model. Groups have attributes to provide further information about the components they aggregate.

## 3.2   Mappings from Other Languages

A key feature of GENTL is its generic nature which allows for easy mapping from other topology definition languages. As an example of this capability, Table 1 contains the mapping between GENTL and Blueprints and TOSCA. More specifically, with respect to the former, a Blueprint offering is similar in purpose to the Topology element in GENTL. Blueprint offerings are distinguished between resource requirements and implementation artefacts. Both these element types can be mapped to Components in GENTL, with elements of each type forming a Group in GENTL, and their properties captured as Component or Topology Attributes. Blueprints also support three types of links between elements: Vertical (denoting deployment dependency), Horizontal (denoting functional dependency), and Resource, for connections to external resources like IaaS offerings. All these links are mapped as Connectors in GENTL, with the three link types modeled as Connector Class elements.

With respect to TOSCA, the mapping between the two languages is rather straightforward. Topology Templates map to Topology elements, Node Templates can be modeled as Components, and Relationship Templates as Connectors. The properties, interfaces, capabilities and requirements definitions of a Node Template are captured as Attributes on the Component, while relationship properties and interfaces are reflected as Connector Attributes. Node and Relationship Types are mapped to Groups and Connector Classes, respectively.

The mapping presented is, of course, unidirectional (from Blueprints/TOSCA to GENTL); bidirectional mapping between topology languages requires ensuring that sufficient information is available on the level of GENTL models. Annotations, as discussed in the following section can be used for this purpose.

## 4   GENTL Annotations

Annotation schemes are used to provide information that is attached, but not directly related to the application topology itself, and which can be used for several purposes like metering, billing, matching, and management. Different languages provide different mechanisms for this purpose, and existing topology annotation schemes can be classified to one or more of the following categories depending on their intended use:

1. *Discovery:* These annotations describe the capabilities or requirements of topologies and/or their elements, ranging from functional interface descriptions to QoS characteristics and semantics annotations, and used for matching purposes.
2. *Provision and Management:* These are used to automate the deployment of applications, and support tasks ranging from simple installation of components to complex system adaptations at runtime.
3. *Design Support:* This type is used to provide decision making support during the design or migration of an application to the cloud. For example, applicable design patterns can be identified and captured through these annotations.

Blueprints, for example, allow for the definition of QoS information in both offerings and resource requirements elements, which are used for discovery of matching offerings. This information is expressed as policies that are attached to the blueprint elements. TOSCA supports both discovery, and provision and management type plans by means of policy types and templates for non-functional characteristics, and management plans expressed in languages like BPEL or BPMN. In [2] we discuss how design support annotations can be used to identify the most cost efficient deployment of the application in the cloud through interaction with the application designer. In addition, and depending on the level of automation in processing the information captured in them, annotations can be *automatic* (intended for processing entirely by machines), *human-oriented* (e.g. in natural language), or *hybrid* as a combination of them. Furthermore, annotations may be *static* or *dynamic*, requiring e.g. input from the user. Discovery annotations, for example, are usually static and automatic annotations, while provision and management annotations combine static and dynamic with automatic or hybrid characteristics.

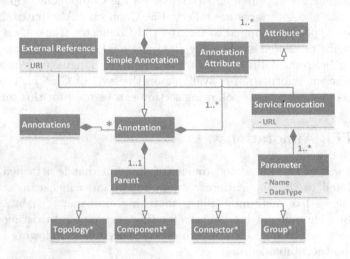

**Fig. 2.** The Annotations Metamodel of GENTL (*Class** refers to Fig. 1)

As discussed in the introduction, the main focus of GENTL is on providing design support, which constitutes the main requirement on the language with respect to its annotation scheme. However, and in order to preserve the generic nature of the language, GENTL Annotations as summarized by Fig. 2 are designed to support all types of annotations discussed above. Following the example of the WS-Policy Framework, GENTL Annotations are defined on a separate document that contains references to the topology definition(s) elements. This allows multiple annotation documents to be created for the same topology, as well as reuse of existing annotations by reorganizing the references to elements. More specifically, an *Annotation* element has one or more *Annotation Attributes* that are of type Attribute (as defined in Fig. 1), and is attached to one *Parent* that can be a Topology element, or any Component, Connector or Group inside a topology model. In addition, an Annotation is one of the following types: a *Simple Annotation* (collection of Attributes), an *External Reference* (a URI referring to a resource actually containing the annotation, e.g. a TOSCA management plan), or a *Service Invocation* (containing a request endpoint, and request *Parameters* for invoking the endpoint). The first two types are static, while the last one is dynamic. The *Annotations* element groups together multiple Annotation elements into one document.

# 5    Tooling Support

Providing the right tooling support is essential for the usability of any topology language. There are some fundamental requirements towards providing an environment for GENTL users, namely: *platform independence*, capability to *import* existing topology models and their annotations from other languages into GENTL, and an easy to use *graphical environment* incorporating automatic graph layout and dynamic interaction functionalities. In the following we discuss how the GENTL Environment that we developed satisfies these requirements.

## 5.1    The GENTL Environment

The GENTL Environment was developed as a Web application, providing platform-independent access by means of most popular Web browsers. For this purpose, a project in the Django framework[6] was created. Django is based on Python and offers an object-relational mapper that enables the definition of data models in Python. The data models are persisted in a built-in database and are accessed either through API calls or SQL statements directly to the database. The resulting Django project consists of the following set of Python applications:

**Topology App:** handles the topology data and is responsible for the graph visualization (using Graphviz[7] and the pydot[8] interface between Python and Graphviz for this purpose). Topology elements are implemented as Python objects and stored in Django's database in tables containing the data model instances.

**Annotation Apps:** implement the annotation model through two different applications — a Static Annotation App for Simple Annotations and External References, and a Dynamic Annotation App for Service Invocation Annotations.

**Transformation App:** bundles the importing functionalities — currently for Blueprint and TOSCA topology models based on the mappings discussed in Section 3.2.

Beyond importing existing topologies, the GENTL Environment allows also for the modeling of application topologies from scratch. Furthermore, it supports exporting GENTL application topology models into a serialized XML format, with exporting to other languages being ongoing work. The source and binary files for the GENTL Environment are available online[9] under Apache License 2.0.

## 5.2    User Interface

The main Graphical User Interface (GUI) of the GENTL Environment is shown in Fig. 3. The top menu allows for the addition of new elements in the topology

---

[6] Django: https://www.djangoproject.com/
[7] Graphviz: http://www.graphviz.org/
[8] pydot: http://code.google.com/p/pydot/
[9] The GENTL Environment: http://www.iaas.uni-stuttgart.de/GENTL

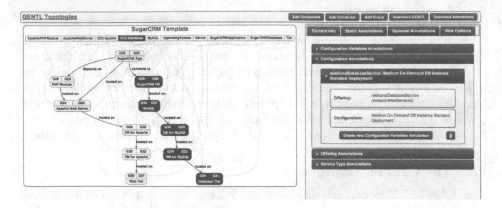

**Fig. 3.** The SugarCRM Application in the GUI of the GENTL Environment

model, exporting the model in a serialized GENTL document, and exporting the annotations (in a separate document). Following the 'GENTL Topologies' link leads to an initial screen that lists all models currently in the database, as well as importing an existing GENTL, TOSCA or Blueprint model (not shown in the figure). The topology model itself is visualized in the left pane of the screen as a graph with Group elements arranged at the top of the pane and connected to individual Components and Connectors with dashed lines to show membership in this group. Selecting a group ('EC2 Database' in Fig. 3) highlights the members of the group. The right pane of the GUI is used to show the element attributes, as well as provide access to the annotations (both static and dynamic) of each element. In the case shown in Fig. 3, the 'EC2 Database' group is annotated with the information that it is (also) deployable on a Medium On-Demand Instance DB (Standard Deployment) of the Amazon RDS[10] service instead of an EC2[11] instance. This dynamic annotation actually builds on the integration with the Nefolog system [2] for identifying and retrieving the details of this offering and can dynamically change to another cloud service offering if the requirements for this group change. Using the cost calculation capabilities of Nefolog, this information can be used to provide a projection of the operational expenses of using alternative deployment groups, as shown in Fig. 4.

## 6   Related Work

Related works in the literature build on application topology models to optimize the distribution of an application across cloud offerings. The optimization involves different dimensions, usually however in combination with operational expenses. For example, the work in [14] presents DADL, a language to describe the architecture, behavior and needs of a distributed application to be deployed

---

[10] Amazon Relational Database Service (Amazon RDS): http://aws.amazon.com/rds/
[11] Amazon Web Services Elastic Compute Cloud: http://aws.amazon.com/ec2/

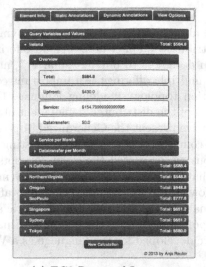
(a) EC2 Reserved Instance

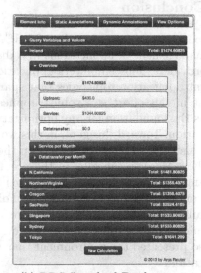
(b) RDS Standard Deployment

**Fig. 4.** Cost Calculation in the GENTL Environment for two AWS Offerings

on the cloud, as well as describing available cloud offerings for matching purposes. Similarly, in [3], the authors propose an approach that matches and dynamically adapts the allocation of infrastructure resources to an application topology in order to ensure SLAs. CloudMig [9] builds on an initial topology of the application that is adapted through model transformation in order to optimize the distribution of the application across cloud offerings. A similar approach is proposed by the MODAClouds work [4] which uses CloudML (see Section 2) for the definition of the application topology model.

The approach in [13] uses a Palladio-based application topology model in order to distribute an application across different cloud providers aiming at optimizing for availability and operational expenses. The MOCCA framework [11] deals with the same problem by introducing variability points in the application topology in order to cope with possible alternative deployment topologies. CMotion [7] uses an approach based on topology modeling, generation of alternative topologies, and consequent evaluation and selection of one of those alternatives based on multiple criteria. The work in [1] uses the notion of typed graphs for similar purposes and proposes a formal framework to support this effort. In a similar approach, MADCAT [10] incorporates to the topology model scalability elements, and refines the topology model from a high-level application topology to a ready for deployment one. While GENTL allows for mapping from different application topology language however, the above works rely on a single topology language. In this respect our proposal offers the means for a more generic approach that decouples from the specifics of each language used.

# 7    Conclusion

The existence of initiatives like TOSCA allow for the automated deployment and management of applications in a distributed manner across cloud offerings and providers. This empowers application designers to pursue "smarter", more efficient application topologies that span multiple offerings. An important component in this effort is a robust application topology modeling language that acts as the foundation for any optimization of the distributed deployment of the application. Toward this goal, in this work we present the Generalized Topology Language (GENTL) which builds on the common characteristics of existing approaches. More specifically, in the previous we presented the main concepts of the language, as well as the mappings that allow transforming topology models from other languages to GENTL. Following on, we discussed the annotation mechanism developed for the language, enabling the addition of both static and dynamic additional information to the topology models in the language. Finally, we also presented the environment that we developed for the language as a Web application.

With respect to the latter, and beyond adding additional mappings from, e.g. CloudML to GENTL, the main task for the immediate future is enabling the automated deployment and management of GENTL application models in a cross-solution manner. For this purpose, we plan to define a language-specific annotation type that will allow application designers to provide the necessary information for the mapping to a deployable language. In addition, in future work we intend to use GENTL as the underlying language for the definition of $\alpha$- and $\gamma$-topologies (application-independent and -specific topology models, respectively) as discussed in [1]. By these means we will be able to provide a comprehensive design support solution to application designers in identifying the most efficient distributed deployment of their application.

**Acknowledgment.** This work is partially funded by the FP7 EU-FET project 600792 ALLOW Ensembles.

# References

1. Andrikopoulos, V., Gómez Sáez, S., Leymann, F., Wettinger, J.: Optimal Distribution of Applications in the Cloud. In: Jarke, M., Mylopoulos, J., Quix, C., Rolland, C., Manolopoulos, Y., Mouratidis, H., Horkoff, J. (eds.) CAiSE 2014. LNCS, vol. 8484, pp. 75–90. Springer, Heidelberg (2014)
2. Andrikopoulos, V., Reuter, A., Mingzhu, X., Leymann, F.: Design Support for Cost-efficient Application Distribution in the Cloud. In: Proceedings of CLOUD 2014. IEEE Computer Society (to appear, 2014)
3. Antonescu, A.F., Robinson, P., Braun, T.: Dynamic topology orchestration for distributed cloud-based applications. In: Second Symposium on Network Cloud Computing and Applications (NCCA), pp. 116–123 (2012)

4. Ardagna, D., Di Nitto, E., Mohagheghi, P., et al.: MODAclouds: A model-driven approach for the design and execution of applications on multiple clouds. In: 2012 ICSE Workshop on Modeling in Software Engineering (MISE), pp. 50–56. IEEE (2012)
5. Armbrust, M., et al.: Above the Clouds: A Berkeley View of Cloud Computing. Tech. Rep. UCB/EECS-2009-28, EECS Department, University of California, Berkeley (2009)
6. Binz, T., Breiter, G., Leyman, F., Spatzier, T.: Portable cloud services using tosca. IEEE Internet Computing 16(3) (2012)
7. Binz, T., Leymann, F., Schumm, D.: CMotion: A Framework for Migration of Applications into and between Clouds. In: Proceedings of SOCA 2011, pp. 1–4. IEEE Computer Society (2011)
8. Ferry, N., Rossini, A., Chauvel, F., Morin, B., Solberg, A.: Towards model-driven provisioning, deployment, monitoring, and adaptation of multi-cloud systems. In: Proceedings of CLOUD 2013, pp. 887–894. IEEE Computer Society (2013)
9. Frey, S., Hasselbring, W.: The cloudmig approach: Model-based migration of software systems to cloud-optimized applications. International Journal on Advances in Software 4(3&4), 342–353 (2011)
10. Inzinger, C., Nastic, S., Sehic, S., Vögler, M., Li, F., Dustdar, S.: Madcat a methodology for architecture and deployment of cloud application topologies. In: Proceedings of SOSE 2014. IEEE (to appear, 2014)
11. Leymann, F., Fehling, C., Mietzner, R., Nowak, A., Dustdar, S.: Moving applications to the cloud: An approach based on application model enrichment. International Journal of Cooperative Information Systems 20(03), 307–356 (2011)
12. Mietzner, R., Unger, T., Leymann, F.: Cafe: A generic configurable customizable composite cloud application framework. In: Meersman, R., Dillon, T., Herrero, P. (eds.) OTM 2009, Part I. LNCS, vol. 5870, pp. 357–364. Springer, Heidelberg (2009)
13. Miglierina, M., Gibilisco, G., Ardagna, D., Di Nitto, E.: Model based control for multi-cloud applications. In: 5th International Workshop on Modeling in Software Engineering (MiSE), pp. 37–43 (2013)
14. Mirkovic, J., Faber, T., Hsieh, P., Malaiyandisamy, G., Malaviya, R.: DADL: Distributed Application Description Language. Tech. Rep. ISI-TR-664, USC/ISI (2010), ftp://www.isi.edu/isi-pubs/tr-664.pdf
15. Papazoglou, M.P., van den Heuvel, W.J.: Blueprinting the cloud. Internet Computing 15(6), 74–79 (2011)

# Cloud Resources-Events-Agents Model: Towards TOSCA-Based Applications

Soheil Qanbari[1], Vahid Sebto[2], and Schahram Dustdar[1]

[1] Technical University of Vienna
{qanbari,dustdar}@dsg.tuwien.ac.at
http://dsg.tuwien.ac.at
[2] Baha'i Institute for Higher Education (BIHE)
{vahid.sebto}@bihe.org
http://www.bihe.org

**Abstract.** The dilemma for domain experts and developers during design time of a cloud application is ensuring the sufficient programming abstractions between them in mapping the business requirements to cloud specifications. Thus, a modeling language is needed to capture and express the business requirements. Resources-Events-Agents (REA) is a well-known business requirement modeling language that decomposes the information system into three constituents with the set of compliant binary collaborations called, *Duality*. This study is a preliminary attempt to employ REA for developing cloud applications. In this study, we define a conceptual mapping between REA model and OASIS Topology and Orchestration Specification for cloud Applications (TOSCA) policies, plans and templates. Based on that, we proceed with the process of building business-driven cloud applications. In support of our model, we implement a cloud REA Modeling tool referred to as CREAM, where business requirements are specified in REA, then corresponding cloud application is composed and built. We describe the underlying mapping strategy as well as the details of our tool in support of the proposed approach.

**Keywords:** Cloud application, Resources-Events-Agents (REA), TOSCA, Business requirements.

## 1 Introduction

The cloud abstraction model delivers a shared pool of configurable computing resources (processors, storage, applications, etc.) that can be dynamically and automatically provisioned and released [1]. This elastic delivery of cloud resources improves business agility by enabling the providers to respond faster to the demanding needs of the markets. Firms benefit from this as an enabler in developing adaptive business models built upon cloud applications that meet both business and customer needs. Thus, they can orchestrate processes, (de)allocate resources, (de)provision services and seamlessly adapt to the constantly changing

M. Villari et al. (Eds.) : ESOCC 2014, LNCS 8745, pp. 160–170, 2014.

requirements of their clients. Cloud adaptive business modeling, poses challenges of performing an ongoing assessments to ensure compliance and alignment between business requirements and system specifications.

In architecting cloud applications, the cloud market-leader, Amazon web services (AWS), offers a *CloudFormation*[1] service where we can create a stack to seamlessly provision the collection of resources required by applications. We can deploy CloudFormation's *templates*[2] or create our own templates to describe the AWS resources with associated dependencies or runtime parameters, required to run our applications. The cloud management platform, *OpenStack* provides a service called *Heat*[3] to orchestrate multiple composite cloud applications using the AWS CloudFormation template format, through both an OpenStack-native REST API and a CloudFormation-compatible Query API. The *Heat* engine's main responsibility is to orchestrate the launching of templates and provide events back to the API consumer. On a similar service, the Ubuntu open-source community, provides Ubuntu JuJu[4], a service orchestration management tool where we can define the technical requirements and specifications of our cloud application and proceed with its deployment. Similarly, the openTOSCA[5] provides a container where we can define and run our TOSCA-based cloud application implementation artifacts composed into the cloud Service Archive (CSAR) file which includes the service topology and its implementation plans.

Suffice to say that these initiatives are more focused on capturing technical requirements rather than business models. Such solutions are appropriate for cloud application developers and pose limitations for business developers who know the domain knowledge best but with limited programming skills. There are several well-established business modeling frameworks,including e3-value [3], Resource-Event-Agent (REA) [4] and the Business Modeling Ontology (BMO) [5]. These models allow shorter development cycles and faster time to products and value. However, at the moment, to the best of our knowledge, there is no engagement between the current business modeling frameworks and cloud computing business models. In this paper, we provide this mapping and ultimately, show how effective our tooling is. In summary, our contribution is twofold as follows:

- Analyzing the contemporary business modeling frameworks on which firms base their service identification, specification, and realization strategies.
- The mapping rules between the REA model and the TOSCA model. We implement a tool in support of these compliance rules.

The paper continues with a background in the cloud REA model in section 2 in support of proper positioning of the CREAM tool. Section 3 introduces the REA business modeling framework as an input model. In section 4 TOSCA specifications as an output model are detailed. Section 5 presents the actual contribution of the paper, the conceptual mapping rules together with their supporting

---

[1] http://aws.amazon.com/cloudformation/

[2] http://aws.amazon.com/cloudformation/aws-cloudformation-templates/

[3] https://wiki.openstack.org/wiki/Heat

[4] https://juju.ubuntu.com

[5] http://www.iaas.uni-stuttgart.de/OpenTOSCA/indexE.php

facts. Next, the CREAM tool architecture is presented in section 6 and a sample use-case scenario is given to support the efficiency and utilization of our tool. Subsequently, section 7 surveys some scientific related work. Finally, section 8 concludes the paper and presents an outlook on future research directions.

## 2    Related Work

In relation to our approach, there are some prominent approaches for defining the cloud value chain reference model[7], like an $i*^6$, a goal-oriented social modeling framework for linking business models to their supporting services and process models by Jaap et al[8] and Ramel et al[9]. In their approach, first, the business requirements are modeled with the $i*$ notation and then business services are derived. In the second phase, the identified services are refined according to these requirements using UML activity and class diagrams. On a similar approach, Gailly et al[10] defined a set of business rules to transform the REA meta-model into a UML class diagram with accompanying OCL constraints. Schuster et al[11] leverages model driven development and provide a mapping from REA to UMM. In support of this mapping, Sonnenberg et al[12], developed a domain specific modeling language called REA-DSL. Another more conceptual approach exploiting service science perspective on REA business modeling is introduced by Roelens et al[13]. The authors specify six design criteria to evaluate the ability of REA business model to create service interaction model. Poels et al[14] propose the Resource-Service-System model adapted from REA as a conceptual model for service science that emphasizes the service systems interaction through the exchange of resource for more utilization. To the best of our knowledge, the existing approaches do not address the cloud computing business models as we aim to do by a mapping from REA modeling language to cloud TOSCA model. Next, we explore each of them as an input and an output models of our mapping process.

## 3    REA – The Input Model

The REA (Resources-Events-Agents) model focuses on the value of business objects exchanged among parties and abstracts away the implementation details of the system to business developers. Figure 1, illustrates the core concepts of REA. Now we delve into the core concepts, their meanings and interdependencies:

◇ **Economic Resource** is a thing that has utility for *Agents*. In fact, users need to deploy, monitor, and utilize the resources. For instance, economic resources can be products, tools, services and humans as well.

◇ **Economic Agent** is a stakeholder or organization capable of having control over economic resources, with an interest in it. Agents deal on resources upon their established service level agreements. Examples of economic agents are consumers, vendors, employees, and third-party enterprises.

---

[6] http://www.cs.toronto.edu/km/istar

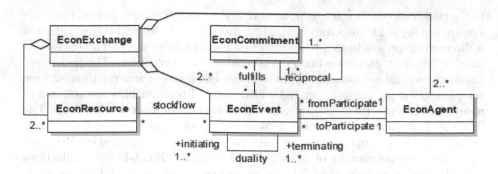

**Fig. 1.** Excerpt of the REA meta-model and core concepts

◇ **Economic Event** represents either an increment or a decrement in the value of economic resources. Some economic events are demand, supply of resources. Events can be classified into two poles of *Take* and *Give*. At least one *take* event and one *give* event exist for each resource. When the event occurs, the provider loses rights to the resource, and the consumer receives the rights.

◇ **Economic Commitment** is a promise or obligation of an economic *Agent* to perform an economic *Event* in the future. For example, line items on a sales order represent commitments to sell goods. Lack of resources leads to unmet demands and, while reflecting the SLA violations, leads to financial consequences and penalties.

◇ **Economic Contract** is a collection of increment and decrement commitments and terms. Thus, the contract can specify what should happen if the commitments are not fulfilled.

In REA, business processes are the orchestration of events that can be triggered by agents affecting the resources. Resources are exchanged through these processes. The notion of stockflow is used to specify in what way an economic event affects a resource. REA identifies five stockflows: *Produce, Use, Consume, Give* and *Take*. For instance, the *Deployment* process of the *Vendor* specifies an *outflow* of *Resources* and *inflow* of *Cash* to the *Vendor*. The model of the *Usage* process from the perspective of the client agent is a mirror image of the vendor's *Deployment* process. The *Usage* pattern of the client specifies the *inflow of Resource* and *outflow of Cash* from the client.

## 4   TOSCA – The Output Model

The Topology Orchestration Specification for cloud Applications (TOSCA) language introduces a grammar for describing service templates by means of Topology Templates and Plans. The root of a TOSCA service is the Service Template. The Service Template contains a directed graph that represents the structure of the service called a Service Topology. Every *service template* has at least one *service topology*. The topology graph is composed of nodes and edges. Edges in a directed graph are links with a direction from node to node. The edges in a Service Topology graph are binary relationships between nodes. The nodes represent the logical components of the service. These nodes and relationships are templates that are patterns for the real nodes and relationships instantiated in a deployed service. Plans orchestrate various aspects of a service life cycle. The TOSCA specification defines *Build* plans and *Termination* plans. Build Plans orchestrate the deployment and installation of a service. Termination Plans orchestrate decommissioning of a service. Designers of TOSCA-based applications can add plan types as needed. The designers can benefit by work-flow notations such as BPMN or BPEL. In our CREAM model, TOSCA embodies the cloud composite application design and its elasticity specifications directly derived from the business requirements model using REA.

## 5    Mapping REA to TOSCA

In this section we describe the mapping from a REA model to TOSCA artifacts. Before we delve into the details of modeling and implementation, it is reasonable to focus on the underlying approaches as we have taken on the mapping process to provide a holistic view about the source model (REA) and target (TOSCA) artifacts. Our approach is twofold: first, we proceed with the conceptual mapping from a meta-level perspective. Second, we define the mapping rules of the two models supported by their implementation scripts in the tool.

### 5.1    Conceptual Mapping

A mapping from the REA business modeling language to the TOSCA artifacts is a first step in the progress of developing business-oriented cloud applications. This section formulates such a mapping. To define a mapping, we first discover the most suitable matches for REA concepts in TOSCA, then we formulate this connection in rules which will be formalized further in the tooling. We start with the eight concepts derived from the REA as core concepts. As listed in Table 1, we identified the following eight rules.

### 5.2    Mapping Rules (M.R.)

◇ **M.R.1**: *Resource*, indicate things that are affected or exchanged in processes. For cloud applications, software services or infrastructure resources express the same semantics. It can be specified by *nodeTemplate* and *nodeType* elements in TOSCA. For instance, a *nodeType* of *ApacheWebServer* can be instantiated by a *nodeTemplate* of *MoodleAppServer*.

◇ **M.R.2**: *Event*, is nested within an economic *Exchange*. These events are initiated by *Agents* affecting a *Resource*. In TOSCA, the *nodeTypes* has element

**Table 1.** Mapping Rules from REA model to TOSCA artifacts

| No | Rules | REA Concepts | TOSCA Concepts |
|---|---|---|---|
| 1 | Resource | Economic Resource | Node Tempalate |
| 2 | Event | Economic Event | Interface Operation |
| 3 | Exchange | Economic Exchange | Relations / Plans |
| 4 | Entity | Economic Agent | Roles |
| 5 | Contract | Contract / Commitment | Policy Types |
| 6 | Duality | Exchange Duality | Relation Types |
| 7 | Links | Stockflow, Inflow, Outflow | Relations Types |
| 8 | Pack | Typification, Grouping | Service Templates |

of *Interfaces* in which each interface includes some *Operations*. For instance, re-leasing or allocating storage resource unit from/to a VM.

◊ **M.R.3**: *Exchange*, is a value or resource *Exchange* with pair of economic *Events* linked by *Duality* relationship. It is mapped to TOSCA *relationType* and *plans* which defines the process models that are used to manage the application life-cycle. In TOSCA, a plan is a set of operations exposed in a sequence flow by the service template. Both concepts contain the business transactions, resource exchange, events, and agents that are necessary to fulfill the business goal. The typical TOSCA plans are *buildPlans*, *terminationPlans* and can be extended to *modificationPlans*.

◊ **M.R.4**: *Entity*, is basically an economic unit or an *Agent* representing an actor and therefore mapped to *Role* in TOSCA plans. The mapping is logical since both concepts share the same semantics. TOSCA roles are oriented on three actors of cloud service *Developer*, *Provider* and *Consumer*. An economic agent in REA and a role in TOSCA are both actors with an interest in a col-laboration. TOSCA *typeArtifact*, *artifactDeveloper* and *applicationArchitect* are the specialization of the service developer role. Cloud *service provider* hosts and operates the application to be used by the *service consumer*.

◊ **M.R.5**: *Contract*, details an agreement reflected in an economic *Event*. The resource delivery is governed by an associated *Contract*, composed of set of *Commitments*. An economic contract comprises agreements, rights and terms made among agents. Commitment fulfills the *exchange-reciprocity* application. In TOSCA, the commitments can be declared by the use of *Policy Types* and *AppliesTo* element. A policy type can express the resource intended behavior or the Quality of Service (QoS) that a *nodeType* is about to expose. A TOSCA Pol-icy can also express diverse things like monitoring behavior, payment conditions, scalability, or availability, for instance. Policies can inherit and apply properties by *derivedFrom* and *appliesTo* elements. Thus a relevant policy type can show the specified behavior of a resource in a *Contract*.

◊ **M.R.6**: *Duality*, also nested within an economic *Exchange* and the *Event* holding this association triggers the resource exchange. Duality can be used to model many-to-many relationships between any two resources. This allows *Give & Take* operations to increase or decrease the amount of resource allocation. Duality implements the elasticity behavior of the cloud application. Thus, the messaging among the resources should be paired via a duality relationship to bind events together with the resource exchange. For instance, *Request & Response, Demand & Allocate, Service Acquisition & Service Provision* and *Pay_per_resource_usage* can be considered as cloud use-cases of *Duality* concepts. In this sense, *Duality* is mapped to TOSCA *relationType* that identifies the corresponding relation of a service provisioning event to a specific request and payment subsequently.

◊ **M.R.7**: *Link*, denotes the semantics behind the links among service encompassed components. The *Stockflow* association denotes the flow of resource exchange triggered by an economic events like increment or decrement resource allocation. The relationship between an increment event and a resource is called *inflow* and the relationship between a decrement and a resource is called *outflow*. For instance, in vendor's *sales* process, the exchange will represent an *outflow* of resource and an *inflow* of cash in return. In TOSCA, the relationship specifies the semantics between nodes of *sourceElement* and *targetElement* in a topology template. The REA relations can be mapped to the TOSCA *relationTypes* like *dependsOn, hostedOn* and *deployedOn* concerning the context.

◊ **M.R.8**: *Pack*, is a course or principle of composition action, adopted by *Grouping* and *Typification* abstractions in the REA application model. Typification implements *a-kind-of* element, grouping realizes *a-member-of* applications. This forms a composite application which will be deployed under certain policies. Hybrid association of *Types* and *Groupings* defines the *Policy Layer* on top of the *Operation Layer* in the model. In TOSCA, a policy type defines the constraints of a property, i.e. data types, allowed values, obligations and authorization requirements in a corresponding template.

## 6   Implementation: CREAM Tool Support

The aim of this toolkit is to provide a framework to facilitate the modeling and deployment of cloud based applications. Our toolkit provides a web interface which hides and abstracts away the cloud implementation details to business developers. CREAM captures the system requirements and their relationships, then builds the cloud application topology in TOSCA. The CREAM is a Java-based web application which is developed in WSO2 Developer Studio[7]. We used *Maven* to resolve its dependencies and deployed CREAM on WSO2 Application Server. Cloud resources are stored in WSO2 Governance Registry in compliance with TOSCA standard. All resources and artifacts are located in "/cream" path

---

[7] http://wso2.com/products/developer-studio

in the registry and categorized in two collections: (i) TOSCA Templates: this collection contains cloud and REA resources. For instance, *Instructor* is mapped to a TOSCA *NodeType* which is located in human resources category (HuaaS). For each resource and collection in ”/cream/ToscaTemplates”, a title is set in registry that will be displayed in CREAM Tool canvas, otherwise the name of the resource will be used. (ii) CSAR: the cloud topologies designed by business and application developers will be stored in this collection. Each designed topology is a TOSCA XML file named with a UUID and contains a *ServiceTemplate*. This contains all required information about services and resources requested by the user.

## 6.1   CREAM Architecture

Now, we detail the architecture. We developed the CREAM Toolkit based on a Model-View-Controller (MVC) design pattern. MVC framework is designed around a *DispatcherServlet* that dispatches requests to handlers. In CREAM, Dispatcher servlet is responsible to handle requests and responses. It delegates requests to controller (i.e., class *CloudApplicationDesignerController*). Controller class is identified by *@Controller* annotation and has methods to handle incoming requests. Each URL is mapped to a method annotated with *@RequestMapping*. This method executes the user requests, generates a model object and returns it to dispatcher. Dispatcher send models to view template which is responsible to render response. Finally dispatcher returns rendered response to user. For the sake of brevity, we only describe the packages and classes to clarify the CREAM architecture as illustrated in Fig 2.

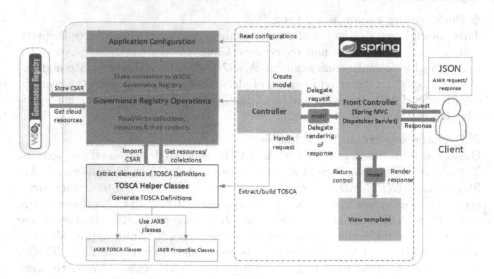

**Fig. 2.** Cloud REA Model (CREAM) architecture

## 6.2   Package Description

In this section, we describe the packages, their bundled classes, and implemented interfaces to support the CREAM architecture.

◇ **Package org.cream.commons**
This package includes exception classes, simple classes for Jakson *ObjectMapper* and other helper classes which are common in whole application. Its core classes are *ApplicationConfiguration*, *ServletContextHelper*, *ResourceObjectMap*, and *DesignedApplicationObjectMapItem*. The *ApplicationConfiguration* is responsible to read configuration file and make its entries accessible by other components of the application. The *ApplicationConfiguration* uses the *ServletContextHelper* class to find the real path of the configuration file. Both classes are designed using Singleton pattern.

◇ **Package org.cream.tosca.model**
This package contains JAXB generated classes from TOSCA XML schema (XSD). It also contains a sub-package `org.cream.tosca.model.properties` which includes JAXB generated classes for our defined properties schema. There are several sub-packages such as `org.cream.tosca.model.properties.` `amazonec2` whereas each package contains JAXB generated classes from a specific properties XML schema file. We use *Properties* element in TOSCA *NodeTemplate* to store specifications of each resource. We have defined these properties elements for each resource with XML schema. For each XML schema, we have generated corresponding classes using Java API JAXB. All packages in `org.cream.tosca.model.properties` corresponds to one schema.

◇ **Package org.cream.wso2.greg**
This package contains helper classes to connect to WSO2 Governance Registry and to retrieve resources and collections. Class *GovernanceRegistryConnector* is responsible to make connection to WSO2 Governance Registry. Method *getRemoteRegistry* returns an instance of class *RemoteRegistry* since the registry data retrieval APIs are defined here. Class *GovernanceRegistryReader* is responsible to read and write resources.

◇ **Package org.cream.tosca.loader**
Classes of this package works with JAXB generated classes. They extract TOSCA elements from TOSCA files and generate TOSCA Definitions and CSAR files. Class *JAXBMetaDataExtractor* uses Java *Reflection* API to extract properties' element names from JAXB property classes. Class *ToscaFileReader* marshals TOSCA Definitions from the given *InputStream*. It also provides a few helper classes for entire application to retrieve needed information about a TOSCA XML file. Class *ToscaBuilder* is responsible to generate final TOSCA definition object from user-defined topology. Finally this class converts the generated TOSCA Definitions to its XML string and stores it in WSO2 Governance Registry.

# 7  Conclusion and Outlook

So far, we have used the REA model to specify the business requirements, constraints and rules for building cloud applications. In support of our approach, we developed the CREAM tool in which, initially does the conceptual mapping and build the TOSCA-based cloud application. As an outlook, our future work includes further extension to the CREAM tool that can also support the REA's structural and behavioral business patterns[15] at policy, operational and aspect layers to provide a more holistic coverage of the various perspectives relevant to application development process. Summarizing, we envision cloud REA Model as a potential cloud value modeling framework for building business-driven cloud applications.

# References

1. Papazoglou, M.P.: Cloud blueprints for integrating and managing cloud federations. In: Heisel, M. (ed.) Software Service and Application Engineering. LNCS, vol. 7365, pp. 102–119. Springer, Heidelberg (2012)
2. Osterwalder, A., Pigneur, Y., Tucci, C.L.: Clarifying business models: Origins, present, and future of the concept. Communications of the Association for Information Systems 16, article 1 (2005)
3. Gordijn, J., Akkermans, H.: e3-value: Designing and evaluating ebusiness models. IEEE Intelligent Systems 16(4), 11–17 (2001)
4. Mccarthy, W.E.: The rea accounting model: A generalized framework for accounting systems in a shared data environment. The Accounting Review 57(3), 554–578 (1982)
5. Iso: Information technology - business operational view - part 4: Business transaction scenarios, iso/iec 2007, iso 15944-4 (2007)
6. Oasis, un/cefact: ebxml - technical architecture specification, version 1.4 (February 2001)
7. Mohammed, A.B., Altmann, J., Hwang, J.: Cloud computing value chains: Understanding businesses and value creation in the cloud. In: Economic Models and Algorithms for Distributed Systems, Autonomic Systems, pp. 187–208. Birkhäuser, Basel (2010)
8. Gordijn, J., Yu, E., van der Raadt, B.: E-service design using i* and e3value modeling. IEEE Software 23(3), 26–33 (2006)
9. Ramel, S., Grandry, E., Dubois, E.: Towards a design method supporting the alignment between business and software services. In: 33rd Annual IEEE International Computer Software and Applications Conference, COMPSAC 2009, vol. 1, pp. 349–354 (2009)
10. Gailly, F., Geerts, G.: Frederik Gailly and Guido Geerts. Formal definition of business rules using rea business modeling language. In: Proceedings of the 7th International Workshop on Value Modeling and Business Ontology, p. 7 (2013)
11. Schuster, R., Motal, T., Huemer, C., Werthner, H.: From economic drivers to B2B process models: A mapping from REA to UMM. In: Abramowicz, W., Tolksdorf, R. (eds.) BIS 2010. LNBIP, vol. 47, pp. 119–131. Springer, Heidelberg (2010)
12. Sonnenberg, C., Huemer, C., Hofreiter, B., Mayrhofer, D., Braccini, A.: The REA-DSL: A domain specific modeling language for business models. In: Mouratidis, H., Rolland, C. (eds.) CAiSE 2011. LNCS, vol. 6741, pp. 252–266. Springer, Heidelberg (2011)

13. Roelens, B., Lemey, E., Poels, G.: A service science perspective on business modeling. In: Proceedings of the 6th International Workshop on Value Modeling and Business Ontology, p. 8 (2012)
14. Poels, G.: The resource-service-system model for service science. In: Trujillo, J., et al. (eds.) ER 2010. LNCS, vol. 6413, pp. 117–126. Springer, Heidelberg (2010)
15. Hruby, P.: Model-Driven Design Using Business Patterns. Springer-Verlag New York, Inc., Secaucus (2006)

# TOSCA in a Nutshell:
# Promises and Perspectives*

Antonio Brogi, Jacopo Soldani, and PengWei Wang

Department of Computer Science, University of Pisa, Italy

**Abstract.** How to deploy and flexibly manage complex multi-service applications in the cloud is one of the emerging problems in the cloud era. The OASIS Topology and Orchestration Specification for Cloud Applications (TOSCA) [1] aims at contributing to solve this problem by providing a language to describe and manage complex cloud applications in a portable, vendor-agnostic way. The objective of this paper is twofold: To provide a compact and easy-to-access introduction to TOSCA, and to discuss possible research directions for TOSCA.

## 1 Introduction

Cloud computing is revolutionizing IT by enabling a convenient, on-demand and scalable network access to shared pools of configurable computing resources. However, current cloud technologies suffer from a lack of standardization, with different providers offering similar resources in a different manner [2]. As a result, cloud developers tend to remain locked in a specific platform environment because it is practically unfeasible for them, due to high complexity and cost, to migrate their applications to a different platform. According to [3], in order to enable the creation of portable cloud applications, the application's components, their relations and management should be modeled in a standardized, machine-readable format. This will also allow the automation of the deployment and management of the modeled application [4].

In this perspective, OASIS recently released version 1.0 of TOSCA, the Topology and Orchestration Specification for Cloud Applications [1]. TOSCA proposes an XML-based modeling language which permits to specify an application's structure as a typed topology graph, and the management tasks as plans. More precisely, TOSCA aims at addressing the following three issues in cloud application management [3]: (O1) automated application deployment and management, (O2) portability of application descriptions and their management, and (O3) interoperability and reusability of components.

Interested readers can browse various documents to get acquainted with TOSCA. The official specification [1] and the primer [5] provide a comprehensive presentation of TOSCA, while several research papers (like [3], [6], and [7]) provide a short recap of the main features of TOSCA. Moreover, recent research

---

* Work partly supported by project EU-FP7-ICT-610531 SeaClouds (www.seaclouds-project.eu).

M. Villari et al. (Eds.) : ESOCC 2014, LNCS 8745, pp. 171–186, 2014.

papers (e.g., [8], [9], [10], [11], [12], [13], and [14]) are proposing various extensions of TOSCA. One of the motivations of this paper is that we believe that the availability of an updated, compact, and easy-to-access description of TOSCA may contribute to the dissemination of this OASIS specification.

In this paper:

(i) We try to provide a compact, easy-to-access description of TOSCA. We reorganize the available information about TOSCA in a compressed overview which outlines the goals of the specification, illustrates the TOSCA modeling language, positions TOSCA with respect to other cloud interoperability standard proposals and describes how TOSCA specifications are processed.

(ii) We analyze TOSCA with the aim of discussing some research perspectives which are leveraged by TOSCA itself. Namely, we discuss (D1) reuse of available specifications, (D2) enhanced and full-fledged implementations of so-called *TOSCA containers*, (D3) implementation of TOSCA tools, (D4) integration of TOSCA with existing standard proposals, and (D5) comparative assessment of TOSCA.

The rest of the paper is organized as follows. Sect. 2 presents an easy-to-access description of TOSCA. Sect. 3 analyzes TOSCA with the aim of highlighting its possible extensions and improvements, while Sect. 4 discusses some research perspectives. Finally, Sects. 5 and 6 discuss related work and draw some concluding remarks, respectively.

## 2    Overview of TOSCA

As previously mentioned, TOSCA [1] is an emerging standard whose main goal is to enable the creation of portable cloud applications and the automation of their deployment and management. In order to achieve this goal, TOSCA focuses on the following three sub-goals [3].

**(O1) Automated Application Deployment and Management.** TOSCA aims at providing a language to express how to automatically deploy and manage complex cloud applications.

This objective is achieved by requiring developers to define an abstract topology of a complex application and to create plans describing its deployment and management [4], [3] (see Sect. 2.1).

**(O2) Portability of Application Descriptions and Their Management.** TOSCA aims at addressing the portability of application descriptions and their management (but not the actual portability of the applications themselves) [3].

To this end, TOSCA provides a standardized way to describe the topology of multi-component applications (see Sect. 2.1). It also addresses management portability by relying on the portability of workflow languages used to describe deployment and management plans [6].

**(O3) Interoperability and Reusability of Components.** TOSCA aims at describing the components of complex cloud applications in an interoperable and reusable way.

Interoperability is the capability for multiple components "*to interact using well-defined messages and protocols*" [1] so that they can be combined independently of the vendor(s) supplying them. TOSCA abstracts from messages and protocols details, and it permits to describe the dependencies between application components (see Sect. 2.1).

Furthermore, TOSCA enables defining, assembling, and packaging the building blocks of an application in a completely self-contained manner (see Sect. 2.2), thus providing a standardized way to reuse them in different applications [3].

Fig. 1 tries to position TOSCA with respect to some other cloud interoperability[1] standards and specifications, namely CAMP [16], CIMI [17], EMML [18], OCCI [19], Open-CSA [20], OVF [21], SOA-ML [22], and USDL [23]. The three numbered sections of the pie represent the aforementioned three main goals of TOSCA, and the position of each label is intended to summarize "how much" the goals of an initiative overlap with TOSCA goals[2]. More precisely, to indicate that a standard is targeting one of the goals, its label covers the corresponding section of the pie. For instance, CAMP aims

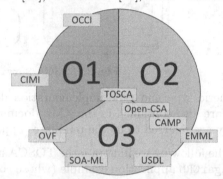

**Fig. 1.** Positioning TOSCA

at addressing both O2 and O3. Furthermore, if a label is not completely contained in the pie, this means that the corresponding standard only partially addresses the covered goals. Consider for instance OCCI. It provides an standardized IaaS interface which can be employed to automatize application deployment and management. Nevertheless, automation is not its real goal and thus OCCI is represented as partially covering the section O1 and partially out of the pie.

## 2.1   TOSCA Modeling Language

To achieve the aforementioned goals, TOSCA provides an XML-based modeling language, whose purpose is to allow formalizing the structure of each cloud application as a typed topology graph, and the management tasks as plans [3].

An application is represented as a `ServiceTemplate` (Fig. 2), which is in turn composed by a `TopologyTemplate` and (optionally) by some management `Plans` [1].

---

[1] A more thorough discussion on the relations between TOSCA and other cloud interoperability initiatives can be found in [15].

[2] Note that all mentioned initiatives target cloud interoperability, while only some of them also target the interoperability of application *components* (viz., O3).

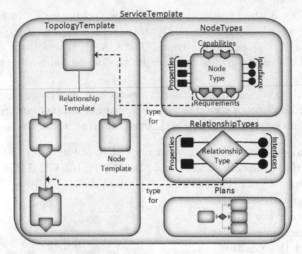

**Fig. 2.** TOSCA `ServiceTemplate`

Generic type and type implementation definitions (which will be discussed later) are also contained in the XML document defining the `ServiceTemplate` as they are referred to by the templates appearing in the topology [5].

In the following we illustrate the TOSCA modeling language with reference to the `SugarCRM` application example (whose complete description can be found in the TOSCA primer [5]), which exemplifies a complex cloud application designed for enabling businesses to manage the relationships with their customer.

**Topology of an Application.** The topology of a multi-component application is represented by means of `TopologyTemplate`s. A `TopologyTemplate` is essentially a typed graph whose nodes are the application components, and whose edges are the relations between these application components [1]. Syntactically speaking, the application components and their relations are represented by

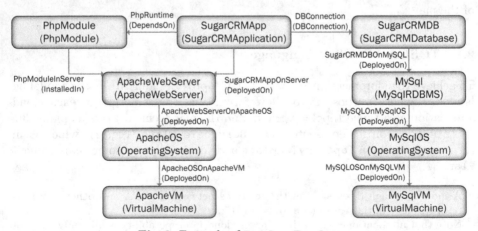

**Fig. 3.** Example of `TopologyTemplate`

means of typed `NodeTemplates` and `RelationshipTemplates`, respectively. A concrete example of an application topology is shown in Fig. 3, which illustrates the `NodeTemplates` and `RelationshipTemplates` composing the topology of the `SugarCRM` application. Fig. 3 also indicates the corresponding `NodeTypes` and `RelationshipTypes` between parentheses.

**Application Components.** As shown in Figs. 2 and 3, each application component appears in the topology as a `NodeTemplate`, and each `NodeTemplate` is in turn typed. This is because the purpose of `NodeTemplates` is to define the application-specific features of components (e.g., actual property values, QoS, etc.), while the purpose of the corresponding types is to describe the structure of the features to be specified.

The structure of the features exposed by an application component is defined by means of `NodeTypes` [10]. More precisely, a `NodeType` specifies the structure of the observable properties of an application component, the management operations it offers, the possible states of its instances, the requirements needed to properly operate it, and the capabilities it offers to satisfy other components requirements. Syntactically speaking, properties are described with `PropertiesDefinitions`, operations with `Interface` and `Operation` elements, requirements with `RequirementDefinitions` (of certain `RequirementTypes`), and capabilities with `CapabilityDefinitions` (of certain `CapabilityTypes`).

An example of a Node-Type is shown in Fig. 4, which illustrates the structure of the properties, requirements and interfaces exposed by the `SugarCRMApp` component.

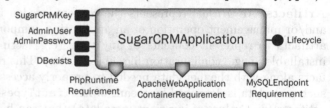

**Fig. 4.** Example of `NodeType`

Note that `NodeTypes` do not specify which are the artifacts required to instantiate and operate application components, since that is the purpose of `NodeTypeImplementations`. Each `NodeTypeImplementation` refers to the `NodeType` whose implementation is under definition and specifies its `DeploymentArtifacts` and `ImplementationArtifacts` [1]. The former are the contents (viz., `ArtifactTypes` and `ArtifactTemplates`) needed to materialize instances of application components, while the latter are those which implement management operations offered by application components [6].

**Relations between Application Components.** Complex multi-service applications require not only to model their components, but also the relations between them [5]. As for components, relations can be modeled by means of `RelationshipTypes`, `RelationshipTypeImplementations`, and `RelationshipTemplates` [1].

A `RelationshipType` defines the structure of a generic relationship between a `ValidSource` (i.e., a `NodeType` or a node's `RequirementType`) and a `ValidTarget` (i.e., a `NodeType` or a node's `CapabilityType`). It also allows to describe the operations which can be performed on the source and on the target of the

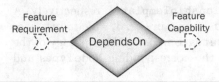

**Fig. 5.** Example of `RelationshipType`

relationship (via `SourceInterfaces` and `TargetInterfaces`, respectively), its observable properties, and the possible states of its instances. For instance, Fig. 5 illustrates the `DependsOn Relationship-Type`, whose `ValidSource` is a `Feature-Requirement` exposed by an application component, and whose `ValidTarget` is a `FeatureCapability` offered by another application component. Such a `RelationshipType` is only one of those modeling the relations between the component of the `SugarCRM` application example.

Each `RelationshipType` requires to be connected with the artifacts implementing the operations it offers. This is the purpose of `RelationshipType-Implementations` [1], each of which refers to a `RelationshipType` and specifies its `ImplementationArtifacts`. More precisely, a `RelationshipTypeImplementation` links each operation offered by a `NodeType` with the `ArtifactTypes` and `ArtifactTemplates` implementing it.

As for nodes, types and type implementations only describe relations in a generic way [5]. Once placed in the topological description of a certain application, they become application-specific and thus require to be described by means of `RelationshipTemplates` (to describe application-specific features).

**Artifacts.** An *artifact* represents the content needed to realize a deployment and/or management operation of an application component [5]. TOSCA allows artifacts to represent contents of any type (e.g., script, executable program, installable image, configuration file, library, etc.). This requires to describe artifacts along with the metadata needed to properly access them. The structure of such metadata is described by means of `ArtifactTypes`, while links to concrete artifacts (and values of invariant metadata) that can be specified by employing `ArtifactTemplates` [1].

**Management Plans.** `Plans` enable the description of application deployment and/or management aspects [14]. Each `Plan` is a workflow combining the operations offered by the nodes in the topology [1]. TOSCA prescribes to use workflows to describe `Plans` (so as to leverage of their suitability to handle errors, exceptions and human interactions [6]), but it does not mandate the use of specific workflow language [3]. Furthermore, `Plans` are distinguished on the basis of their `planType`. There are only two predefined types of plans: the `BuildPlan` type models plans which initially create a new instance of a service template, while the `TerminationPlan` type is for plans used to terminate the existence of a service instance [1].

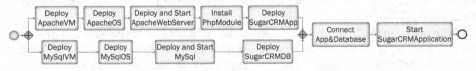

**Fig. 6.** Example of `Plan`

A concrete example of a TOSCA Plan is shown in Fig. 6, which illustrates a possible (BPMN) BuildPlan for the SugarCRM application example.

**Application "Boundaries".** A ServiceTemplate can also describe the functional and non-functional features it exposes externally. More precisely, the (optional) BoundaryDefinitions element allows to specify the properties, capabilities, requirements and operations of internal components which are externally visible. It also allows to expose management plans as operations and to describe the non-functional properties of the complex application.

**Non-functional Features of an Application (Component).** TOSCA employs policies to describe non-functional behavior and/or quality-of-service (QoS) that an application and its components can declare to expose [3]. Similar to the other entities in the TOSCA standard, a policy has an abstract PolicyType definition and is instantiated by defining a PolicyTemplate. While the PolicyType describes the structure and required parameters of a policy, the PolicyTemplate is used to define a specific policy instance [1].

ServiceTemplates (via BoundaryDefinitions), NodeTemplates, and RelationshipTemplates can then declare their non-functional features by referring the PolicyType and/or PolicyTemplate describing them [13].

## 2.2   Packaging and Processing of Application Specifications

TOSCA also prescribes the format to archive application specifications along with the installable and executable files needed to properly instantiate the specified applications. This is because the modeling language illustrated in the previous section only allows developers to specify the application topology and its management and to give it in a Definition.tosca document. Such document must be packaged together with the artifacts implementing its components so as to make all such artifacts available to the execution environment.

**Packaging of Application Specifications.** The TOSCA specification defines an archive format called CSAR (*Cloud Serivce ARchive*) to package application specification together with concrete implementation and deployment artifacts [1]. A CSAR is a (compressed) zip file containing at least the Definitions and TOSCA-Metadata directories.

The Definitions directory contains one or more Definitions.tosca documents. These documents contain the TOSCA definitions describing the cloud application. More precisely, exactly one of them must contain the ServiceTemplate defining the structure and behavior of the whole cloud application, while the others can be devoted to supporting definitions (so as to modularize the application specification). Additionally, CSARs can also be devoted to contain TOSCA definitions to be reused in other contexts. For instance, a CSAR might be used to provide a set of NodeTypes (with their corresponding implementations) to be employed as building blocks while specifying new cloud applications.

A TOSCA-Metadata directory contains the TOSCA.meta file. Its purpose is to describe metadata about the other files in the CSAR by means of blocks, which in turn consist of a set of name-value pairs. More precisely, the first block of the `TOSCA.meta` file provides metadata about the CSAR itself (e.g., version, creator, etc.), while each other block points to a file in the CSAR and describes its metadata.

**Processing of Application Packages.** An application specification is packaged (along with the concrete artifacts implementing its components) in a CSAR archive with the purpose of deploying it on TOSCA-compliant cloud platforms. A cloud platform is TOSCA-compliant if it offers a TOSCA container (e.g., OpenTOSCA [8]) which is an engine able to process CSAR archives, and thus to deploy and operate the applications they contain.

TOSCA containers can deploy applications by processing the CSAR archives in two different ways [5]. On one hand, *imperative processing* takes the CSAR and deploys the application according to the workflow defined as a `BuildPlan` in the corresponding `ServiceTemplate` (e.g., the `BuildPlan` shown in Fig. 6). On the other hand, *declarative processing* deploys the application by trying to automatically excerpt a deployment plan from the application's `TopologyTemplate`. In the latter case, the CSAR engine (a) first deploys the nodes without requirements on other nodes, and then (b) until all nodes have been deployed, it searches the nodes whose requirements are satisfied (by the capabilities of the already deployed nodes) and deploys them. For instance, if we consider the topology in Fig. 3, the *declarative processing* works as follows. First, it deploys the node templates `ApacheVM` and `MySqlVM` since they have no dependencies on other nodes. Second, it deploys `ApacheOS` and `MySqlOS` since the node templates they depend on have been deployed. Then, it proceeds in repeating steps analogous to the second one until all the node templates in the topology have been deployed.

TOSCA containers not only have to support application at deployment time, but also at run time. They are indeed in charge of ensuring that the implementation artifacts (corresponding to management operations) are available [14]. They should also be able to properly operate such artifacts as well as the management plans provided by the application specification [3].

## 3    Analysis of the TOSCA Approach

In the previous section, we illustrated how TOSCA permits to describe the topology and management behaviour of multi-component cloud applications. It allows application developers to describe their solutions by clearly separating topology and management concerns. In this section we analyze the TOSCA approach for describing an application's topology and management, with respect to its declared main goals.

### 3.1    Topology Aspects

One of the main advantages of TOSCA is its suitability to (easily) represent the structure of (even complex) cloud applications. Each multi-component application is indeed modeled as a graph, in which typed nodes correspond to the application's components, and typed relationships represent the dependencies between these components.

The availability of an abstract topology description is necessary to achieve the goal of automating the deployment of applications [4]. The topology description (along with the artifacts connected to each component) indeed allows TOSCA containers to automatically excerpt the declarative plans needed to deploy the specified application [5]. The automated management also benefits from the topology description. Imperative management plans can indeed be implemented by orchestrating the operations offered by the nodes in the topology.

Furthermore, the topology description is portable [6]. Despite application developers have all the freedom in choosing the types of the elements composing a topology, this is understandable to every container (provided that also the type definitions are available to the same container). This is because TOSCA, with the aim of giving flexibility to application developers in deciding the types to be used, only prescribes how to *structure* the definition [1].

Finally, TOSCA enhances reuse. Each TOSCA definition may indeed be referred by more than one specification (in order to be reused) [5]. Consider, for instance, the definition of a server component. By defining `ServerType`, we can specify (abstractly) its observable properties, capabilities, requirements, and management operations. The `ServerType` can then be referred by `Server-Template1`, ..., `ServerTemplateN`, which are different templates whose structure has been defined only once. The same holds for `ServerType` implementations. Different providers can offer different `ServerTypeImplementations`, each of which implements this `ServerType` according to the provider's running environment. Furthermore, type definitions can be refined through derivation [3]: If one needs an Apache server component, then she can reuse the definitions in `ServerType` by extending them into an `ApacheServerType`.

The above mentioned features come at the price of defining a bunch of (XML) TOSCA elements. For instance, to define the above mentioned server component, an application developer must specify a `ServerType`, a `ServerTemplate`, and a `ServerTypeImplementation`. The latter in turns needs the definition of a set of `ArtifactTypes` and `ArtifactTemplates` corresponding to the set of artifacts implementing the `ServerType`. Since all the previously mentioned definitions are required for a single component of an application, it is not difficult to imagine how many definitions are required for a complex, multi-component application. The heaviness of the specification can be however mitigated mainly by leveraging reuse of TOSCA definitions, and by employing graphical tools (like Winery [12]) while defining new application components.

## 3.2 Management Aspects

TOSCA enables the automated application deployment and management by capturing the knowledge of the application developers via the modeling of their management proven best practices [3]. More precisely, application developers can model their application management at two different levels of abstraction. `DeploymentArtifacts` and `ImplementationArtifacts` are used to implement deployment and management operations of a single application component, while Plans allow to express higher level management tasks [14]. For instance, an artifact may implement the pausing of an application module, while a plan may pause the multi-component application (by employing such artifact).

Artifacts can be implemented in whatever programming language the application developers like. Analogously, application developers have all the freedom in choosing the workflow languages to model (both declarative and imperative) plans. Ideally, the employed workflow languages should satisfy the following requirements, as BPMN4TOSCA does [14]: (i) they should provide ways to access and modify properties of nodes and relationships, (ii) they should enable management plans to access TOSCA topology model, (iii) they should ease the selection of management operations offered by nodes, and (iv) they should support an easy and comfortable way to execute scripts on nodes.

The freedom given to application developers makes TOSCA really flexible. On the other hand, to ensure "portability of applications and their management", TOSCA containers must be able to process the set of artifacts and plans needed to execute the management operations and to instantiate component instances [1]. In other words, TOSCA containers must pay the cost of supporting a bunch of languages and of being able to bind management of analogously defined operations to different kinds of artifacts.

## 3.3   Other Aspects

Besides topology and management aspects, TOSCA also allows application developers to specify the non-functional properties of their applications. Non-functional properties are expressed in TOSCA by means of policies, which in turn can be written with whatever policy language an application developer likes. This empowers the flexibility of TOSCA, but at the price of requiring TOSCA containers to support a bunch of policy languages.

Furthermore, the purpose of policies is to declare which non-functional properties an application offers. Thus, to specify what an application requires, application developers are asked to employ policies in a somewhat counter-intuitive way (by mixing what the application offers and what it requires). We argue that to split policies in *non-functional capabilities* and *non-functional requirements*, similar to functional requirements and capabilities could be a better alternative.

The flexibility of TOSCA is even more visible in the possibility of deploying CSAR archives both *imperatively* and *declaratively*. This gives freedom to application developers, by allowing them to either explicitly specify how to deploy their applications, or to ask containers to excerpt deployment plans from the application topology. This freedom comes at the price of requiring TOSCA containers to support both ways of processing.

In summary, TOSCA achieves its goals — automated application deployment and management, portability of application descriptions and their management, and interoperability and reusability of components — by also trying to be as much flexible as possible. On one hand, such a flexibility gives application developers freedom in choosing languages and types to be used while specifying their applications. On the other hand, it obviously requires TOSCA containers to support a bunch of languages, and this complicates the development (and potentially also the operation) of TOSCA containers.

## 4  Research Directions

In the previous section we discussed the TOSCA approach for describing topology and behaviour of cloud applications. In this section we exploit such an analysis to try to identify a set of possible interesting research directions.

**(D1) Fostering the Reuse of TOSCA Specifications.** Cloud applications can share some management infrastructure. For instance, web applications (independently of their purposes) share an underlying topology whose top component is the web server needed to run them. If the underlying topology (and the related management) is already somehow available, it can be included in the specification and then suitably configured. In this way, the time and complexity required for application specification could be considerably decreased. It is thus interesting to identify reusable (fragments of) specifications so as to speed-up the development of new ones.

**(D2) Enhanced and Full-fledged Implementations of TOSCA Containers.** TOSCA aims to achieve its objectives by remaining as much flexible as possible. This also means to not prescribe (i) how to select whether to process a CSAR archive either declaratively or imperatively —if both are possible—, (ii) how to decide which build plan is to be invoked to imperatively processed when more than one are available, and (iii) how to select the proper type implementation when multiple are present. While issue (i) can easily be fixed by extending the TOSCA specification issues (ii) and (iii) may not be satisfactorily solved by simply extending the TOSCA specification, since they involve the development of proper selection criteria, and the implementation of mechanisms and tools which operate these criteria. Thus, it may be worth investigating issues (ii) and (iii) so as to gain smart and effective solutions.

**(D3) Implementation of TOSCA Tools.** Another interesting research direction is obviously the development of tools capable of working with TOSCA specifications (e.g., visual editors, analyzers, etc.) which can contribute to a widespread adoption of TOSCA.

**(D4) Integration of TOSCA with Existing Standard Proposals.** Another interesting direction is to investigate how TOSCA can be integrated with other initiatives. For instance, it is interesting to understand whether and how TOSCA can be integrated with CAMP, another emerging standard targeting the management of cloud applications. It is also interesting to understand which of the existing workflow modeling languages (e.g., BPMN, WS-BPEL, etc.) may be more suited for writing TOSCA plans.

**(D5) Comparative Assessment of TOSCA.** Since TOSCA is emerging, it still has to be accepted as the *de-facto* standard for the management orchestration of cloud applications. It is thus really interesting to devote further investigation to comparatively assess TOSCA with respect to other proposals that permit to specify cloud applications (e.g., CAMP). Such an assessment may be performed in terms of the expressive power of the language, the heaviness of the specifications, and the exploitability of the specification for analysis and verification.

We shall now expand the discussion regarding the above mentioned research directions. Due to space limitations, we will mainly focus on (D1), which is the scope of our immediate future work.

The reuse of TOSCA specifications can be fostered from two different perspectives: (i) (flexible) matching of available topology fragments with required node types, and (ii) identification of common management patterns. In this way, application developers become able to model their application without taking care of the underlying infrastructure. Once the application is modeled, they can indeed look for TOSCA nodes corresponding to PaaS offerings, select the most suited one (possibly on the basis of desired QoS), and then just include it as a single node in their application specification.

Informally speaking, (i) consists of determining a fragment of an available application specification that can become a standalone TOSCA service to be included in place of a desired node type while specifying new cloud applications. This may be done only from a functional perspective, or also by including non-functional features of desired nodes and available applications.

In case of (ii), starting from a bunch of cloud application specifications, it may be interesting to identify recurring substructures (modeling the same node types) and to export them as *management patterns*. The identified management patterns could then be merged with other patterns and definitions so as to build-up whole applications. This requires to solve two main issues, namely: how to merge the topologies, and how to merge the deployment and management plans. The former issue has already been studied [9], but the provided solution is no longer applicable (since it thoroughly employs GroupTemplates, which are no longer supported by TOSCA). So, there is a need for new solutions that can either be based on the available approach [9] or not. The merging of plans has not yet been studied in the TOSCA context, but it is strongly related to the research work on web service composition. Some available solutions can then be employed in order to solve this new, TOSCA-related issue.

The above discussion about the reuse of available definitions implicitly assumes the ability to detect the TOSCA definitions corresponding to needed components. However, it is worth noting that TOSCA models application components from a management perspective, while application developers search them from an operational viewpoint. For instance, an application developer needing a web server searches a middleware component able to run web applications, rather than a component which offers the server-related management features. Thus, a mechanism to map an application developer's operational needs to TOSCA management definitions is an interesting research perspective.

Such a mechanism would allow to build-up a repository which lets application developers satisfy their (operational) needs with available TOSCA (management) definitions. TOSCA will benefit from such a repository, since the availability of easy-to-find, reusable definitions will strongly simplify the specification of applications in TOSCA, and thus exponentially decrease the time needed to do it. Furthermore, a repository of official definitions also empowers the portability of application specifications because TOSCA containers should support all of them.

Portability and reusability of application specifications are even more effective if the repository addresses the issue of having application components offering the same management features with similar (but different) names. A solution may be to provide a super-type standardizing the name of common features to be implemented by all derived definitions (maybe according to emerging API standardization like CAMP [16]), so that containers can uniformly understand them. Another solution may be to make the repository able to match available specification with respect to needed ones, and to suitably adapt them [10].

## 5    Related Work

At the time of writing, TOSCA [1] is a hot research topic. This is witnessed by the amount of research work which has already been produced, despite the young age of TOSCA.

On the one hand, some research efforts are targeted at illustrating what TOSCA is and how to use it. The primer [5] illustrates how TOSCA should be employed to specify complex applications and their management. More precisely, it identifies the three possible usage roles (viz., *application architect*, *type architect*, and *artifact developer*) and shows how they should employ TOSCA. The primer also discusses how CSAR archives are declaratively and imperatively processed. Binz et al. [3] outline the main goals of TOSCA and then discuss how it achieves them. The discussion starts with a very high-level overview of TOSCA, and then proceeds by illustrating how TOSCA achieves its goals. Lipton [7] and Binz et al. [6] overview TOSCA a bit more in detail, with the aim at highlighting the portability of TOSCA specifications, thus showing how TOSCA avoids the cloud vendor lock-in problem. Each of the aforementioned efforts discusses general aspects of TOSCA, either focusing on the modeling language or on other aspects like the processing of specifications or its goals (and sub-goals). In this paper, we tried to reorganize the aforementioned available information in a compact, easy-to-access description which comprises both the TOSCA modeling language and the other aspects.

On the other hand, several researches are related to TOSCA, but do not target at illustrating TOSCA itself. These researches can be considered in line with the research directions individuated in this paper. Brogi et al. [10] aim at instantiating desired node types by reusing existing service templates, and thus define four types of matching between service templates and node types (and show how to adapt service templates, if needed). Since [10] illustrates how to match and adapt available TOSCA definitions, this can be considered in line with (D1). Binz et al. [9] are also strongly related with (D1), since they show how to improve resource sharing by merging the topologies of available cloud applications. OpenTOSCA [8] and Winery [12] are a container and a visual editor for TOSCA, respectively. Thus, OpenTOSCA is related to (D2), while Winery is in line with (D3). Kopp et al. [14] and Cardoso et al. [11] work in the direction (D4), by trying to integrate TOSCA with BPMN and USDL, respectively. Finally, Waizenegger et al. [13] illustrate two possible mechanisms for automatically processing policies expressed according to TOSCA, which are in line with (D3), since they can be easily implemented as a TOSCA tool.

## 6  Conclusions

As mentioned in the Introduction, interested readers can browse various documents to get acquainted with TOSCA. In this paper, we reorganized the available information so as to provide a compact, easy-to-access description of TOSCA which may speed-up the learning process of this promising OASIS specification, thus leveraging its widespread acceptance.

We have also discussed how TOSCA achieves its goals — automated application deployment and management, portability of application descriptions and their management, and interoperability and reusability of components — by also trying to be as flexible as it can. We also discussed how a reduction of such a flexibility (e.g, by reducing the number of supported plan/artifact languages) may empower the portability of application descriptions across different TOSCA containers.

In this paper, we also individuated some research perspectives, namely: (D1) reuse of available specifications, (D2) enhanced and full-fledged implementations of so-called *TOSCA containers*, (D3) implementation of TOSCA-about tools, (D4) integration of TOSCA with existing standard proposals, and (D5) comparative assessment of TOSCA. (D1) and (D5) are scope of our future work.

As a final remark, it is worth highlighting that TOSCA is not the *de-facto* standard for the interoperable specification of cloud applications. Its widespread adoption depends not only on its potential, but also on commercial and economical decisions. In this perspective, TOSCA may leverage of the set of big companies (e.g., Alcatel-Lucent, CA Technologies, Fujitsu, Huawei, IBM, SAP) which are active members of the OASIS TOSCA WG[3].

## References

1. OASIS: TOSCA 1.0 (Topology and Orchestration Specification for Cloud Applications), Version 1.0 (2013),
   http://docs.oasis-open.org/tosca/TOSCA/v1.0/TOSCA-v1.0.pdf

---

[3] The full list of OASIS TOSCA WG members can be found at
https://www.oasis-open.org/committees/membership.php?wg_abbrev=tosca.

2. Armbrust, M., Fox, A., Griffith, R., Joseph, A.D., Katz, R., Konwinski, A., Lee, G., Patterson, D., Rabkin, A., Stoica, I., Zaharia, M.: A view of cloud computing. Commun. ACM 53, 50–58 (2010)

3. Binz, T., Breitenbücher, U., Kopp, O., Leymann, F.: TOSCA: Portable automated deployment and management of cloud applications. In: Bouguettaya, A., Sheng, Q.Z., Daniel, F. (eds.) Advanced Web Services, pp. 527–549. Springer, New York (2014)

4. Wettinger, J., Andrikopoulos, V., Strauch, S., Leymann, F.: Enabling dynamic deployment of cloud applications using a modular and extensible PaaS environment. In: 2013 IEEE Sixth International Conference on Cloud Computing (CLOUD), pp. 478–485 (2013)

5. OASIS: Topology and Orchestration Specification for Cloud Applications (TOSCA) Primer Version 1.0 (2013),
http://docs.oasis-open.org/tosca/
tosca-primer/v1.0/tosca-primer-v1.0.pdf

6. Binz, T., Breiter, G., Leymann, F., Spatzier, T.: Portable Cloud Services Using TOSCA. IEEE Internet Computing 16, 80–85 (2012)

7. Lipton, P.: Escaping Vendor Lock-in with TOSCA, an emerging Cloud Standard for Portability. CA Technology Exchange 4, 49–55 (2013)

8. Binz, T., Breitenbücher, U., Haupt, F., Kopp, O., Leymann, F., Nowak, A., Wagner, S.: OpenTOSCA – a runtime for TOSCA-based cloud applications. In: Basu, S., Pautasso, C., Zhang, L., Fu, X. (eds.) ICSOC 2013. LNCS, vol. 8274, pp. 692–695. Springer, Heidelberg (2013)

9. Binz, T., Breitenbücher, U., Kopp, O., Leymann, F., Weiss, A.: Improve Resource-Sharing through Functionality-Preserving Merge of Cloud Application Topologies. In: Desprez, F., Ferguson, D., Hadar, E., Leymann, F., Jarke, M., Helfert, M. (eds.) Proceedings of the 3rd International Conference on Cloud Computing and Service Science, CLOSER 2013, Aachen, Germany, May 8-10, 8 pages. SciTePress (2013)

10. Canal, C., Villari, M. (eds.): ESOCC 2013. CCIS, vol. 393, pp. 218–232. Springer, Heidelberg (2013)

11. Cardoso, J., Binz, T., Breitenbücher, U., Kopp, O., Leymann, F.: Cloud computing automation: Integrating USDL and TOSCA. In: Salinesi, C., Norrie, M.C., Pastor, Ó. (eds.) CAiSE 2013. LNCS, vol. 7908, pp. 1–16. Springer, Heidelberg (2013)

12. Kopp, O., Binz, T., Breitenbücher, U., Leymann, F.: Winery – A Modeling Tool for TOSCA-Based Cloud Applications. In: Basu, S., Pautasso, C., Zhang, L., Fu, X. (eds.) ICSOC 2013. LNCS, vol. 8274, pp. 700–704. Springer, Heidelberg (2013)

13. Waizenegger, T., et al.: Policy4TOSCA: A policy-aware cloud service provisioning approach to enable secure cloud computing. In: Meersman, R., Panetto, H., Dillon, T., Eder, J., Bellahsene, Z., Ritter, N., De Leenheer, P., Dou, D. (eds.) ODBASE 2013. LNCS, vol. 8185, pp. 360–376. Springer, Heidelberg (2013)

14. Kopp, O., Binz, T., Breitenbücher, U., Leymann, F.: BPMN4TOSCA: A domain-specific language to model management plans for composite applications. In: Mendling, J., Weidlich, M. (eds.) BPMN 2012. LNBIP, vol. 125, pp. 38–52. Springer, Heidelberg (2012)

15. Pahl, C., Zhang, L., Fowley, F.: Interoperability standards for cloud architecture. In: Desprez, F., Ferguson, D., Hadar, E., Leymann, F., Jarke, M., Helfert, M. (eds.) CLOSER. SciTePress (2013)

16. OASIS: Cloud Application Management for Platforms (CAMP) Version 1.1 (2014),
http://docs.oasis-open.org/camp/camp-spec/v1.1/camp-spec-v1.1.pdf

17. DMTF: Cloud Infrastructure Management Interface, CIMI (2013),
    http://www.dmtf.org/sites/default/files/
    standards/documents/DSP0264_1.0.0.pdf
18. Open Mashup Alliance: Enterprise Mashup Markup Language, EMML (2011),
    https://en.wikipedia.org/wiki/EMML
19. Open Grid Forum: Open Cloud Computing Interface, OCCI (2013),
    http://occi-wg.org/about/specification/
20. OASIS: Open Component Service Architectures, Open-CSA (2007),
    http://www.oasis-opencsa.org/specifications
21. DMTF: Open Virtualization Format, OVF (2014),
    http://www.dmtf.org/sites/default/files/
    standards/documents/DSP0243_2.1.0.pdf
22. OMG: Service Oriented Architecture Modeling Language, SOA-ML (2012),
    http://www.omg.org/spec/SoaML/1.0.1/
23. W3C: Unified Service Description Language, USDL (2011),
    http://www.w3.org/2005/Incubator/usdl/XGR-usdl-20111027/

# Author Index